AF559859

LINES and LIVES

Lines and Lives

Stories of Conflict, Resilience and Hope from Jammu and Kashmir Borderlands

Edited by

Mohita **Bhatia**
Rekha **Chowdhary**
Sandeep **Singh**

Orient BlackSwan

LINES AND LIVES: STORIES OF CONFLICT, RESILIENCE AND HOPE FROM JAMMU AND KASHMIR BORDERLANDS

ORIENT BLACKSWAN PRIVATE LIMITED

Registered Office
3-6-752 Himayatnagar, Hyderabad 500 029, Telangana, India
Email: centraloffice@orientblackswan.com

Other Offices
Bengaluru, Chennai, Guwahati, Hyderabad,
Kolkata, Mumbai, New Delhi, Noida, Patna

First published by Orient Blackswan Private Limited 2024

ISBN 978-93-5442-740-4

039307

Typeset in
Sabon Lt Std 11/13.5
by Manmohan Kumar, Delhi

Printed in India at
Thomson Press, New Delhi 110 020

Published by
Orient Blackswan Private Limited
3-6-752 Himayatnagar, Hyderabad 500 029, Telangana, India
e-mail: info@orientblackswan.com

CONTENTS

ABBREVIATIONS

AGPL	Actual Ground Position Line
BADP	Border Area Development Programme
BJP	Bharatiya Janata Party
BJS	Bharatiya Jana Sangh
BSF	Border Security Force, Central
CRPF	Reserve Police Force
CBM	Confidence-Building Measures
CFL	Ceasefire Line
EU	European Union
IAJK	India-Administered Jammu and Kashmir
IB	International Border
IGNOU	Indira Gandhi National Open University
IMD	India Meteorological Department
J&K	Jammu and Kashmir
LoC	Line of Control
NDA	National Democratic Alliance
PAJK	Pakistan-Administered Jammu and Kashmir
POJK	Pakistan-Occupied Jammu and Kashmir/Pakistan-Controlled Jammu and Kashmir
POK	Pakistan-Occupied Kashmir
PoKDP	Pakistan-Occupied Kashmir Displaced People
ReT	Rehbar-e-Taleem
RTCs	Round Table Conferences
SAARC	South Asian Association for Regional Cooperation
SC	Scheduled Caste
SP	Superintendent of Police
WPR	West Pakistan Refugees

PUBLISHERS' ACKNOWLEDGEMENTS

The publishers would like to thank the Centre for Dialogue and Reconciliation (CDR), New Delhi, India (website: www.cdr-india.org) for permission to reproduce excerpts of the report titled 'Bordered People: Impact of Conflict on the Lives of People living on the Border in J&K: A Case Study of Arnia Belt' (2012) by Rekha Chowdhary. This report has shaped the essence of Chapter 3 of the present volume.

The publishers are indebted to the Centre for Dialogue and Reconciliation (CDR), New Delhi also for permission to reproduce excerpts from the work titled 'Living Close and yet Apart: Divided Families and Border' by Mohita Bhatia. This has formed the basis of Chapter 4 of the present volume.

I

Conflict and Borderlands in Jammu and Kashmir

A Conceptual Analysis

Mohita Bhatia, Rekha Chowdhary
and Sandeep Singh

The theoretical understanding of borders has changed over the years as they are no longer seen as geometrical lines or territorial markers existing at the edges of the nation-state. Instead, borders are viewed as diffused processes present at various places, intangible spaces and moments such as 'in airports distant from the "edge" of the territory and, more significantly, in databases that may not even be "in" the country in question' (Cooper 2020: 24) While this dispersion of borders has occurred to some extent in the South Asian societies as well, this book argues through an exploration of Jammu and Kashmir (J&K) borderlands that this diffusion does not supersede the territorial significance of borders in these societies. Territorial borders and demarcations at the nation's edges still have an exceptionally powerful presence, both for the state and for the people inhabiting those spaces. Geometrical fantasies and imaginaries still stand strong, making these national peripheries extremely significant sites of violence, ridden with contestations over securitisation, negotiation and refuge. These continue to be remarkable zones for the assertion of state sovereignty and authority as well as for nation-making. This book thus examines the various J&K borders and their multiple contestations to bring the attention back to territorial delineations in the South Asian context, even while recognising borders at national edges as processes and practices rather than static state-oriented reality. It goes on to fuse these territorial understandings with non-tangible, abstract and more diffused socio-cultural border practices. However, restoring focus on territorial spaces is not meant to reinforce the state-oriented, canonical conceptualisation of borders; in fact, the objective of this book is to bring forth a polysemic, fluid and processual notion of these borderlands.

South Asian borders, though peripheral in a territorial context, are central to defining the idea of a nation-state, its territorial, symbolic as well as absolute authority. In the words of Hastings Donnan and Thomas M. Wilson (1999: 1), 'Borderlands are sites and symbols of power'. Such power is clearly reflected through the 'guard towers' and 'barbed wires' which are common sights at borders. These and many other symbols such as the presence of the military, constant surveillance, checking of identity cards and no-entry zones that distinguish the borderlands from the mainlands are the 'extreme examples of markers of sovereignty which inscribe the territorial limits of the state' (ibid.). Delineating, demarcating, defining and defending national borders are the most significant processes symbolising states' fantasies and exclusive control (ibid.; van Schendel 2005). In this context, Benjamin H. Johnson and Andrew R. Graybill (2010: 2) state,

> National borders represent the territorial embodiment of a bundle of ideas that modern states have propagated and enforced. They tell us that all of humanity is divided up among discrete nation-states; that these nations have sovereign powers over particular territory to the exclusion of other nations; and that, collectively, nations exercise this sovereignty over all the earth.... The mere fact of living within a nation's borders implies that one is the product of that nation's past, and that one's own fate is inextricably linked to that of one's fellow countrymen above all others.

In South Asian societies where the territorial notion of nations assumes phenomenal significance, especially for the state, 'the meanings attributed to such borders are inward-oriented'. This implies that borders 'are closely related to the ideological state apparatus, ideological practices such as nationalism and related nationalist identity narratives' (Paasi: 2011). Borders and boundaries thus become significant mediums through which the narratives of national identity are produced. Here, the power of the state, symbolised through borders, is thus not simply the coercive power represented by the armed forces stationed at the borders but also the ideological power as represented by the contexts of identity. Bordering and clearly making a distinction between 'us', who are part of this identity and 'them', who live across the border, forms a broader nationalist ideology that is constantly evoked, reinforced and reiterated.

Since such a conceptualisation of national identity essentially draws strength from embedding people within the physical boundaries and providing sanctity to these boundaries, the very history of the nation-state itself reflects the double processes of 'closures'—'on the one hand, the closure of geographical space by borders; on the other hand, the closure of membership' (Mau et al. 2012: 5). It is thus inevitable for the modern nation-state with its concept of citizenship to draw a line between those who were 'included' in and those who were 'excluded' by the state. Those included were the privileged 'citizens' who were differentiated from 'outsiders' or 'aliens'. Border controls, therefore, are integral to enforcing this differentiation and regulating the entry of the latter. As the case of Jammu and Kashmir borders illustrate, these controls and border markers become extremely militarised, contentious and violent when the neighbouring nation-states have belligerent relations and have pasts immersed in memories of violence, bloodshed and Partition. The state uses its ideological and cultural apparatus—cultural nationalism, educational practices, national symbols and popular culture—to emphasise and reiterate these demarcations and closures (Wastl-Walter 2011: 14).

Borders, in their conventional definition, are limiting, restrictive and constraining. The state ideology of border is thus characterised by its fixity and permanence. Borders are projected as natural and eternal. However, as the anthropological and cultural studies have emphasised, borders can be seen as 'constructs' that can not only be defined and redefined, but also be traversed. Despite their function of containment, borders are being crossed, contested and re-constructed in many ways. Borders are associated with the constant migration, mobility and displacement of refugees and migrants, even at great risk to their lives. The 'illegality' associated with crossing of borders by people or economic goods are questioned and often not complied with. In short, the attempts by the nation-states to 'fix' borders have always been contested and breached, even when these struggles have involved huge human costs. Even the most militarised, securitised and sealed borders, such as that of Israel–Palestine, are fiercely contested.

In this book, we look at borders as an 'ironic' reality—one that is often breached, reconstructed and contested, and yet assumes a non-permeable, constraining reality. It is viewed differently by the nation-state, nationalist ideologues, and the people of the border areas. In the case of Jammu and Kashmir borders, its paradoxical character is reflected in the fact that on the one hand, the nation-state makes it impossible to permeate and considers it a rigid, non-negotiable boundary. Many non-state actors or ordinary people residing in the mainstream of the Indian nation, and who passionately adhere to the Indian nationalist ideology, also unyieldingly uphold and reiterate the stand of the nation-state. Yet on the other hand, many residents of the borderlands find these borders, particularly the LoC to be restrictive, separating them from their land and families. These differing interpretations of the borders make them ambiguous and paradoxical in character, despite the unyielding performances of the nation-state.

These paradoxes and differing interpretations of borders, despite their obstinate existence, also enable a shift away from the canonical analyses. They open more possibilities that point to a varied imagery of peripheral borders—borders as political or cultural discourses formulated by the residents of borderlands; borders as an imagined boundary of the state visualised by these residents; borders as a tool of political resistance; borders as processes of reinforcing or contradicting narratives of national identity; or borders as performances, conducted differently by state- and non-state actors, state agents and political actors. It is through these discourses, performances and resistant imagination that alternative meanings of borders are produced and lived.

As mentioned above, a focus on the Jammu and Kashmir borderlands points to the most constraining, violent and securitised borders that are almost impossible to cross and yet are most fiercely contested. This contestation politics takes many different forms. To begin with, the contestation is rooted at the level of the state itself, as is clearly reflected from both the states' treatment of the Line of Control (LoC) as the 'Border'. The peculiar situation of J&K entails that besides having a settled border with Pakistan, recognised as the International Border (IB), it also has a rather not-so-settled border in the form of the LoC. The LoC divides J&K into two parts, each of which is under the respective control of India and Pakistan. The irony of considering the LoC as a border lies in the fact that neither India nor Pakistan officially recognises the division as final and both lay claim over the whole of J&K.[1] In this way, the division (of Jammu and Kashmir) is neither officially accepted nor is the border legally recognised. To assert its own claim over the whole of J&K (as well as to negate Pakistan's claim), India makes symbolic efforts from time to time. For instance, in 1994 the Indian Parliament passed a resolution by which it declared the whole of J&K, including the part under the control of Pakistan, as part of India. [2] More recently in 2019, the Government of India officially drew up an Indian map which shows the areas under Pakistan's control as part of India (*Mint* 2019). To make its claim appear more assertive, the Indian state has started including the major towns of Pakistan-occupied Jammu and Kashmir (POJK) in its 'weather bulletin'.[3]

Apart from the state, the contestation over borders has also been taking place at other levels. Besides the India–Pakistan contestation over the J&K borders, another layer of contestation has been emanating from Kashmir's conflict politics. The protagonists of conflict politics make a case for the 'whole of Jammu and Kashmir' as one unit across the two sides of the LoC. What is interesting is that in this whole process, the idea of LoC as the border gets fully dismissed. It is a different matter that the conflict politics in itself is contested within Kashmir as well as beyond it. While in Kashmir, such a contestation has been coming from the mainstream, pro-India political class; beyond Kashmir, there have been strong contesting voices in Jammu and Ladakh.

There is yet another significant context of the contestation of the LoC which involves the border residents of the districts adjoining the LoC. These are the people who have been directly impacted by the division of the state. Their cultural context as well as their familial linkages across the border makes them question the absurdities of the border. Forming a very significant part of stakeholders in this conflict-ridden state, they have been looking for any opportunity to unify the two sides of Jammu and Kashmir—whether physical or notional. They comprise families arbitrarily divided by the borders in 1947 or in the later period, and the refugees who were forced to migrate from across the LoC, leaving their homes and land on the other side. These residents of the border areas demand a blurring or softening, if not dissolution, of borders so that members of divided families can visit one another. It is in humane acknowledgement of their stories that the cross-LoC bus service was initiated to facilitate interactions across the border. This was one of the most important confidence-building measures (CBM) offered by the Indian and the Pakistani states during the post-2004 peace process.[4] Ironically, even when the peace process collapsed, the bus service (along with the cross-LoC trade) continued till 2019.[5]

Paradox exists, as this above episode shows, even in the response of the state towards the borders. Though heavily mined, fenced and excessively securitised, borders can also acquire a 'softness', 'flexibility' and even 'irrelevance'. While starting the cross-LoC bus service and initiating cross-LoC trade, all these terms were used and sufficient enthusiasm was shown by the state in redefining the Line of Control as the 'Line of Peace' or 'Line of Trade'. Although the borders still remain sealed and heavily surveilled and are projected as symbols of nationalist affirmation, they also represent zones of contestation, negotiation and cross-border interactions. What adds to the peculiar and ironical nature of the Jammu and Kashmir borderlands is the fact that on most occasions, people of the borderlands are engaged in both reinforcing some aspects of a nationalist performance and challenging many other symbols of nationalist authority.

The paradoxical nature of the border in J&K, as we will see in this book, gets reflected in various other ways. One such paradoxical situation is reflected in the context of the relationship between security personnel and local residents. No clear black-and-white relationship exists between the security personnel or army men and the locals. A vernacularisation of the military–local relationship takes places at the border areas where both sides get used to one another, may collaborate in viewing borders as mechanisms of economic opportunities, come to help each other, and may see one another as part of everyday life in the borderlands. While antagonism and suspicion define one aspect of the relationship between local residents of border areas and the security personnel located in these spaces, other facets of their everyday interactions also point to utilitarian interests and a normalisation of their relationship. In the case of borderlands in Jammu, the army is seen everywhere—camping around the houses in villages and in residential areas in towns; inside the parks and monuments; close to schools and adjoining offices. It permeates all aspects of the daily life of locals in these border areas. Such a pervasive presence of the army may be, at times, resented by locals, yet its presence is also 'normalised' and often viewed as providing security to them from outside infiltrators, or offering infrastructural support in terms of opening of army schools and providing employment avenues to the people of border regions. Madeleine Reeves (2018: 42–56), in her work on Central Asian borders, coins the term 'intimate militarism' to describe a routinised closeness between residents and the military. 'A critical aspect of intimate militarization, then is not just the routinization of military presence, but rather the normalization of appeal to threat of force to resolve habitual disputes,' she states.

In this book, we look at borders as 'being' and 'becoming' rather than as mere existing territorial lines at the edge of a national space. Viewing borders as a process enables us to not only look at them from people's perspectives, but also to explore the interactions among the state, people, communities and physical spaces. It offers a more holistic understanding of the bordering realities and the way these realities are made, re-made, resisted or reinforced, as opposed to the linear state versus people analysis of borderlands. Some of the chapters in the book also examine borders in terms of performances—everyday lived lives of border residents; performance of nationalism in material, symbolic and coercive terms; events that unfold in the borderlands; security and state performances of authority; and contestation or reinforcement of the bordering processes. We focus on the cross-border dynamics and interactions to examine the fluidity of borders despite their 'closed' or 'sealed' character. A focus on the lives of the residents living close to the borders, war-prone zones, divided families, cross-border movements, or nationalist performances at these spaces offer a visualisation of the process of bordering. We focus on these processes to demonstrate that boundaries that seem unchanging in the short term are in fact constantly being reconstructed at spatial, political and cultural levels in the longer duration.

South Asian Specificities: The Case of Jammu and Kashmir Borderlands

A focus on the Jammu and Kashmir borderlands also points to the specificities of South Asian borderlands that are a consequence of colonial intervention and thus, in many ways different from the borderlands of the West. Globalisation processes triggered the visualisation of a borderless world in the West and influenced the theorisation of borders and boundaries. What is offered here as an example is the European model with its invisible borders and free movement of people. The dissolution of the European Union (EU) border changed the whole perspective on borders. Rather than borders as a concept signifying 'inclusion' and 'exclusion' and therefore important for maintaining the identity of the state, they were now seen 'as challenges to communication and movement to be overcome, and increasingly also, as lines of reference to define identities and belongings in relation to others' (Herrschel 2011: 15).

Theories of borders and nations coming from the most volatile regions in South Asia, such as Jammu and Kashmir, depart from the 'borderless world' or 'global village' theorisations. While Western theories of borders have also questioned the 'global village' argument and illustrated that borders may be simultaneously open to some (the educated, highly-skilled) and closed to others (refugees, low-income groups), most vociferous contestations of these theories emerge from the Asian and South Asian context of borders that still represent the most sealed off, volatile and militarised zones. Many of these borderlands are prone to frequent cross-border firing, shelling and mining, often causing the displacement of families living close to the border areas and even loss of lives. A borderless world does not comply with South Asian realities where 'national sovereignty' and 'national boundaries' are still apocalyptic political issues. It may be argued that the theorisation of borders and the national imagination emerging from the West must also be supplemented by the theories emerging from the most securitised and sensitive borderlands located in South Asia. The latter illustrate the continuing importance of territorial borders in contemporary times, being constantly guarded and affecting directly the lives of people living close to these places.

The most recent contribution to the theory of borders is Étienne Balibar's thesis (2002)—'borders are everywhere'. Many scholars have used and extended Balibar's argument to shift the notion of borderlands away from territorial borders that lie at the edges of the nation-state to a more diffused and pervasive sense of physical, symbolic, subjective and mental borders as well as forms of surveillance and control that exist in many forms at various places, including cities and mainstream spaces. Extending Balibar's thesis, Chris Rumford (2008) has offered a useful terminology—'borderwork'—to demonstrate that borders are not just pervasive in our social lives but are being made and unmade by ordinary people, and not just imposed by the nation-state in geopolitical terms. Explaining the term 'borderwork', Rumford (ibid.: 22) states:

> Citizens, entrepreneurs, and 'civil society' actors, amongst others, can engage in bordering, or what is here termed borderwork, the efforts of ordinary people leading to the construction, dismantling or shifting of borders. The borders concerned are not necessarily those (at the edges) of the nation-state; they can be found at a range of sites throughout society: in towns and cities, in local neighbourhoods, in the countryside.

As argued previously, while these insights have contributed significantly in advancing the theories of borders and shifting interpretations away from territorial explanations and towards broader, diffused meanings of borders, these dispersed multiple meanings also tend to deflate the continued significance of cartographic demarcations and territorial delineations that South Asian nation-states vociferously engage in. The 'everywhere' theories take attention away from the experiences of those who are living at the territorial edges of the nation-state and often bearing violent consequences specific to these outer spatial boundaries. Similarly, the concept of 'borderwork', though commendable and appropriate in a wider and diffused context of borders, does not accurately capture the power dynamics between state and local actors living literally in the territorial border regions. The concept tends to depict the autonomous power of ordinary people in creating, collapsing or changing borders; such autonomy is not completely possible along the violent territorial borders of South Asia, where the state still maintains an upper hand in controlling borders. Though local residents do engage in processes of bordering in various ways and also contribute in influencing, shifting or breaching these boundaries in the long term, the concept of 'borderwork' cannot be applied here as the term does not attend to power asymmetries between people and the state. There are clear inequities of power between the state and residents of territorial border areas.

While partially concurring with Balibar's 'borders are everywhere thesis', the South Asian realities demonstrate that borders are particularly affective and consequential near the edges of the nation. Borders might be omnipresent in the form of surveillance, CCTV cameras, airport check points, or even gated communities, yet the most consequential, violent and life-threatening boundaries are still the territorial national borders in a South Asian context. To reiterate, the aim here is not to move towards the nation-state's geopolitical interpretation of borders. Rather, the idea is to emphasise the continued relevance of border studies that focus on the distinct nature and intensity of border conflicts, and negotiations or collaborations that are taking place at the peripheries of the nation-states in South Asia.

Taking the case of Jammu and Kashmir borderlands, this book has two broad aims: One, it seeks to demonstrate the South Asian situation of constantly volatile and sensitive borderlands and the continued fixation of the state (and of many mainstream non-state actors) with the idea of 'nation' as the supreme identity. Two, this book aims to point out the specificities of the J&K borderlands, which, in relative contrast to many other border zones (Sindh–Rajasthan, India–Bangladesh, India–Bhutan, India–Nepal) are constantly facing violence, instability and even contestation. The Line of Control in J&K is one of the borderlands in the region that still represents a temporary, contested and provisional India–Pakistan border.

The book also attempts to offer a holistic understanding of what is called 'the Kashmir conflict'. Till now, most works on the conflict have exclusively focused on the Kashmir region and the conflict politics emerging from this Valley. The voices of those living in border areas—who have been caught up in the conflict only due to their location along the India–Pakistan boundary—are completely obscured in these works. This book aims to foreground the voices and lives of people living in these borderlands to illustrate the ways in which these lives are intricately connected to the Kashmir conflict.

Borderlands in J&K do not simply materialise in the form of fences, walls and barbed wires. In fact, various components of the national sovereignty and its enforcement make borders appear sensitive and alive—security guards alert not just along the fenced areas but inside the villages and towns of the border zones as well (to watch out for silent infiltration of militants); symbols and signs prohibiting entry at various points in public spaces; military patrolling of various monuments, buildings, parks and even schools; limited mobility and various check points. All these everyday symbols and processes lead to the materialisation of borders. Additionally, the daily lives of the residents of these areas make these borders lively and dynamic by complying with and reinforcing the nation's boundaries as well as by challenging these territorial markers.[6] Borders are experienced through a synthesis of these symbolic, lived, processual and physical realities. This book will focus on diverse physical, symbolic and everyday performances at the borders. It will also look into diverse themes that characterise J&K borderlands—fencing and war at the borders; politics and culture of resistance; divided families; refugees; women living in borderlands; and everyday nationalism.

Every Border is Distinct

Despite studies on different kinds of borders, the theory on borderlands does not reflect much on the distinctness and diversity of borders. While the theories discuss the multiple usages or meanings of borders and boundaries, there is not much debate on the heterogeneity of borderlands and the conditions contributing to these differences. There are a few exceptions, such as Oscar Martinez's classification of borderlands (Martinez 1994) into four broad categories, contingent on the nature of interactions along borders—alienated, co-existent, interdependent and integrated borders. While these classifications provide useful criteria to understand and differentiate borderlands, the these categorisations are too broad and general to analyse and describe the diversity and uniqueness of border areas. South Asian borders are, for instance, viewed homogeneously, as violent, closed and militarised, without delving into the uniqueness and diversities of these borders.

In this book, we attempt to examine the diversity of borderlands within J&K. We look at two main kinds of borders that adjoin J&K—the international border and the Line of Control (which is the provisional and disputed border). These two kinds of borderlands within J&K are distinct in character and performance, and together they are also different from other South Asian borders. To reiterate, given the India–Pakistan conflict over the territory of J&K, their borderlands are constantly surveilled, politicised and heavily militarised, more so than many other borders in India or South Asia. These borderlands are fiercely contested in comparison to other relatively stable India–Pakistan borders, for instance the borders on the western periphery of India—the Rajasthan–Sindh border. Through an exhaustive study of the two main kinds of borders in Jammu and Kashmir and the different ways in which they impact their residents, this book aims to open up a debate on the diversity within the borderland discourse.[7]

This book seeks to highlight the implications of the ever-continuing volatility of borders, both the settled International Border or the not-so-settled LoC. It focuses on the impact that the arbitrary bordering (in the wake of the tribal invasion of 1947[8]) had on the lives of people; the way they were uprooted and forced to live the life of refugees for the rest of their lives; the trauma of their rehabilitation and the challenges they faced, including living around the border areas again and continuously facing its volatility. What is unique about the contributions in this book is their focus on the untold stories of the people who have become invisible and silent victims, not only of the hostilities between India and Pakistan but also of the official state positions and nationalist stances. It also seeks to underline the exceptional situation caused by the 'division' of the state between the Indian- and Pakistan-administrated areas. The experience of division for the people affected by it is quite like the experience of the Partition of the Indian subcontinent in 1947 and the creation of the two states of India and Pakistan, but with a difference. Unlike the Partition, the 'division' of J&K has not had its closure.[9] Partition has continuous and unending implications for the people—be they the refugees, the divided families, or those settled on the J&K borders. Several of the chapters reflect on the continuities of Partition and the transience of borders. Thus, one is given a fair idea as to how Partition conflict continues in varied forms, and how it is impacting the present-day lives and identities of people. All chapters in this edited volume focus on border areas that lie on the Indian side of J&K.

The focal point of this study is the erstwhile State[10] of Jammu and Kashmir as it existed before its reorganisation in 2019. At that time, it consisted of three main divisions—Kashmir, Jammu and Ladakh. In August 2019, the Government of India took the significant decision of reorganising the state by bifurcating it into two Union Territories—the Union Territory of Jammu and Kashmir and the Union Territory of Ladakh.[11] Notwithstanding the division of the state and the administrative separation of Ladakh from Jammu and Kashmir, we continue to focus on all the three divisions of the state as they existed from 1947 to 2019.

The book opens with a chapter by Rekha Chowdhary and Mohita Bhatia, titled 'Life in the Margins: Specificities of Borders in J&K (Chapter 2). This chapter flows out of this introductory chapter and focuses on the logic of the book. It highlights the specificities of borders in this erstwhile state and explains the distinct implications that the bordering process has on various kinds of people. It specifically emphasises the vast canvas of the border in this state and points out the distinction between the settled IB and the unsettled LoC It also focuses on the division of the state and the drawing of the ceasefire line, and the emergence of new categories of people affected by the division, such as the border people, the divided families and the POJK refugees. All three categories of people, as the chapter explains, face the consequences of the specific nature of the conflict and the resultant specific nature of the border in this erstwhile state, that is, not only the volatility of borders during war time or peace time, but also the transient and the contested nature of borders. It is this transient nature of the border that has led to innumerable miseries for thousands of people living close to borders, has resulted in keeping the issue of the rehabilitation of POJK refugees open, and has arbitrarily divided villages, communities and families into two hostile nations lacking normal channels of communication.

In Chapter 3, titled 'Bordering, People and Identities: International Border in Arnia', while analysing the history of the 'bordering' of an area that comes under IB, Rekha Chowdhary highlights the implications of the volatility of all the borders in J&K. She particularly argues that given the conflict situation in which J&K has been embroiled, all distinctions get dissolved here—whether between the unsettled or settled border, or between borders in war time or peace time. The 'settled' International Border is as militarised, unpredictable and volatile as the 'unsettled' LoC. Though Arnia is part of the settled border, it faces constant hostile activity in the form of firing and shelling, which displaces people quite often. This volatility, along with the mining and fencing, makes the day-to-day life of people quite difficult. Arnia is part of the area in Jammu and Kashmir that has endured a history of intense Partition trauma. Arnia's horrors of Partition and violence led to the mass migration of Muslims towards Pakistan as well as to an inflow of Hindu and Sikh refugees from the other side, who faced similar horrors accompanying the division of the state and were relocated to this area. For these Hindu and Sikh refugees, uprooted from their homes in 1947, their relocation to the border areas reflects their sheer marginality and helplessness, which gets doubly compounded by not only the constant uncertainties of the border but also by the lack of proper rehabilitation—many of them continue to face land-related insecurities as they do not enjoy ownership of the land given to them for cultivation.

Chapters 4 and 5 focus on divided families—Mohita Bhatia's study of divided families located in the border district of Rajouri ('So Close, Yet Far Apart: Borders and Divided Families in Rajouri and Poonch') and Seema Shekhawat's study of divided families in Kargil, a remote border district of Ladakh ('Contested Borders: Divided Families in the Kargil Region').

Both chapters focus on the continued trauma experienced by families arbitrarily divided between two hostile nations, with no easy access to communication or travel across the LoC. These chapters take the context of conflict beyond the Kashmir dispute. They tell us a different story of conflict being thrust upon border inhabitants and argue that while 'Kashmir' represents one dimension of conflict, 'border' represents another. Both the authors seek to show us how the story of division and separation that started in 1947 has continued to play out for the third generation, even while the members of the first generation of the divided families have passed away without fulfilling their desire to visit their homes and meet their close relatives. The story, as Bhatia informs, has various layers that speak of the multiple senses of belonging that cannot be defined in the limited discourse of nationalism. Apart from the ambiguities about the 'nationalist' sense of belonging, there remains confusion about the relationship between the sense of belonging to the land, and being part of the family and kinship group. In the complexity of their movement from one side to the other, what gets challenged are the institutionalised meanings of 'nation' and 'national imagination'.

A very interesting point made by Bhatia relates to the role played by the divided families in constructing, challenging as well as reinforcing borders and border-related activities. She argues that though 'bordering practices' is a top-down project, many bordering practices entail an engagement and participation of divided families. What is remarkable is the 'border terminologies' of members of the divided families that often influence the state to modify or reconstruct border-related practices. Using the example of the demand for opening the borders, Bhatia explains how their discourse offers a dialogic opportunity to the state and therefore helps the state to reduce the intensity of conflict.

The focus of Shekhawat's chapter is on the divided Shia families located in Kargil. She explains how the creation of borders was based on no particular principle other than the fact that the line of separation represented the respective state's control on the day of the ceasefire, be it the India–Pakistan war of 1948 or the wars of 1965 or 1971. The ceasefire line passed not only through valleys and mountains but also through villages and houses, leading to the division of thousands of families along the newly created borders. This is almost a permanent division of society. But there is much more to this division—it is a division not merely of villages but of a common history, cultures, markets and narratives.

An important point made by Shekhawat is that this division is not the result of any planned political understanding but one that has been thrust upon the people. The people were abruptly caught in the situation and remained stuck on either side of the border. On the basis of the various stories of separation, she refers to borderland as a pool of 'emotions, fears and memories'. Borders in J&K, she concludes, have a painful past, a traumatising present, and an uncertain future.

Continuing with the story of the ongoing implications of Partition is the story of what is commonly referred to as the POJK refugees or refugees who came from Pakistan-controlled Jammu and Kashmir to the Indian side of the state in 1947. Mohita Bhatia and Mamta Sharma in Chapter 6, 'Internally Displaced or Refugees?: Politics, Identities and Citizenship Experiences', note the intricate connection of the past with the present. The events of 1947 have not only continued to form the memories of POJK refugees, but have also continued to shape their present subjectivities, concerns and citizenship narratives. Suffering from the fear of loss of their cultural and political identities, they hold on to their identity and also idealise their past and pass on their memories to succeeding generations. Partition, therefore, lives and thrives in their memories and takes on multiple expressions. It is their complaint that their concerns do not fit in with the priorities of the local government. Feeling excluded from local Kashmiri politics, these refugees have been identifying strongly with Indian nationalism as well as viewing their victimisation, concerns, rights and sufferings from a religious standpoint. However, despite their strong identification with the Indian government and its nationalist narrative, they feel betrayed. As the state remains mired in broader territorial aspects of conflict, the POJK refugees feel marginalised and used by the political parties, whether national or local, who seek only to serve their political agendas.

Chakraverti Mahajan and Sandeep Singh's chapter (Chapter 7), 'Marginalisation and Borders: What Does it Mean to Live on the LoC?', examines how the division of the Jammu and Kashmir State into Jammu and Kashmir on the Indian side and POJK, symbolised by the LoC, has altered and distinctively affected the quotidian lives of the people living in border areas. The authors focus on the twin border districts of Poonch and Rajouri in Jammu and foreground the specific experiences of people who endure socio-economic uncertainties, unresolved land ownership issues and multiple displacements due to wars or everyday cross-border firing and shelling. However, they argue that a more profound impact of the bordering practices and numerous displacements has been the separation of these people from their kin, siblings and relatives residing on the other side. A large number of families in the borders areas of Poonch and Rajouri are part of the phenomenon of divided families, and many of them spend their entire lifespan without being able to meet their separated families.

An extremely interesting part of this chapter is the illustration of the experiences of people living in the 'sandwiched villages' that lie between the fencing and the actual LoC. These people view fencing as an important security aspect that protects them from infiltrators, and yet they feel extremely constrained and harassed by these surveillance measures. The authors argue that '[w]hile in the imagination of the rest of the country, the borders are romanticised as the symbols of national power, in reality the people residing in the border areas are rendered invisible'.

Chapter 8, titled 'Irrelevance of Borders? Cross-LoC Interactions, 2005–2019', by Rekha Chowdhary, is located in the realm of possibilities that lie between the apparently hardened state positions regarding borders and the situation in which the bordered people, especially the divided families, are stuck. While dealing with the cross-LoC interactions that were put in place in the wake of the 2004 peace process between India and Pakistan, she seeks to analyse the implications of 'softened borders' for various categories of people, especially the divided families. Unrealistic as it may seem in the present, when the hostility between India and Pakistan has reached a new peak and nationalist emotions have overtaken the desire for establishing peace, the chapter serves as a reminder that both India and Pakistan had invested huge efforts, goodwill and political resources in initiating confidence-building measures (CBM) related to cross-LoC interactions, and that this CBM had proved to be quite successful and productive, and had also had the approval of many stakeholders in J&K.

The purpose of including this chapter is not only to remind ourselves of the implication that this CBM had for the large number of people who could travel across the two sides of LoC but also to indicate the possibilities lying buried beneath the maximalist positions and hard stances of Indian, Pakistani and Kashmiri nationalist politics.

All the chapters in this book draw on qualitative methodology, mainly semi-structured and conversational interviews, focus group interviews and narrative analysis. The contributors have conducted fieldwork at different periods and phases between 2010–2014. However, they revisited their fieldwork in the last couple of years (2021–2023), either virtually or by making in-person trips to their respective areas of study. Bhatia, for instance, after revisiting her field of study in Poonch, Rajouri and Jammu in 2016–2017, conducted a few interviews over Skype and WhatsApp during the pandemic period of 2020–2021. Similarly, Chowdhary conducted various stints of fieldwork in the past 10 years, and relied on online interviews for additional information in the last couple of years. Other contributors have similarly engaged in fieldwork in person as well as through online conversations and interviews to substantiate and update their data. Mahajan and Singh also made a few visits to the field sites of Poonch and Rajouri border belt in 2021 to understand if there have been any changes due to the reorganisation of J&K and the reading down of Article 370. Virtual interviews as well as in-person field visits[12] reveal that the recent political changes have not made much of a difference in the quality of life of the people living close to the borders or being impacted by bordered situations. In fact, months after the changes, in 2020, the volatility of borders had increased, with more ceasefire violations and intensified firing and shelling (*Hindustan Times* 2020b).

Notes

1. On the Indian side, time and again, the official position is that by the Instrument of Accession signed by Maharaja Hari Singh, ruler of the erstwhile princely State of Jammu and Kashmir, on 26 October 1947, the whole of Jammu and Kashmir is an integral part of India. The 'whole of Jammu and Kashmir' includes the part that remains in the control of Pakistan, irrespective of the fact that LoC is the functional border that divides the part on the Indian side from the part that is under the control of Pakistan.

2. On 22 February 1994, following increasing terrorist violence and Pakistan's attempts to highlight the Kashmir dispute, both houses of the Indian Parliament unanimously adopted a resolution, parts of which are as follows (Available at https://www.satp.org/satporgtp/countries/india/document/papers/parliament_resolution_on_Jammu_and_Kashmir.htm [accessed December 2023]):

> This House note[s] with deep concern Pakistan's role in imparting training to the terrorists in camps located in Pakistan and Pakistan Occupied Kashmir, the supply of weapons and funds, assistance in infiltration of trained militants, including foreign mercenaries into

> Jammu and Kashmir with the avowed purpose of creating disorder, disharmony and subversion ....

The resolution strongly called upon 'Pakistan to stop forthwith its support to terrorism, which is in violation of the Simla Agreement and the internationally accepted norms of inter-State conduct and is the root cause of tension between the two countries'. The resolution also declared that '[t]he State of Jammu & Kashmir has been, is and shall be an integral part of India and any attempts to separate it from the rest of the country will be resisted by all necessary means' and demanded that 'Pakistan must vacate the areas of the Indian State of Jammu and Kashmir, which they have occupied through aggression'.

3. The India Meteorological Department (IMD) started mentioning areas under POJK (or Pakistan-occupied Jammu and Kashmir, which presently includes the districts of Muzaffarabad, Mirpur and parts of Poonch and Gilgit-Baltistan) in its daily weather bulletin. 'The India Meteorological Department (IMD) has been issuing weather bulletin for entire Jammu & Kashmir and Ladakh area. We are mentioning Gilgit-Baltistan, Muzaffarabad in the bulletin as they are the parts of India,' news agency ANI quoted IMD Director General Mrutyunjoy Mohapatra as saying (*Hindustan Times* 2020a).

4. During the peace process that was initiated between India and Pakistan, then Prime Minister Manmohan Singh held a number of Round Table Conferences and established five working groups. Of these groups, the working group on strengthening relations across the LoC was an important one. This working group suggested various measures to open up interactions among people living on both sides of the LoC. Apart from the availability of the cross-LoC bus service for the divided families, this group also suggested the extension of the bus service to groups visiting places of religious and tourist attractions, and opening of various other routes in J&K. See, the *Report of the Working Group* (2007).

5. It was in April 2005 that the first cross-LoC bus service was started. As per the 2005–2006 Report of the Home Ministry, in a short period (i.e., by the time the 2005–2006 Report was written), 'there have been 18 bus trips from Srinagar to Muzaffarabad and an equal number of trips from Muzaffarabad to Srinagar. 317 Indians visited Muzaffarabad, out of whom 265 have returned. Similarly,

365 Pakistanis visited Srinagar from PoK/Pakistan out of whom 324 have returned' (GoI 2006).

Initially it was a fortnightly bus service which was converted into a weekly bus service in 2008. As per the Annual Report of the Ministry of Home Affairs 2017–2018 (GoI 2018), by the end of 2017, a total of 10,666 passengers from the Indian side and 23,695 passengers from POJK had crossed the LoC.

6. Referring to borders in J&K, Sumona Dasgupta notes, 'whether "guarded" and "fenced" on the territorial landscape or faultlines that are imprinted on people's mindscapes—can collide and coalesce, creating myriad patterns that offer room both for creative dialogues as well as violent encounters' (Dasgupta 2012: 83).

7. If one seeks another unique case of borders which has its own complexities based on the context of cultural continuities on the one hand and conflict politics on the other, one can refer to the Northeast borders. They have its own unique issues related to economic marginalisation as well as insurgency and militancy. Though much has been written on these borders, no comparative analysis of the Northeast and Jammu and Kashmir has been attempted so far. For some understanding of border-related issues in the Northeast, one can refer to Barua (2020); Dutta (2002); Ghoshal (2020); Gogoi (2020); Sharma and Banerjee (2020).

8. Immediately before the Accession of the State of J&K with India, the NWFP tribals, with the support of Pakistani armed forces, invaded the state, as a result of which a large part of J&K came under the control of Pakistan. Although India succeeded in liberating many parts from Pakistan's control after the first war between India and Pakistan in 1947–1948, after the ceasefire Muzaffarabad, Mirpur and Poonch continued to be in Pakistan's control. For the people affected on two sides of the Ceasefire Line that took the shape of LoC later, it was a sudden and arbitrary bordering process.

9. The division of J&K between the Indian side and the Pakistan-controlled areas remains conflictual and since neither India nor Pakistan recognises the division, its dissolution is also not possible. On the contrary, people have to face the implications of the division on an almost daily basis.

10. Throughout this book, 'erstwhile state' refers to the State of Jammu and Kashmir before its reorganisation into Union Territories in 2019.

11. This decision to bifurcate the erstwhile State of Jammu and Kashmir along with the decision to abrogate the special constitutional status of the state as guaranteed by Article 370 of the Indian Constitution was taken by the Bharatiya Janata Party (BJP)-led NDA-II government. Article 370 mandated that only Article 1 and Article 370 applied to this state. For the rest of the provisions of the Indian Constitution to be extended to the state, there was a requirement of consent by the state. There was also a restriction on the application of the laws made by the Union Parliament, even though these laws could be extended to the state with the approval of the latter. In reality, however, the special constitutional status of the state was quite compromised. By various Presidential Orders passed since 1954, several provisions of the Indian Constitution were extended to the state. Though the state had its own Constitution, yet in the structure of its governance, the state was brought almost at par with the other Indian states. The autonomy underlying Article 370 had been hollowed out, and its spirit now existed mostly in symbolic terms (such as the state having its own Constitution, its flag and its residence law). However, whatever little autonomy was enjoyed by the state was taken away in August 2019, as the clauses restricting the application of the Constitution of India (as also the application of the central legislations) to this state were deleted from Article 370.

Both these changes—the revocation of the special constitutional status of J&K and the reorganisation of the state—have been the responses of the BJP government to the conflict situation in which this erstwhile state has been embroiled since 1947. The BJP, since its earlier avatar of the Bharatiya Jana Sangh (BJS), has been ideologically opposed to the special constitutional status of J&K and has been demanding the withdrawal of Article 370 since the 1950s. The non-applicability of the Constitution of India in its entirety to this state, as accorded by Article 370, has been seen as incomplete sovereignty of the Indian State and therefore as a threat to national security. Syama Prasad Mukerjee, the founder of the BJS, entered into a debate with Jawaharlal Nehru and Sheikh Abdullah on this issue in a series of correspondence (see Grover and Arora [1999] for 'Mookerjee-Nehru-Abdullah Correspondence [9 January 1953 to 23 February 1953]'). The BJS also supported a local agitation in Jammu demanding the abolition of Article 370 in 1952 (Baxter

1969). Even though Article 370 and the constitutional autonomy of J&K had been diluted by successive Indian governments since 1947, the BJP had continued to demand the abolition of the Article in an absolute sense. It had always proclaimed its intent to abolish Article 370 once it came into power. The party has been linking the militant separatist movement in Kashmir region with the special constitutional status of the state, holding Article 370 responsible for the separatist psyche in this region.

12. Names of all the respondents mentioned throughout this book have been changed to protect their identity.

References

Balibar, E. 2002. *Politics and the Other Scene*. London: Verso.

Barua, Sanjib. 2020. *In the Name of the Nation: India and its Northeast*. California: Stanford University Press.

Baxter, Craig. 1969. *The Jana Sangh: A Biography of an Indian Political Party*. Philadelphia: University of Pennsylvania Press.

Cooper, Anthony. 2020. 'How do We Theorise Borders, and Why Should We Do It?: Some Theoretical and Methodological Challenges'. In Anthony Cooper and Seren Tinning (eds), *Debating and Defining Borders: Philosophical and Theoretical Perspectives*. London: Routledge.

Dasgupta, Sumona. 2012. 'Borderland and Borderlines: Re-negotiating Boundaries in Jammu and Kashmir'. *Journal of Borderland Studies* 27(1): 88–93.

Donnan, Hastings and Thomas M. Wilson. 1999. *Borders: Frontiers of Identity, Nation and State*. Oxford: Berg Publishers.

Dutta, Sristidhar. 2002. *Cross-Border Trade of North-East India: The Arunachal Perspective*. Kolkata: Maulana Abul Kalam Azad Institute of Asian Studies.

Ghoshal, Anindita. 2020. *Refugees, Borders and Identities: Rights and Habitat in East and Northeast India*. Oxon and New York: Routledge.

Gogoi, Dilop. 2020. *Geopolitics of Borderland and Transnational Interactions*. Oxon and New York: Routledge

GoI. 2006. *Annual Report 2005–06*, Ministry of Home Affairs. Available at https://www.mha.gov.in/sites/default/files/AnnualReport_05_06.pdf (accessed February 2024).

———. 2018. *Annual Report 2017–18*, Ministry of Home Affairs. Available at https://www.mha.gov.in/sites/default/files/AnnualReport_17_18.pdf (accessed February 2024).

Grover, Verinder and Ranjana Arora (eds). 1999. *50 Years of Indo-Pak Relations: Chronology of Events, Important Documents from 1947 to 1998*. New Delhi: Deep & Deep.

Herrschel, Tassilo. 2011. *Borders in Post-Socialist Europe: Territory, Scale, Society.* Farnham, UK: Ashgate Publishing.

Hindustan Times. 2020a. 'Areas in Pakistan occupied Kashmir now in weather department's forecast', 7 May. Available at https://www.hindustantimes.com/india-news/areas-in-pakistan-occupied-kashmir-now-in-weather-department-forecast/story-vpnunRAqwvnYFubyxTfJyJ.html (accessed December 2023).

———. 2020b. 'J&K: Highest number of ceasefire violations by Pak in 2020 since 2003 truce'. Available at J&K: Highest number of ceasefire violations by Pak in 2020 since 2003 truce | Latest News India – Hindustan Times (accessed February 2024).

Johnson, Benjamin H. and Andrew R. Graybill (eds). 2010. *Bridging National Borders in North America: Transnational and Comparative Histories*. Durham and London: Duke University Press.

Martinez, Oscar J. 1994. *Border People: Life and Society in the US–Mexico Borderlands*. Tucson: University of Arizona Press.

Mau, Steffen, Hause Brabandt, Lena Laube and Christof Roos (eds). 2012. *Liberal States and the Freedom of Movement: Selective Borders, Unequal Mobility*. Houndmills, UK: Palgrave Macmillan.

Mint. 2019. 'PoK in UT of Jammu and Kashmir, Gilgit-Baltistan in Ladakh in new map of India', 2 November. Available at https://www.livemint.com/news/india/pok-in-ut-of-jammu-and-kashmir-gilgit-baltistan-in-ladakh-in-new-map-of-india-11572714194790.html (accessed February 2024).

Paasi, Anssi. 2011. 'A Border Theory: An Unattainable Dream or a Realistic Aim for Border Scholars?' In Doris Wastl-Walter (ed.), *The Ashgate Research Companion to Border Studies*. Farnham, UK: Ashgate Publishing.

Reeves, Madeleine. 2018. 'Intimate Militarism: Domesticating the Border in Rural Central Asia'. In Alexander Horstmann, Alessandro Rippa and Martin Saxer (eds), *Routledge Handbook of Asian Borderlands*. Oxon and New York: Routledge.

Report of the Working Group. 2007. *Strengthening Relations Across the Line of Control*, January.

Rumford, C. 2008. *Cosmopolitan Spaces: Europe, Globalization, Theory*. New York: Routledge.

Sharma, Chandan Kumar and Roshni Banerjee (eds). 2020. *Fixed Borders, Fluid Boundaries: Identity, Resources and Mobility in Northeast India*. Oxon and New York: Routledge.

van Schendel, Willem. 2005. *The Bengal Borderland: Beyond State and Nation in South Asia*. London: Anthem Press.

Wastl-Walter, Doris (ed.). 2011. *The Ashgate Research Companion to Border Studies*. Farnham, UK: Ashgate Publishing.

II

Life in the Margins

Specificities of Borders in J&K

Rekha Chowdhary and Mohita Bhatia

Borders in Jammu and Kashmir: Settled and Unsettled

The erstwhile State of Jammu and Kashmir, now turned into a Union Territory, could be defined as a 'border state' as borders ran along a substantial part of its three divisions, whether in the form of the International Border (IB), Line of Control (LoC) or Actual Ground Position Line (AGPL). The IB is the settled border between India and Pakistan, while LoC is the unsettled border.[1] The AGPL runs through the Siachen sector in Ladakh. While the LoC forms a larger part of the border (around 788 kms), the IB measures 210 kms, and the AGPL is around 150 kms.

The extensive coverage of the borders within J&K is reflected in the fact that, of the 22 total districts of the undivided State of J&K, the border ran through 10 districts. Of these, five districts fall in Jammu division, namely Jammu, Samba, Kathua, Rajouri and Poonch. Meanwhile, both the districts of Ladakh—Leh and Kargil—are border districts. In Kashmir division, the border runs through three districts—Badgam, Baramulla and Kupwara. Table 2.1 provides district- and block-wise details of borders in J&K state before it was bifurcated.

Since, apart from the recognised and settled border, a large part of the border that passes through this erstwhile state

Map 2.1: Map of UT Jammu & Kashmir and UT of Ladakh

Source: GoI (2019).

is unsettled, it becomes important to make the distinctions regarding the border very clear.

The IB is the recognised or settled boundary between India and Pakistan that was demarcated by the Radcliffe Award. Following the division of the country, the boundary between the two countries was demarcated and approved by the Boundary Commissions of India and Pakistan and named after Sir Cyril Radcliffe, the joint chairman of the two commissions. It is the Radcliffe Line that is known as the International Border that passes through Jammu and Kashmir and extends towards other states, namely Punjab, Rajasthan and Gujarat.

The IB that runs through J&K is located mainly in the Jammu division. This border runs along the River Ravi in the south of Jammu region to Mannawar Tawi in the north. It runs

Table 2.1: Details of Borders in J&K State*

District	No. of Blocks	Name of Blocks	Nature of the Border
Jammu and Samba	8	Samba, Vijaypur, Bishnah, RS Pura, Satwari, Marh, Akhnoor, Khour	IB and LoC
Kathua	4	Ghagwal, Hiranagar, Barnoti, Kathua	IB
Rajouri	4	Sundarbani, Nowshera, Rajouri, Manjakote	LoC
Poonch	4	Balakote, Mendhar, Poonch, Mandi	LoC
Badgan	1	Khag	LoC
Baramulla	7	Booniyar, Gurez, Tangmarg, Baramulla, Ruhama, Uri, Dangiwacha	LoC
Kupwara	9	Tangdhar, Kralpora, Trehgam, Kupwara, Sogam, Langate, Rajwar, Ramahal, Teethwal	LoC
Kargil	3	Drass, Kargil, Shaker, Chikten	LoC
Leh **	2	Khaltsi, Nubra	LoC
Total	42		

Notes: *Districts and Blocks as these existed before reorganisation of the State of J&K. **Besides these, there are two blocks in Leh (Nyouma and Durbu) which share a border with China.
Source: Compiled from various district profiles of Jammu and Kashmir.

through three districts of Jammu—Kathua, Samba and Jammu. Rivers and rivulets mark the border as well. Two important rivers that run across the borders are the River Basentar that runs from Samba in Jammu towards Pasrur in Pakistan, and the River Aik that runs around Arnia town in Jammu towards

Sialkot in Pakistan.[2] The city of Jammu is only 28 kms away from the IB and is situated only 40 kms away from Sialkot, an important town in Pakistan.

One major feature of the IB that needs to be noted is that even before it was recognised as the International Border in the pre-Partition period, there already was a marked boundary between the princely State of J&K and the neighbouring province of Western Punjab. Since Western Punjab joined Pakistan during Partition, the boundary between J&K and Punjab came to be recognizes as the International Boundary. Due to its proximity to the plains of Punjab, the areas near the IB mostly share the topographic features of Punjab, particularly the fertile land as well as the relative prosperity of the area. Compared to the mountainous terrain of the LoC, the IB area is much more accessible, connected and semi-urban in nature. Another peculiarity of the IB is the sociological and demographic character of the area. The area falls in the Dogra belt and is comprised of Dogri-speaking people in the districts of Jammu, Samba and Kathua. Before 1947, it had a large population of Muslims; however, after the Partition violence affected this area, it now comprises a predominantly Hindu population. But a large population that has been settled around the IB is comprised of one or the other kind of 'refugees'. These 'refugees' , who lack a formal status, are displaced people, many of whom were displaced from the princely State of Jammu and Kashmir that came under the control of Pakistan. They are known as POJK refugees, that is, those who had migrated from Pakistan-controlled Jammu and Kashmir. Another category of refugees includes those who came from outside the princely State, mainly from the undivided Punjab, and are known as West Pakistan Refugees (WPRs).

Quite distinct from the IB is the Line of Control (LoC). LoC is not the formal border between India and Pakistan but rather a *de facto* border marking the internal divide between two parts of Jammu and Kashmir—Jammu and Kashmir on the Indian side and Pakistan-controlled Jammu and Kashmir (POJK). Emerging after the tribal invasion of Jammu and Kashmir in 1947 and the subsequent war between India and Pakistan in 1947–1948, it is unsettled and in the nature of a working border, representing only the control of the two countries over the respective areas. The LoC is therefore not only an unsettled border but also a mark of the ongoing conflict between India and Pakistan over Jammu and Kashmir (Shukla 2013).[3]

This dividing line was initially the one around which ceasefire took place after the 1948 war between India and Pakistan. Known therefore as the Ceasefire Line, it was 'drawn on the basis of positions held by the combatants at the time of [when] fighting between them ended' (Wirsing 1998: 62). Though it was supposed to be a 'temporary' border, pending the resolution of the conflict, it has continued to serve as the *de facto* or the working border that divides the two sides of Jammu and Kashmir and Ladakh. After the subsequent wars between India and Pakistan in 1965 and 1971, there were some minor alterations in this line. However, it was formalised and renamed as the Line of Control (LoC) after the 1971 war.

One specificity of LoC lies in its transitory nature. To reiterate, compared to the settled border of IB, it is seen more as a working boundary that signals a dispute over its status. Awaiting a final resolution, it lacks the legitimacy of the International Border. Ranabir Samaddar argues that rather than being recognised as a settled border, it remains 'merely a line of control functioning as a border, but lacking its sanctity' (Samaddar 2004: 86). Happymon Jacob also refers to its transitional nature. Unlike the IB, the LoC, in his words, is a 'notional line rather than an actual one' (Jacob 2017).

Being an arbitrarily drawn line, the LoC has not only divided the princely State of Jammu and Kashmir but has also divided the people. People belonging to the same kinship groups, communities and even the same families came to be divided almost on a permanent basis. The effect of division was felt by people all over the state. While a large part of Jammu came to be divided by the LoC, the division also affected Ladakh and parts of Kashmir.[4]

Despite all the distinctions that exist between the two kinds of borders—the IB and LoC—what remains common is the volatility of borders. Both borders have witnessed the implications of four wars[5] and two war-like[6] situations (Samaddar 2004: 79). Beyond the times of war, the times of peace have also been marked by firing and shelling. The situation during the last three decades has been more precarious, with armed militancy providing a new context to the conflict situation.[7] Since most of the militants infiltrated from the Pakistan side of the LoC to the Indian side, the borders became more active. As Pavan Nair notes about the period of militancy, shelling and exchange of fire became the order of the day. Infiltration by militants was accompanied by artillery, mortar and small arms fire from the Pakistani side, thus adversely affecting normal life. A few odd casualties of soldiers as well as civilians were a daily occurrence around the border (Nair 2013). It was only during a brief period after 2003, when a ceasefire agreement was put in place between India and Pakistan, that people could have a sense of relief and could pursue normal life. The ceasefire was a part of the peace process that had been informally initiated in 2003 by then Indian Prime Minister Atal Bihari Vajpayee and formally launched in January 2003.[8] Though the peace process was preceded by aggressive hostilities between the two nations—in the form of the Kargil War in 1999 and the stand-off between the forces of the two sides following the 13 December 2001 militant attack on the Indian Parliament—it was quite a successful agreement, at least in the initial years.

However, this ceasefire could not last for a long time. Frequent ceasefire violations started taking place after 2007.[9] The cases of violation started increasing by 2013 and assumed dangerous proportions by 2017 and 2018[10] (Krishnan 2019). Ceasefire violations continued in 2020. In fact, 2020 turned out to be year with the highest number of ceasefire violations.[11]

With so many ceasefire violations, life becomes really difficult for the people living close to the border. This is specifically so for Jammu region (especially along the IB in Jammu, Kathua and Samba districts as well as along the LoC in Poonch and Rajouri districts). To begin with, such a large number of ceasefire violations led to a large number of killings, not only of security persons but also of civilians. As we can see from the official data, every year since 2015, the number of killings of civilians as well as security forces has been increasing. Thus in 2015, 10 security personnel and 16 civilians were killed; in 2016, 13 security persons and 13 civilians were killed; in 2017, 19 security persons and 12 civilians were killed; and in 2018, 38 security persons and 31 civilians were killed (Krishnan 2019). Apart from those killed, there are large numbers of injured people. In 2018, for instance, more than 250 people were injured due to cross-border firing and shelling (*The Hindu Businessline* 2019). The number of killings and injuries was quite high in 2020 as well. As per PIB (2021) , 71 civilians and 126 security personnel were injured in ceasefire violations in 2020.

So dangerous becomes life around the border areas that many people are forced to migrate from their places of residence to safer places. In May 2018, for instance, there was such heavy shelling and firing on the IB in Jammu, Samba and Kathua districts, that in all 76,000 people had to flee from their own homes and move to makeshift camps (see *India Today* 2018; Pargal 2018a; Sharma 2018). Though not located at the zero line, the town of Arnia was so impacted that all the people had to be evacuated to safer places.

Conflict in J&K: The Peculiar Historical Context of the Border

The 'border' context of conflict in Jammu and Kashmir had remained away from the gaze of political analysts and researchers. The conflict situation in the state has been the focus of numerous studies, but most of these studies have been centred around the 'Kashmir context' or the Kashmiri separatist movement and have not analysed areas and issues beyond it. There is no doubt that issues related to Kashmir form the core context of conflict, whether seen from internal or external perspectives. Yet it is pertinent to emphasise that conflict has a complex multilayered nature. Beyond Kashmir, there are many layers and dimensions of conflict which remain invisible. 'Border' is one such dimension which has either not been given due attention by political analysts or, if analysed, is seen from the perspective of the state. As mentioned, this volume seeks to analyse the 'border' context of conflict from the perspective of the people whose lives have been linked with it in one way or another. The common thread that runs through these chapters relates to the context of conflict in J&K, beyond its conventional understanding.

Focusing on borders as the conflict zones/spaces, this volume highlights a) the specificity of the border context of conflict; b) the peculiar nature of the borders of J&K; and c) the specific issues faced by the people in these borders.

As mentioned earlier, the borders of J&K, have peculiar characteristics—quite different not only from other borders that India shares with countries other than Pakistan, but also different from the India–Pakistan border in states like Punjab and Rajasthan. What distinguishes the border of J&K from the borders in these states is the very context of conflict in which the former has been embroiled.

The specific situation of conflict in J&K was the result of developments that took place during the 1947–1948 period. As one of the largest princely states of India, this state acceded to India on 26 October 1947 (much after the deemed deadline of August 1947) in the midst of an invasion by tribals from the NWFP area of Pakistan (supported by Pakistan's armed forces) on the one hand and internal turbulence within some parts of Jammu region, especially in the Poonch and Mirpur areas, on the other. A full-fledged war between India and

Pakistan that followed the accession ultimately resulted in pushing the tribals and Pakistan's forces back from many parts of the state, although a substantial part remained under the control of Pakistan. By the time the ceasefire was formalised in 1949,[12] a whole belt of Jammu region comprising the districts of Muzaffarabad and Mirpur, and a large part of Poonch district remained under the control of Pakistan. The ceasefire line drawn at this time formed the temporary border that came to be known as the Line of Control after the Shimla Agreement.[13] With Pakistan contesting the accession of the state with India and India claiming the whole of J&K, including the part under Pakistan's control, J&K has been a bone of contention between India and Pakistan with not only a number of wars fought between the two countries,[14] but also continuous tensions on the borders, during times of both war and peace.

Much of the bordering process has been violent and has resulted in huge material, economic and human loss. This has been more so in the case of LoC. In fact, the very division of the state and the emergence of this border was in itself a violent phenomenon. In the backdrop of this border being drawn in the form of the Ceasefire Line in 1949, there was a lot of disruption in the normal lives of people. The tribals occupied large parts of the state, including the districts of Muzaffarabad and Mirpur, and controlled most parts of Poonch district as well. There were areas which witnessed massive violence. Thus, there was a lot of bloodshed in all these areas with many people killed and many others forced to evacuate. There were towns that were under siege for months together. Poonch town was isolated from the rest of J&K and was under siege by the tribals for 14 months. Rajouri town was similarly under siege for nine months. Both these towns along with many other parts of J&K, including those in Ladakh, were liberated by Indian forces in 1948. However, many other areas could not be liberated.

As things stood at the time of ceasefire, the state was divided between India and Pakistan. While most parts of Kashmir region (with the exception of areas beyond Uri and Kupwara, which came under the control of Pakistan) remain unaffected, the other two regions of the state were heavily impacted. Ladakh lost the entire Gilgit-Baltistan area and the area beyond Kargil, including Skardu, Hunza, Nagar, Astore. These areas went to the Pakistan side. In Jammu region, the western region was severely impacted. While Poonch and Rajouri towns were liberated, areas beyond these—Kotli, Mirpur, Bhimber, Muzaffarabad, Haitian, Kishenganga or Neelam Valley, Poonch Haveli, Bagh, Sudhnoti—were under the control of Pakistan and now formed the POJK.

This conflict has made both the settled IB and the not-so-settled LoC quite difficult and complicated. This is more so in the case of the LoC that divides the two sides of this erstwhile princely state. Even when the state has been divided and the LoC has been operating as a working border between the Jammu and Kashmir (India) and POJK, both India and Pakistan refuse to see these as final/settled borders. Both have been making claims over the territory beyond the borders. This leads to an exceptional situation of borders—being very much present and yet not officially acknowledged as such. The border not only has a 'transient' nature and an unresolved character, but also an 'open' situation which often accentuates the very context of conflict and at the same time impacts the lives of the people in so many ways.

A significant number of people have been impacted by this context of conflict and the peculiar nature of these borders. In fact, the period saw the emergence of new categories of people—categories which did not exist earlier, like of 'border people', POJK refugees, or the 'divided families'. Each category comprises of a group of people who were impacted by the conflict in a particular way. For instance, the border people lived close to the border, and their lives, livelihood, mobility, and living conditions were all impacted by the contentious nature of the borders. The category of refugees comprised of all those people who were forced to leave their homes in Pakistan-controlled Jammu and Kashmir and were now waiting to be rehabilitated on the Indian side of Jammu and Kashmir. The category of divided families comprised of those families living on the Indian side of Jammu and Kashmir, with close relatives in POJK.

The border story has generally remained invisible and therefore the voices of all these categories of people have remained subordinated to either the larger statist perspective of conflict or the Kashmir-centric perspective. That the perspective of people on the volatile borders needs its own voice has been emphasised in a recent work by Anam Zakaria (2018), who has analysed the issue from the people's perspective on the other side of the LoC. In her ethnographic work titled *The Great Divide: A Journey into Pakistan Administered Kashmir*, Zakaria studies the impact of the division of the princely State of J&K and the volatility of borders on people, particularly women and children. Challenging the statist narrative, she makes important points about the common suffering of people on both sides of the LoC as well as the common demand for peace and stability in the region. As she argues, 'violence' and 'migration' as the Partition-linked phenomenon have continued to impact people in the region—whether it is the divided families or the people living in villages on the border.

More peculiar is the silence around the issues related to women. As one goes to the field in the border areas, one does understand that women were not only the worst victims of sexual violence during 1947, but they also continued to bear the brunt of various implications of the post-1947 situation, particularly the process of bordering. However, despite a clear-cut gendered dimension of division and bordering in J&K, there seems to be a total silence in the literature on this aspect. In recent times, some efforts have been made to focus on the gender dimension of conflict in J&K, such as in Sumona Dasgupta's study (2012) and Anuradha Bhasin Jamwal and Shuchismita's study (2012). Focusing on borders from the gender perspective, both studies, seek to bring women to the centre of border analysis.

As our study also shows, the statist perspective on borders has suppressed the voices of the people affected by the continued hostility between India and Pakistan. It is because of the maximalist positions taken by both countries and their emphasis on 'territorial sovereignty' that the people in the border regions of J&K have continued to suffer during the last seven-and-a-half decades. The saga of people's trauma started in 1947 and continues in one form or the other even now.

Bordering and its Consequences: An Ongoing Process

The very process of 'bordering' was quite volatile—not only for the LoC drawn arbitrarily, but also for the IB that was otherwise formalised and settled. Similar to the Partition of the Indian subcontinent, the partition of J&K also witnessed chaos, riots and violence. People fell prey to religion-based violence on both sides of these boundaries. Many lost their lives and many more were uprooted and lost their homes. With the exception of the valley of Kashmir,[15] which was spared the trauma of being 'bordered', most areas of the state went through the anguishing 'Partition' spectacle—communal frenzy, looting, killing, abduction and dislocation. Similar to the other areas impacted by Partition-related violence elsewhere in the Indian subcontinent, women had to face sexual violence and many of them were abducted.[16] While, for the rest of the subcontinent, the 'Partition' was soon to acquire the status of history, for J&K, the trauma continued. With their rehabilitation and relocation in India, the Partition victims, though deeply bruised, were given closure. But for the J&K refugees, there was neither a process of final rehabilitation nor a closure. Partition, therefore, was not a settled history, but a living problem that continued with unsettled and contested borders. Since both India and Pakistan recognised the LoC as a working border but also simultaneously contested it, the border here became a zone of ambivalence and uncertainty.

This ambivalence was reflected not only in the approach of the respective states, but also in the response of the people affected by it. Despite acquiring a heavily securitised character, the borders were porous and there was continuous movement of people across the 'border'. Even though the largest movement of people on both sides took place in the 1947–1948 period, the movement of people from one side to the other continued for many years after that. There was no particular direction of movement—people could be moving on any side, going from the Indian side of Jammu and Kashmir to the Pakistani side or vice versa, depending not so much on love for a particular nation as for pragmatic reasons of land and livelihood on the one hand and being close to their families and relatives on the other. Even when it was difficult to the militarised borders, their movement from one side to the other could not be stopped. And for quite a long time, they continued to maintain their social bonds. Cross-LoC marriages therefore continued to take place. Of course, the routes used were not the legal ones, but the ones that passed through the mountains and forests.

The year 1965, marked by the India–Pakistan war, saw another major movement of people, mainly in the background of the mass infiltration of Pakistani *Razakars*. Much before the war started, the Pakistan army had sent its infiltrators to organise local insurgency, both in Kashmir Valley and in the border areas of Poonch in Jammu division. While these infiltrators could not succeed in organising a local rebellion against the Indian state in Kashmir Valley, in the border areas of Poonch, they could establish limited 'liberated areas' with the locals managing administration and, to some, even extent supporting the Razakars (Choudhary 2012). However, fearing retaliation by the army, many of them went across to the

Pakistani side in large numbers. Many of them returned later, over the years, but many could not.

Till 1965, it was not uncommon for people to visit across the border and come back. However, after the 1965 war, borders started becoming stringent. This started affecting the families divided on both sides. However, the crossing was not stopped altogether, and despite all the difficulties, some people continued to cross. Marriages also continued to take place between the two sides. While many of the people took recourse to the visa route, many others continued to take the traditional local but 'illegal' routes. It was only after the onset of Kashmiri separatist militancy in the 1990s that movement was totally curbed. By this time, border surveillance had become much more intense and almost the entire border was fenced and sealed.

Divided Families

It was in this process of bordering and movement of people that families were divided and blood relations came to acquire different 'national' and even religious identities. Worse consequences were to follow as these 'divided families' across the border were unable to communicate with each other. Being part of two antagonistic countries, they had to bear the burden of hostility between these countries. While the entire State of J&K was impacted by the phenomenon of divided families, the twin border districts of Poonch and Rajouri in Jammu region were more intensely affected. Almost every Muslim family in these districts has relatives across the LoC. The impact of the division has also been felt in Kargil in Ladakh. Here, a large number of people of the Balti race were separated from their close relatives across the border in Baltistan. Similarly, one finds a significant number of divided families in the Baramulla-Kupwara border sector in Kashmir.

Till 1965, there was some possibility of communication through telephones and letters. This became difficult later. The only possibility to meet their relatives was through the long and cumbersome official route of applying for visas to Pakistan. To visit their relatives living in the vicinity of around 50–100 kms, they had to take a longer visa route. The nearest visa route that passed through the neighbouring state of Punjab (Amritsar-Lahore) would take a minimum of three to four days. The visa requirements meanwhile were quite the hassle. People had to apply a number of times and even then, they would not succeed in getting it. With too many procedures and legalities, it was almost impossible to meet their relatives or even communicate with them. As direct communication was almost stopped after 1965, much of the correspondence would take place through any third country, that is, via the relatives and friends who might have settled there. A lot of such communication would pass through the UK or Dubai, for instance. That is why even the news of the death of a close relative would at times reach the other side of the border after months.

The irony of the situation is best understood in the case of Teetwal village on the Indian side and Chilean village in Pakistan. Between the two villages flows the river Kishenganga/Neelum. The people in these two villages are close relatives and can see each other across the banks of the mighty 100-metre wide roaring river from their respective sides. They wave their hands and signboards, but cannot do more than that. There is a convenient bridge in between (Teetwal bridge) which had been constructed in 1931 and could be used, but due to the blocked communication, it is rarely used now.

Kinship provides a very strong bond that keeps the divided families close to their relatives across the LoC. Living the trauma of separation, these people have such a strong desire to be connected with their relatives across the border, that they take an ambivalent view of the borders and national distinctions. Rather than defining distinct national identities, borders are seen as barriers that need to be crossed. This is a complex phenomenon which has been explained by Radhika Gupta in her study of Balti divided families in Kargil, in terms of contradictory emotions of 'belonging' and 'longing' (Gupta 2013: 47–71). The 'longing' to be with the kinship group is different from the 'sense of belonging' as members of a nation. For the divided Balti families on the Indian side of the LoC, there is simultaneously 'a strong sense of belonging to India and at the same time, a longing for Baltistan (in Pakistan).' She makes it very clear that this longing for Baltistan has nothing to do with their choice of 'political membership' of India as a nation. But this is an emotion which is linked with their urge to be with their kin without the obstacle of borders and their various hassles.

Displaced and Dislocated people

It was not only the people of 'divided families' who were caught up in the peculiar border situation of Jammu and Kashmir. Many others were also dislocated and displaced. The process of dislocation that started in 1947 continues till date.

Since the division of the state resulted in the largest dislocation of people, by the time the first war between India and Pakistan ended and the ceasefire line was drawn in 1948, the demography on both sides of the divided state had changed drastically. While a large part of the Muslim population migrated from the Jammu division towards Pakistan and Pakistan-controlled Kashmir, the Hindus from Pakistan-controlled Kashmir, particularly from Mirpur, Kotli and Muzaffarabad, migrated to Jammu region.

Displacement, however, did not end with the 1947 'disturbances' but continued in the later period. During every subsequent war, the people residing in the border areas had to move out for long periods of time. In the wake of the 1965 war between India and Pakistan, a large number of people had to migrate from the areas closer to the borders. As stated above, one of the larger migrations at this time took place in the twin districts of Poonch and Rajouri. However, the classic case of dislocation is that of Chhamb refugees. Chhamb, a town in the Aknoor sector in the western region of the LoC, was ceded by India to Pakistan after the 1971 war. Since the inhabitants were mostly Hindus, they were relocated to the Indian side. As many as 4,300 families were relocated and were later settled in Jammu district around the International Border.[17]

Border-related displacement continued in later periods. More particularly, during the Kargil War between India and Pakistan in 1999, as per the Government of J&K data, over 35,000 families were displaced (Press Trust of India 2013). Though the actual fight took place in Dras and Kargil areas of Ladakh region, the army was mobilised all around the border areas and hence civilians were evacuated from these areas. Again, there was a massive mobilisation of armed forces in the border regions of J&K after the 2001 attack on the Indian Parliament, once again leading to the evacuation and dislocation of people. As per Ministry of Home Affairs (2005), about 30,771 families comprising 1,53,131 persons were displaced from border areas of Jammu.[18]

Refugees—An Ambivalent Term

Many among those displaced in 1947 from the areas that came under the control of Pakistan term themselves 'refugees', but their 'refugee' status is ambivalent. For all practical purposes, these are the people who are at par with the Indian Partition refugees of Punjab or Bengal. Just like the Indian Partition refugees, they have suffered violence and have been uprooted from their villages, lands and homes. They could not return to their homes and had to pick up the threads of their lives in their new adopted homes. However, the similarity between the two cases ends at this point. Unlike the Partition refugees, they have not been rehabilitated by the state. No assessment of their losses has ever been made and no proper rehabilitation attempted by the state. At the most they have been given some land to settle down on and to cultivate, but without any proprietary rights. They have been denied the status of 'Partition refugees' because they belong to the area in Pakistan-controlled Jammu and Kashmir that India has claimed as its own. So they are considered internally displaced rather than Partition refugees. Even though they share the same Partition experiences of violence, killing, losing their homes, lands and livelihood, they have not had the closure that the other Partition refugees have had.

Living in the Borderland: Everyday Struggle

'Partition' for these POJK refugees, as for the 'divided families', is not a 'past situation' from which they have 'moved on' but an ever-continuing present with which they struggle on a day-to-day basis. But these are not the only people who have fallen victim to the conflict politics in which the State of Jammu and Kashmir has been embroiled for the last seven decades. There are many others who reside on the border and experience the conflict situation 'live'. With the exception of a brief period in 2003–2009 when ceasefire was properly enforced, volatility has defined the borders.[19] Regardless of whether it is a time of war or peace, people on the borders have been unable to live their lives in a relaxed manner. Peace and normalcy can be disrupted at any time by provoked or unprovoked firing and shelling. People here have to face a number of hazards, including stray bullets and shells, or mine-related accidents. Almost every war or warlike situation leads to mines being laid in large areas, and despite a process of de-mining, a lot of mine-related accidents occur, leading to loss of life or injuries. The process of mining also leads to a loss of control over cultivable land. Besides mining, fencing has kept a large portion of cultivable land out of bounds for the border residents. As a fallout of armed militancy and the infiltration of a large number of militants from various parts of the porous border, a project to fence the whole border area was undertaken. However, due to resistance from across the border, the fence was at many places constructed way inside the zero line, bringing the cultivable land of many people inside the fence. This land is now not only 'fenced' but also 'gated', thus allowing people access through the gates that are opened for a restricted period during the day. That has many implications for the people whose agricultural land falls within the fence, especially those whose livelihood is dependent on this land.[20]

These issues apart, there are other problems faced by the people in the border areas. The securitisation of the border generates its own problems. The militarisation of borderlands has had implications for the people residing there. There is such an overwhelming presence of security forces that many towns in the border areas of Jammu, like Akhnoor, Sundarbani, Nowshera, Rajouri and Poonch, almost seem like large military cantonments. Apart from the ever-present visibility of the army with its paraphernalia, there are also other implications of the army's presence in these areas. A huge land area under the control of the army is generally out of bounds for the local residents; there are various restrictions, including those related to movement. Referring to the plight of the border residents, Jamwal (2011: 75) notes:

> On both the sides of the dividing line, people in these border areas have borne the brunt of the hostility between the armies of India and Pakistan, during wars and the so-called peace times. These border areas are too heavily militarized for any semblance of normalcy and normal life. The levels

> of violence are not always visible, often not reported but felt psychologically due to the build-up of troops, excessive restrictions, fenced and mined areas. The huge military presence imposes restrictions on their movement, often ends up in harassment and keeps the civil administration away, forbidding any development to penetrate.

Conclusion: A Way Out?

Given the background discussed above, there arises a crucial question—Is a resolution possible that would be satisfactory for most stakeholders? With India and Pakistan taking maximalist positions and 'nationalist sentiments' being invoked around the borders on an everyday basis, the only way out is through the reconceptualisation of 'border' itself. This would require a softening of borders, making them irrelevant so that the movement of goods and people becomes possible.

Given the extremely aggressive stance that India and Pakistan have been taking, one cannot imagine any softening of the borders at the moment. And yet, one cannot simply dismiss this idea as it was earnestly experimented with in the 2003–2007 period. This was the time when the leadership, both in India and Pakistan, had decided to move beyond their hostilities and engage with each other. A formal agreement for a ceasefire was made and later, it was decided to open some of the traditional routes on the LoC and allow the movement of people for cross-border travel and trade. This confidence-building measure related to cross-LoC interactions lasted for a limited time, yet for as long as it lasted, it proved to be one of the most successful measures undertaken by the Governments of India and Pakistan.[21] Its success can be gauged from the fact that despite the revived hostilities and aggression between the two countries, this CBM remained intact until quite recently. Travel and trade were 'suspended' only in 2019 following the abrogation of the special constitutional status of J&K. Even now, officially, the CBM has not been 'withdrawn' and remains in a state of 'suspension'.

These border-related peace initiatives, presented as the 'irrelevance of borders' (including the ceasefire, and travel and trade between the two sides of LoC) served many constituencies—not only India and Pakistan, but also the people of the state—the Kashmiris, the people in Jammu, the people living close to the borders, the divided families. The guns fell silent for the first time, allowing the people on the borders to lead a 'real normal life'. The bus service between the two sides of the LoC allowed thousands of members of divided families to meet each other. The trade, though following only 'political' rather than economic logic, linked the people of both sides in an unprecedented manner.

On the whole, this concept of 'irrelevance of borders' reversed the way borders were imagined. From being 'obstacles' to the movement of people, borders became 'facilitators' of peace and goodwill. While the application of this concept helped ease the trauma of the divided families, it also resulted in various intangible political advantages. For the people of J&K, it was satisfying to have the status quo with regard to J&K since 1947 changed, and the 'notional unity' of the whole state across the two sides of LoC was recognised. It also helped to redefine the roles of India and Pakistan beyond their respective militarised image. It is interesting to note how both countries invested in 'facilitating' cross-LoC exchanges—not only thinking outside the box but also adopting a humanitarian approach to the problems faced by people on both sides of the border.

Though the concept (of irrelevance of borders) has taken a backseat now, its relevance in providing a long-term solution from the perspective of the people is not diminished. One can hope that whenever hostilities between the two countries are eased and an attempt is made to address the problems of the people affected by the LoC, the concept will find its takers among policymakers.[22]

Notes

1. Of the total border that India shares with Pakistan, a very substantial part was located in this State. As per the Ministry of Home Affairs, 'India shares, 3,323 Km (including Line of Control in Jammu & Kashmir sector) of its land border with Pakistan. This border runs along the States of Gujarat, Rajasthan, Punjab and Jammu and Kashmir.' Of the total 3,323 kms, one-third of the India–Pakistan border, that is, 1,225 kms, runs through the former State (Lok Sabha Secretariat 2016).

2. The administrative local units named 'tehsils', which border Pakistan, include the tehsils of Samba, Vijaypur, RS Pura, Satwari, Marh, Akhnoor and Khour in Jammu and Samba districts, and Ghagwal, Hiranagar, Barnoti and Kathua in Kathua district.

3. Defining the complex nature of the border, Ajay Shukla (2013) notes that India's boundaries seem to be drawn in abbreviations: 'The LAC is the 3,488 kms long, de facto border with China. The LoC or Line of Control, is the unsettled 776-kms de facto border with Pakistan (distinct from the settled 2,308-kms border from Gujarat to Jammu). Then there is AGPL, or Actual Ground Position Line, which is the 110-kms long de facto border between India and Pakistan in the Siachen sector'. He further notes that the LAC has three sectors: the 'western sector' between Ladakh and the Aksai Chin; the 'central sector' between Uttarakhand and Tibet; and the 'eastern sector' which divides Sikkim and Arunachal Pradesh from Tibet.

4. How the division has impacted the people of the state can be seen from the position of the LoC as it passes through each of the three regions. While in Jammu region the LoC passes all through the two present-day districts of Poonch and Rajouri, in Ladakh, it passes through the district of Kargil and parts of Leh and in Kashmir, it touches the present-day districts of Baramulla, Kupwara and Badgam. Predominantly Muslim (with the exception of certain Tehsils of Rajouri), the LoC is comprised mainly of Paharis and Gujjars. The terrain here is mostly mountainous and remoteness and backwardness characterise the areas around the LoC in all three regions of the state.

5. The four wars include the 1947–1948 India–Pakistan war, the 1965 India–Pakistan war, the 1971 India–Pakistan war and the 1999 Kargil War.

6. The two warlike situations refer to the 2001–2002 India–Pakistan standoff after the terrorist attack on the Indian Parliament and the 2008 India–Pakistan standoff after the 2008 Mumbai attacks.

7. A new phase of conflict in Kashmir was started with the onset of armed militancy and separatism in the 1989–1990 period. While initially, it was internal factors, mainly the flawed democratic process, that led to this phenomenon, the process soon came to be sponsored and controlled by Pakistan. Not only did Pakistan provide material support to the militancy, but the major militant organisations were also controlled by the ISI, the intelligence agency of Pakistan (Chalk 2001; EFSAS 2017).

8. Initially, on the occasion of Eid, a unilateral ceasefire was announced by Pakistan's Prime Minister Mir Zafarullah Khan Jamali on the Line of Control. After India responded positively to this initiative, a formal agreement took place between the Directors-General of Military Operations (Pargal 2018b). As per this agreement, India and Pakistan formally agreed to observed ceasefire on the IB, LoC and the AGPL.

9. Violations started taking place after 2007, leading to loss of lives in the border areas. In 2009 there were 28 cases of ceasefire violations, which increased to 44 in 2010, 62 in 2011 and 114 in 2012 (Majid 2021).

10. In 2013, there were as many as 347 ceasefire violations which further increased to 583 in 2014. These violations continued in the same form in 2015 and 2016 (405 and 449, respectively). While there were 971 cases of ceasefire violations in 2017, in 2018 there were a total of 1,629 incidents of ceasefire violations (*Hindustan Times* 2020). As per the latest data, as many as 3,168 violations of ceasefire were recorded in 2019 (Singh 2020).

11. As per a statement made by Rajnath Singh, Defence Minister of India, there were 5,133 incidents of ceasefire violations in 2020 in LoC and IB, with a total of 46 casualties of security forces personnel (*NDTV* 2021).

12. The ceasefire between India and Pakistan was a result of protracted negation between the two countries. It was in an UN resolution laid out in August 1948 and formally adopted in January 1949 that the terms of ceasefire agreement were detailed. A ceasefire line (CFL) was drawn. The basis of this line was the actual position on which the respective forces were standing at that time.

13. It was after the India–Pakistan war in 1971 that the Shimla Agreement was signed between Indira Gandhi, the then Indian Prime Minister, and Zulfiqar Ali Bhutto, the then Prime Minister of Pakistan. It was an important peace-building initiative between the two countries that committed them to resolve the problems bilaterally. The inviolability of the LoC was emphasised by this Agreement. With relation to this Line, it was emphasised that 'Neither side shall seek to alter it unilaterally, irrespective of mutual differences and legal interpretations. Both sides further undertake to refrain from the threat or the use of force in violation of this Line' (Shimla Agreement, 2 July 1972, Ministry of External Affairs, Government of India, https://www.mea.gov.in/bilateral-documents.htm?dtl/5541/Simla+Agreement [accessed June 2024]).

14. With the exception of the 1971 war, which was fought for the liberation of East Pakistan (that became Bangladesh), all other wars have been fought around Jammu and Kashmir (though borders here faced all the severity of war even at this time). The 1965 war was fought after Pakistan sent infiltrators into Kashmir with the purpose of creating local insurgency in Kashmir under a systematic military programme named Operation Gibraltar. The Operation failed in Kashmir as most of the infiltrators were handed over by the Kashmiris to the Indian forces; however, India responded by launching a full-scale war against Pakistan that lasted for 17 days. There was another war in 1999 between the two countries, which was limited to Kargil only. This war followed the occupation of Kargil heights by Pakistani forces. Unlike the other wars between India and Pakistan that involved all the borders, this war was limited to the LoC in Kargil area only. Though there was no war in 2001 following the terrorist attack on the Indian Parliament, forces were mobilised and were placed in close proximity for as long as 19 months. Apart from the clear-cut war situations, there has been a continuous situation of 'proxy war', with Pakistan pushing in trained militants (Kashmiris as well as non-Kashmiris, including Pakistani and foreign militants) into J&K (*Deccan Herald* 2014; *Rediff.com* 2015).

15. While the rest of the state was impacted by the tribal invasion and division of the state, the Valley of Kashmir remained mostly intact. This was as much due to the geographical insularity of the Valley as much as its politics. Even when the tribals entered the Valley, they were ultimately pushed back by the Indian forces. However,

the areas that had come under the control of Pakistan's forces in Jammu and Ladakh regions could not be completely recaptured by the Indian forces, though there were areas like the towns of Poonch and Rajouri in Jammu region or Kargil town in Ladakh which were liberated by the Indian forces. But there were large areas which could not be recaptured.

16. Though the stories of abduction of women during the Partition violence had been the subject of novels written after 1947, one can refer to two books which present a systematic focus on the impact that Partition had on women. These include Ritu Menon and Kamla Bhasin's *Borders and Boundaries: Women in India's Partition* (1998), and Urvashi Butalia's *The Other Side of Silence: Voices from the Partition of India* (1998).

17. Referring to their plight, Jamwal (2004) notes, 'The displaced families had to be kept in tented camps at Manwal, about 60 kms from Jammu. The government did provide them with some land and cash doles in 1976 but their demands of adequate rehabilitation are still pending.'

18. For women-specific issues related to displacement, one may refer to the work of Dasgupta (2012) and Jamwal and Shuchismita (2012).

19. On the basis of official data provided by the Indian government, Jacob has given the comparative figures of ceasefire violations before the 2003 Ceasefire Agreement, in the period when this agreement was effective and later when the number of ceasefire violations (CFV) started increasing. Thus, he notes that there were 4,134 CFVs in 2001, 5,767 in the year 2002 and 2,841 in 2003. The number drastically fell after the 2003 Agreement. Thus, there were only 4 CFVs in 2004, 6 in 2005, 3 in 2006, 21 in 2007, 86 in 2008 and 35 in 2009. Even in 2010 and 2011, the number of CFVs was relatively smaller, at 70 and 62, respectively. Ceasefire violations started increasing after 2012. While in 2012, the CFVs were 114, these increased to 347 in 2013, 583 in 2014, 405 in 2015 and 449 in 2016 (Jacob 2017: 12). The number of CFVs increased further after 2017. As per a press release of the Press Information Bureau, Government of India, there were 2,140 CFVs in 2018, 3,479 in 2019 and 5,133 in 2020. See https://pib.gov.in/PressReleasePage.aspx?PRID=1741907 (accessed February 2024).

20. The adverse implications of fencing on agricultural activities have been analysed by studies on Punjab borders. In his study of

fenced agricultural land in four border districts of Punjab, Jagroop Singh Sakhon has talked of the unintended consequences of fencing meant to stop the infiltration of militants. He refers to the agriculturalists of the fenced land as the structured victims of the division of the country and their victimisation as 'forced deprivation'. The fenced land remains unattended for the large part and is both underutilised and undervalued (Saikhon 2014: 237–252). A similar study of the impact of fencing in Amritsar and Ferozepur by Harpreet Kaur has noted how fencing remains an obstacle to the rural economy. It has generated exclusions and resulted in a poor quality of life for marginal sections, including women and the lower castes (Kaur 2014: 218–236).

21. Referring to the success of the cross-LoC movement and trade, in a ground report undertaken by Conciliation Resources, several authors emphasised the 'improved movement of populations—people previously separated for over 60 years—through the two LoC crossing points opened so far'. These, as per the contributors of the Report, 'are important for ground level understanding of differences.' The Report summarised that trade is 'showing itself to transcend ethnic and religious divides.... Families divided for decades are reunited. Employment opportunities, direct and indirect, are developing to provide the services required to operate the trade'. (Conciliation Resources 2010: 5).

22. Though the concept seems unique, in the context of cross-LoC trade, it has a parallel in the Northeast borders of India that have links with four countries—China, Nepal, Bangladesh and Myanmar. Here, the local state governments have been insisting on opening the borders. And it is on the basis of their advocacy that India has officially adopted the 'Look East Policy' (Das and Thomas 2016; Hazarika and Raghavan 2011; Muni and Mishra 2019).

References

Butalia, Urvashi. 1998. *The Other Side of Silence: Voices from the Partition of India*. New Delhi: Penguin Books.

Chalk, Peter. 2001. 'Pakistan's Role in the Kashmir Insurgency', 1 September. Available at https://www.rand.org/pubs/

commentary/2001/09/pakistans-role-in-the-kashmir-insurgency.html (accessed February 2024).

Choudhary, Zafar. 2012. 'Locating Jammu Muslims in Kashmir Conflict: An Alternative Narrative of Kashmir Conflict'. New Delhi: Centre for Dialogue and Reconciliation and Federich Naumann Foundation.

Conciliation Resources. 2010. 'Jammu and Kashmir—Trade Across the Line of Control: Discussion Papers', December. Available at https://rc-services-assets.s3.eu-west-1.amazonaws.com/s3fs-public/JammuandKashmir_DiscussionPapers_201012_ENG.pdf (accessed December 2023).

Das, Gurudas and C. Joshua Thomas. 2016. *Look East to Act East Policy: Implications for India's North East*. London: Routledge.

Dasgupta, Sumona. 2012. 'Borderland and Borderlines: Re-negotiating Boundaries in Jammu and Kashmir'. *Journal of Borderland Studies* 27(1): 88–93.

Deccan Herald. 2014. 'Pak's unending proxy war', 25 November. Available at https://www.deccanherald.com/opinion/paks-unending-proxy-war-2226454 (accessed June 2024).

EFSAS (European Foundation of South Asian Studies). 2017. 'Proxy War in Jammu and Kashmir', Study Paper, May. Available at https://www.efsas.org/publications/study-papers/proxy-war-in-jammu-and-kashmir/ (accessed February 2024).

GoI. 2019. 'Maps of newly formed Union Territories of Jammu Kashmir and Ladakh, with the map of India', 2 November. Ministry of Home Affairs. Available at https://pib.gov.in/PressReleasePage.aspx?PRID=1590112 (accessed February 2024).

Gupta, Radhika. 2013. 'Allegiance and Alienation: Border Dynamics in Kargil'. In David N. Gellner (ed.), *Borderland and Lives in Northern South Asia*. Durham: Duke University Press.

Hazarika, Sanjoy and V. R. Raghavan (eds). 2011. *Conflicts in the Northeast: Internal and External*. New Delhi: Vij Books.

Hindustan Times. 2020. 'J&K: Highest number of ceasefire violations by Pak in 2020 since 2003 truce', 29 December. Available at https://www.hindustantimes.com/india-news/j-k-highest-number-of-ceasefire-violations-by-pak-in-2020-since-2003-truce/story-TJ7teyXb88dheysDqEgWCN.html (accessed February 2024).

India Today. 2018. '4 killed, 23 injured as Pak shells dozens of Indian villages, border outposts in Jammu', 23 May. Available at https://www.indiatoday.in/india/story/4-killed-23-injured-as-pak-shells-dozens-of-indian-villages-border-outposts-in-jammu-1239275-2018-05-22 (accessed February 2024).

Jacob, Happymon. 2017. *Ceasefire Violations in Jammu and Kashmir: A Line on Fire*. Peaceworks, United States Institute of Peace.

Jamwal, Anuradha Bhasin. 2004. 'Homeless and Divided in Jammu and Kashmir'. *Refugee Watch* 23, December.

———. 2011. 'Women's Voices: From Jammu and Kashmir'. In Paula Banerjee and Anusua Roy Choudhury (eds), *Women in Indian Borderlands*. New Delhi: Sage Publications.

Jamwal, Anuradha Bhasin and Shuchismita. 2012. 'Women's Voices from Jammu and Kashmir', *Journal of Borderland Studies* 27(1): 95–104.

Kaur, Harpreet. 2014. 'No Man's Island? Exclusion in Borderland of Punjab'. In Paramjit S. Judge (ed.), *Mapping Social Exclusion in India: Caste, Religion and Borderlands*. Delhi and New York: Cambridge University Press.

Krishnan, Varun B. 2019. 'Crossing the line: Ceasefire violations by Pakistan'. *The Hindu*, 1 March. Available at https://www.thehindu.com/news/international/ceasefire-violations-by-pakistan/article26405645.ece (accessed December 2023).

Lok Sabha Secretariat (LSS). 2016. 'Border Management and Counter Insurgency: Challenges and Strategies', Parliament Library and Reference, Research, Documentation and Information Service, February. Available at http://parliamentlibraryindia.nic.in/writereaddata/Library/Reference%20Notes/India's_Border_Management.pdf (accessed February 2024).

Majid, Zulfikar. 2021. 'Ceasefire Violations by Pakistan along J&K Border declined sharply in 2021'. *Deccan Herald*, 24 December. Available at https://www.deccanherald.com/india/ceasefire-violations-by-pakistan-along-jk-border-declined-sharply-in-2021-1064192.html# (accessed February 2024).

Menon, Ritu and Kamla Bhasin. 1998. *Borders and Boundaries: Women in India's Partition*. New Delhi: Kali for Women.

Ministry of Home Affairs. 2005. *Annual Report 2004–05*. New Delhi: Government of India. Available at https://www.mha.

gov.in/sites/default/files/AnnualReport_04_05.pdf (accessed June 2024).

Muni, S. D. and Rahul Mishra. 2019. *India's Eastward Engagement: From Antiquity to Act East Policy*. New Delhi: Sage Publications.

Nair, Pavan. 2013. 'Skirmishing on the Line of Control'. *Economic and Political Weekly* 48(4).

NDTV. 2021. '5,133 Ceasefire Violations By Pak In 2020: Rajnath Singh', 8 February. Available at https://www.ndtv.com/india-news/5-133-ceasefire-violations-by-pakistan-in-2020-rajnath-singh-2365786 (accessed July 2024).

Pargal, Sanjeev. 2018a. 'Tension flares-up on IB again, BSF jawan, 4 civilians dead; 15 injured', *Daily Excelsior*, 19 May. Available at https://www.dailyexcelsior.com/tension-flares-up-on-ib-again-bsf-jawan-4-civilians-dead-15-injured/ (accessed February 2024).

———. 2018b. 'India, Pak agree to stick to peace on LoC, 2003 ceasefire agreement', *Daily Excelsior*, 14 November. Available at https://www.dailyexcelsior.com/india-pak-agree-stick-peace-loc-2003-ceasefire-agreement/ (accessed February 2024).

PIB. 2021. 'Ceasefire Violations and Terrorist Attacks', Ministry of Home Affairs, 2 February. Available at https://pib.gov.in/PressReleasePage.aspx?PRID=1694506 (accessed June 2024).

Press Trust of India. 2013. 'Over 35,000 families were displaced during Kargil War: J&K Government', 1 April. Available at https://www.news18.com/news/india/over-35000-families-were-displaced-during-kargil-war-jk-govt-600242.html (accessed June 2024).

Rediff.com. 2015. 'Pakistan continues to bleed India', 23 March. Available at https://www.rediff.com/news/column/pakistan-continues-to-bleed-india/20150323.htm (accessed June 2024).

Samaddar, Ranabir. 2004. *The Politics of Dialogue: Living Under the Geopolitical Histories of War and Peace*. London: Routledge.

Saikhon, Jagroop Singh. 2014. 'Farmers at the Borderbelt of Punjab: Fencing and Forced Deprivation'. In Paramjit Singh Judge (ed.), *Mapping Social Exclusion in India: Caste, Religion and Border Lands*, 237–252. New Delhi: Cambridge University Press.

Sharma, Arun. 2018. 'Incessant ceasefire violations by Pakistan derail life in Kashmir's border towns as India struggles to protect locals', *Firstpost*, 28 May. Available at https://www.firstpost.com/india/incessant-ceasefire-violations-by-pakistan-derail-life-in-kashmirsborder-towns-as-india-struggles-to-protect-locals-4485843.html (accessed February 2024).

Shukla, Ajai. 2013. 'The LAC is not the LoC', *Business Standard*, 21 January. Available at https://www.business-standard.com/article/opinion/ajai-shukla-the-lac-is-not-the-loc-112091800050_1.html (accessed February 2024).

Singh, Sushant. 2020. 'Pakistan tries to heat up LoC, 41 militants killed this month in stepped-up J&K ops'. *Indian Express*, 30 June. Available at https://indianexpress.com/article/india/pakistan-loc-militants-killed-in-jammu-and-kashmir-6482353/ (accessed February 2024).

The Hindu. 2018. 'Cease fire: on India–Pakistan LoC tensions', 9 February. Available at https://www.thehindu.com/opinion/editorial/cease-fire/article59780821.ece (accessed February 2024).

The Hindu Businessline. 2019. 'J&K records 2936 cases of ceasefire violations by Pakistan in 2018, highest in 15 years', 7 January. Available at https://www.thehindubusinessline.com/news/national/jk-records-2936-cases-of-ceasefire-violations-by-pakistan-in-2018-highest-in-15-years/article25932363.ece (accessed February 2024).

Zakaria, Anam. 2018. *Between the Great Divide: A Journey into Pakistan administered Kashmir*. New Delhi: Harper Collins.

Wirsing, Robert G. 1998. *India, Pakistan and the Kashmir Dispute: On Regional Conflict and its Resolution*. USA, India: Palgrave Macmillan.

III

Bordering, People and Identities

International Border in Arnia

Rekha Chowdhary

The concept of border is quite ambiguous and can be viewed from different perspectives. As we have been discussing, these perspectives range from a conventional understanding of the border being a line on a map separating two states to the border being a process, always in a flux, in the process of being constructed (and challenged). As per the geographical/cartographic concept, borders denote the limits to a state; here, emphasis is placed on territory, sovereignty, citizenship and national identity. Seen from this perspective, borders lie at the remote end of the state and are characterised by fixity and permanence on the one hand, and concepts like inclusion/exclusion and 'us *vs.* them', on the other.

The dynamic concept of 'bordering' holds that borders are constantly being 'made through ideology, symbols, cultural mediation, discourses, political institutions, attitudes and everyday forms of border transcending and border confirming' (Scott 2012: 86–87). Rather than the fixity and assignation of borders, this concept focuses on the continued 'construction' processes involving accommodation, negotiations and contestations. Instead of setting the limits of the state, borders here seem to be deconstructing the very notion of the state itself. As David Newman notes, the very notion of border is linked with the 'process': 'Demarcation is not simply the drawing of a line on a map or the construction of a fence in the physical landscape. It is the process through which borders are constructed and the categories of difference or separation created' (Newman 2007: 35).

In view of this vast spectrum of the concept of borders, how does one approach the study of borders? One would certainly like to understand borders by centring the lived experience of the people living there. Arguing that borders are not given but '(re)produced through modes of affirmation and contestation', one would agree with Nick Vaughan-Williams (2009: 1) that 'borders are not natural, neutral nor static but historically contingent, politically charged, dynamic phenomena that first and foremost involve people and their everyday lives.' It is in the process of affirmation and reproduction of borders that states get involved. The 'border technologies' therefore become important. Referring to these, Thomas Nail (2016: 7) notes, 'If anything, borders are more like motors: the mobile cutting blades of society. Just like any other motor, border technologies must be maintained, reproduced, refuelled, defended, started up, paid for, repaired, and so on.'

Seen from this perspective, even when people are placed at the centre of border studies, one cannot ignore the 'harsh materiality of the borders'. As Sandro Mezzadra and Brett Neilson (2020) note, 'geopolitical borders are today sites of some of the most intense and often lethal conflicts that we witness in many parts of the world.' This is certainly true of borders in South Asia, particularly the India–Pakistan borders as these pass through Jammu and Kashmir. In fact, these borders fit in the category of 'alienated borderlands', as cited by Oscar Martinez (1994) in his famous four-fold classification. This classification, based on 'a different degree of cross-border interaction and prevailing tendencies in a borderland', refers to four differentiated models of borderlands—alienated borderlands, coexistent borderlands, interdependent borderlands and integrated borderlands.

The alienated borderlands are impacted by tension, violence and instability and reflect almost no interaction between people on both sides of the border. The coexistent borderlands provide some basis of formal and limited interaction between the two sides. In contrast to these two models, the model of interdependent borderlands represents a very dynamic cross-border interaction. A stable international environment as well as a favourable economic scenario facilitates interaction between the two sides. The fourth model of integrated borderlands represents a close interaction, both between the states and the people of the two bordering countries. Following this definition, borders in Jammu and Kashmir can be placed in the first group of 'alienated borderlands'. To further elaborate, by 'alienated borderlands' Martinez (1994: 6) means such borders that operate in 'extremely unfavourable conditions', which includes warfare, political disputes, intense nationalism, ideological animosity, etc. Such conditions lead to 'militarization and establishment of rigid control…'. There is neither any possibility of routine cross-border interactions nor of normal lives for the people:

> To say the least, such a tension-filled climate seriously interferes with the efforts of local populations to lead normal lives. International trade and substantial people-to-people contacts are very difficult, if not impossible to maintain. The ever-present possibility of large-scale violence keeps these areas sparsely populated and underdeveloped (ibid.: 6).

Despite the distinctions that he draws in his four-fold classification, Martinez holds that borders remain borders, at the edge of the state and presenting a case of 'differing' and 'special circumstances'. To quote him,

> By nature all borderlands, regardless of their location or level of interaction, function in an environment … that springs from boundary-related phenomenon. As the peripheries of nations, borderlands are subject to frontier forces and international influences that mould the unique way of life of border landers, prompting them to confront myriad challenges

> stemming from the paradoxical nature of the setting in which they live. Borders simultaneously divide and unite, repel and attract, separate and integrate. These opposing forces have the effect of pulling borderlands in different directions, causing stress in both the private and public domains... (Martinez 1994: 25).

While looking at the material reality of the borders of Jammu and Kashmir and analysing these as 'alienated borders' following Martinez, one cannot see borders merely from the territorial perspective. Since people form an important part of border studies, this chapter therefore treats borders as dynamic and focuses on the way in which borders relate to people and the way people confront these borders in their day-to-day life. The approach therefore is to focus on the process of reproduction and affirmation of the border by the state on the one hand, and the border as a zone of contestation, accommodation and negotiation by the people, on the other.

Rather than following an either/or approach and focusing either on the state *or* on the people and their lived experience, this chapter seeks to bring both the state *and* the people into focus. This approach is already followed by ethnographies analysing the anthropology of borderlanders. They 'narrate the experiences of people who are tied culturally to many other people in the neighbouring states' and simultaneously focus on states 'in their efforts to control the social, political, economic and cultural fields which transcend their borders' (Wilson and Donnan 1998). The emphasis is therefore both on permeability and on the permanence of borders on the one hand, and the adaptability and rigidity of the border people on the other hand.

This chapter, focusing on the International Border (IB) located in the Arnia sector of Jammu region, is meant to be illustrative of the borderlands in J&K and explores the lived experiences of the people of the borderland. This sector that lies on the IB comprises of Arnia town and numerous villages that are located nearby. At a distance of around 25 kms from the city of Jammu, this whole sector is a part of Jammu district.

As discussed earlier, the IB is the settled border between India and Pakistan and besides J&K, runs through the states of Gujarat, Rajasthan and Punjab. This border can be differentiated from the Line of Control (LoC), which is the working or the unsettled border between the two countries, and actually reflects the division of the state between Jammu and Kashmir and Pakistan-controlled Jammu and Kashmir (POJK). Much of the IB runs through the Jammu region, touching the districts of Kathua, Samba and Jammu. Arnia is an important sector of the IB that lies in the Jammu district and touches the Sialkot sector on the Pakistan side.

Though the study focuses mainly on Arnia (which was earlier known as the biggest village in this area and now has become a town), it also covers a few villages located on the zero line,[1] especially Allah, Devi Garh, Treva and Pindi Charkan. This chapter is based on field study and extensive interviews with the people living in these areas during 2010–2012 and again in 2017–2022.

The choice to study the town of Arnia and the nearby villages has been made to understand the intricacies of the bordered lives of people. As the study clearly shows, though people all through this belt have been adversely impacted by the conflict situation in general and border problems in particular, there is a marked difference in the ways in which such impact is felt by the people on the zero line and those who are somewhat at a distance from the zero line.

The central point that this study intends to understand is the impact that the conflict situation (in which J&K has been entangled since 1947) has had on all kinds of borders, including the settled border of J&K. Irrespective of the fact that unlike the LoC, the IB is not a matter of contestation between India and Pakistan, the nature of its volatility is similar to that of the LoC. The Arnia sector has remained in the news for border infiltration, abrupt firing and shelling even during peace time, dislocations and the like. As late as 2018, this sector was so volatile that it created headlines in the national and international media. In the summer months, there were such fierce attacks that the whole area was evacuated and people not only in the villages on the zero line but also in the town of Arnia were forced to seek refuge in Jammu city and other nearby places. The intense mortar shelling faced by people here was described as the worst since the 1971 war (PTI 2018). Ceasefire violations have continued in the last few years and even in 2021, after a fresh ceasefire agreement between India and Pakistan (PIB 2021), there have been a few cases of such violations and people in Arnia have borne the brunt of them.

Explaining the Field

Arnia is a town and notified area in Jammu district, with a mostly Hindu population. There are a few Sikh and Christian families. The total population of the town, as per the 2011 Census, is around 9,000 and comprises a mix of upper castes and lower castes or Dalits (Scheduled Castes, or SCs). Among the upper castes are the Sainis and Brahmins.[2] Dalits actually form more than one-third of the population of the town.[3] Agriculture is the main source of livelihood. The largest landholding class is that of the Sainis. The SCs, like elsewhere in India, have been socially oppressed and still form the lower strata of the society. Though many Dalits are also landholders as they have benefitted from the land reforms in the post-1947 period,[4] not all the SCs are landowners in the region or in this area. There are many who still work on the farms as part of the labour.[5] Located in one of the less-developed localities of the town known as Mahasha Mohalla, they are cramped in the small *kuchha-pucca* (semi-concrete) houses.

Apart from agriculture, the other source of livelihood is the service sector. A sizeable chunk of the population is employed in government offices of various kinds. There are also people employed in the security forces—including the Army, Border Security Force (BSF), Central Reserve Police Force (CRPF), and the state police.

Although there are a few people who have served in high official positions as bank managers (three), university professors (one), Superintendent of Police (one), principals of higher secondary schools (six), Deputy Director, Government of J&K (one), Army Captain (one), most of the employed people in government jobs are working at lower levels, like linesmen, tubewell operators, etc. The employment in the 'security forces' is also low.

As far as the public infrastructure is concerned, there are three government schools (one higher secondary, one high school and one middle school), lots of private schools (including two higher secondary, five high schools, one middle school and one primary school), one Primary Health Centre, one community hall and one guest house. In more recent years, the town has acquired a cricket stadium, namely the Ted Rose Cricket Stadium.

Being part of the fertile belt of Jammu, there is a relative sense of prosperity in this town, and yet there are large numbers of the poor.[6] Though the poor are spread across the caste divide, their numbers among the SC are the largest.

Allah is a village close to the border in the Arnia belt. As per the information provided by the respondents, it was a twin village called Allah–Charwah. Charwah is now in Pakistan. Allah, like the other villages of Pindi Charkan and Kathar, witnessed much of the communal violence in 1947. While many Hindus and Muslims were killed here, many Muslims fled to Pakistan.

Being a village on the border, it has been designated as a model village. As per the norms of the model village, a number of facilities have been provided here. Unlike urbanised Arnia, which is well-connected to Jammu, Allah is rural in nature and has all the characteristics of a 'remote' area. The village is not very poor and there are *pucca* houses. However, there is no sewerage system here. SCs form a very large part of the population. Other castes include Rajputs, Brahmins, Jats and Mahajans.

Devigarh, like Allah, is the last village on the Indian side near the border. A farm before 1947, this was left vacant after Partition and its land came under the custody of the state. It was inhabited in the 1960s by the new settlers, the Chhamb refugees. These refugees were relocated from the Meera Sahib area where they had settled after their displacement. The total population of the village is around 1,000. The level of poverty in this village is reflected in the kuccha houses and low level of literacy. There is no gazetted officer from this village.

Apart from Arnia, Allah and Devigarh, the study includes the village Treva and village Pindi Charkan. Treva village lies at a distance of 5 kms from Arnia. Home to 5,000 people, it is quite close to the zero line. Pindi Charkan Kalan, as it is formally named, is similarly located on the border at a distance of 8 kns from Arnia. As per the 2011 Census, its population was less than 2,000. The SCs, numbering 622, formed one-third of the total population.

Bordering of Arnia Belt

Before 1947, Arnia was a Hindu-dominated village in an area with a mixed population. The whole belt was part of Jammu district, which itself had a mixed population. Though Hindus dominated this district, Muslims also formed a substantial part of the population. As per the 1941 Census, of the total population of Jammu district (431,362), 170,789 (60.41 per cent) were Muslims and 260,573 (39.59 per cent) were non-Muslims. However, while the village Arnia had a majority of Hindus, the villages around Arnia had large Muslim populations.

Arnia sector (including the Arnia town and villages around it) was part of one of the most fertile areas of Jammu with an abundance of agricultural produce. Being part of the area where the world-famous Basmati rice is grown, it was economically quite prosperous. Describing the life of the area, and especially Arnia village during the pre-Partition period, an elderly respondent, Ram Rattan (name changed),[7] thus informed:

> It was a fertile land and lots of things were produced. Apart from Basmati, there was production of *dhangar* (a kind of pulse) and *san/patsan* (jute crop) and other food-related items. Almost everything that was required as food item was produced here. We would only buy salt. Pathans travelling through Punjab would come to sell salt here. There were also local crafts based on patsan. Beautiful furniture was made using this material, especially the *charpoys* (jute bed).

A Different Kind of Border before 1947

The Arnia belt, including the village of Arnia and other villages like Allah, Devigarh, Treva and Pindi Charkan (the villages where we based our study), were linked with Sialkot city located in the Province of Punjab in undivided India before 1947. The belt, therefore, even before 1947, was a border belt, but it was a different kind of border. Rather than the IB between India and Pakistan as is the situation now, it was the border between the princely State of J&K and the Province of Punjab. As per the information provided by an elderly retired teacher and resident of Arnia, known as Master Chander, there used to be an excise post at this border. Customs duty was charged for 'exporting' tobacco from J&K to Sialkot and 'importing' sugar from Punjab. To quote him:

> It was a rice producing belt and there was a restriction on 'export' of rice from the state to Punjab, so there were a number of excise posts to check if *mujjhi* (rice) was being taken out. There was a post each in Jabba, Allah and Chakrohi. But the largest excise post was in Suchetgarh.

Therefore, before 1947, 'border' signified more an economic barrier rather than a securitised/militarised barrier. The concerns of the state related to border were also economic. Master Chander noted, 'Across the border was the "*angrez illaqa*" (area under British control). Since rice was not allowed to be imported, it was smuggled out because better rate was offered in the market there.' Hence, it was through the 'excise posts' that the state's control of borders was symbolised. Other than these, the border between the State of J&K and Punjab did not mark any controls. The people of both the Arnia belt and mainland Jammu had many linkages with Punjab, especially with the adjacent town of Sialkot. It was the most vibrant town in the whole vicinity and apart from being a major trade centre, it was also a cantonment that was established by the British in 1852. Connelley Park, which also served as the cricket ground, Scotch Mission College, also known as Murray College, and shopping areas made this city an attractive option for people in Jammu, not only to visit but also to look for employment and trade opportunities.[8] Ilyas Ahmad Chattha has noted the vibrancy of Sialkot during the pre-1947 period. In his opinion, it was the most industrialised centre of the Punjab Province and attracted people from many nearby towns, including Jammu (Chattha 2009: 51–75). Many considered it a twin city of Jammu. Khalid Hasan, a well-known journalist of Pakistan who had been a resident of Jammu and shifted to Pakistan after 1947, thus noted that one could see the Vaishno Devi hills from the rooftops of Sialkot on clear days (informal conversation with Khalid Hasan). The link between Jammu and Sialkot was established by road and train, though *tonga* (horse-drawn carts) used to be the popular mode of travel for lots of people.[9] The proximity of Jammu with Sialkot resulted in a close interaction of people from both cities. This gets reflected in the fact that many Dogri-speaking people had come to settle in this town. According to Chattha, Dogri was one of the spoken languages of Sialkot and around

9 per cent of the people of the town were Dogri-speaking (Chattha 2009: 84).

For the people of Arnia belt, Sialkot was more special. In actual distance, it was closer to them than Jammu city. The life of people here was therefore intricately linked with it. For a large population of skilled and unskilled labour, this city provided lot of opportunities. 'There was a sugar mill in Sialkot and lots of people from this belt were employed there,' informed Master Chander, who in his younger days would visit Sialkot more often than Jammu town. Arun, another middle-aged respondent, stated that he was informed by his father that there was a very big menthol factory in Chakrohi and a lot of people from Arnia worked there. Referring to the nearness of Sialkot to Arnia, he stated: 'Sialkot was certainly closer to people here than Jammu. If you see from the rooftops, you will see the lights of Sialkot, which are much closer than the lights of Jammu.'

It was not economy alone which linked the people of this belt with Sialkot, but the socio-cultural contiguity. 'We also had strong social linkages with Sialkot. Marriages were performed with people on that side and we had a lot of relatives there,' informed Arun, the school teacher. Many people that I talked to in this belt said that they had a lot more relatives in Sialkot and other nearby towns of Punjab than in Jammu.

The Sialkot route, the nearest route for the people going to Punjab, was lost to people after 1947. With the International Boundary being drawn, the route was closed in 1947. Arun informed,

> My father's sister was married in Gurdaspur. Before 1947, our people did not have any problem reaching there. We would go there via Sialkot and it was quite near. But after Partition, we had to take the circuitous route from Jammu, to Pathankot and then reach Gurdaspur. Same was the story of visiting Amritsar. Amritsar via Sialkot is just two hours. But again for visiting

> Amritsar, one would go via Jammu and Pathankot and that would take us around seven to eight hours.

For the people of Arnia, therefore, the process of 'bordering' meant an abrupt cultural disruption. The International Border that was now put in place was in no way like the earlier 'custom' barrier between J&K and Punjab. It was a hard border which meant a closure of any relationship with the most proximate city that they were economically, socially and culturally attached to. From now onwards, this 'city' was to be seen not as the city one could easily walk into, but as part of 'enemy country' with no civilian contact whatsoever. Irrespective of the cultural continuity with this city and its people, interaction with its people was a closed chapter for all times to come.

However, the abrupt closure of the border did not in any way mean that the attraction for the city and its people also ended. Not only for the people in Arnia but also in the whole Jammu city, 'Sialkot' remained a point of 'nostalgia' and represented good and pleasant memories of the past. Generations after the Partition, people would fondly talk of the city and what it represented for them. People would remember how they would visit Sialkot for shopping and the best dress material; or how they would just go there to watch a movie! With only two movie theatres in Jammu, the choice for watching movies was larger in Sialkot and it also seems that some movies would release earlier in Sialkot than in Jammu (Bhasin 2012). There was a very strong attachment to the old railway station in Jammu city from where the train would go to Sialkot and while passing through it, would refer to their journeys to the town in the good old times. To give one example of this nostalgia for train travel from Jammu–Sialkot, one can refer to a write-up by a resident of Jammu, Yash Bhasin:

> Sports industry was localised in Sialkot, where a large number of workers from villages in RS Puma Teshil and other adjoining

> areas were engaged. They would travel to and fro daily by train running between the two cities. The rail fare from Jammu to Sialkot was only 4 annas, equivalent to 25 paisa of today. A special small train comprising one large coach having carrying capacity of 200 passengers, would make few sorties [trips] between the two cities. The passengers travelling between RS Pura Tehsil and Sialkot had to pay only 1 Anna as fare.

The nostalgia is not only among residents of Jammu visiting Sialkot but also for people from Sialkot visiting Jammu city. Bhasin (ibid.) notes,

> During summer months, on Sundays in particular, many groups of people from Sialkot would come to Jammu for picnic at the Ranbir Canal bands where they would have [a] dip in the icy cool water of the canal to beat the heat. Bringing with them buckets of mangoes and milk in the bottles, they would cool these in [the] canal and enjoy consuming the same.

And even after experiencing hostility and numerous wars, there has always been a demand to open the border in this area. In the 2005–2008 period when roads were opened for the cross-LoC interaction, there was a demand to open the Jammu–Sialkot border for trade purposes. The demand is raised not only from the forums of trade and chambers of business, but also by the common people.

Inter-Community Relations before 1947 and the impact of Partition

Almost everyone we talked to remarked about the idyllic inter-community relations before 1947. The elderly respondents who had spent time with Muslims before Partition stated that there was no tension on the basis of religious differences. There was goodwill among the communities and a sense of sharing of happiness and grief. Ram Rattan informed us that there was no acrimony at the level of the people, although some tension was generated by the presence of fundamentalists belonging to the Muslim League. He further informed that there were Hindu organisations and leaders who were equally fundamentalist and were responsible for creating a communal divide, especially a few years prior to the Partition. Prem Pandit, however, was more nostalgic about the pre-1947 period and told us about the shared life of his village and interdependence on the communities in his village Allah. He specifically made mention of 'Massan Telan', a Muslim woman who used to help in marrying off Hindu girls of poor families:

> She was like a headwoman of the village ['*Panch-Kharpanch*', in his terminology] and was quite rich. The generosity of this woman was so appreciated that the stories about her have been carried over from generation to generation. And even now when there are no Muslims left in the village, these stories are still told.

The Partition of India left a huge impact on the people in these areas. Due to its proximity with the Punjab border, the Jammu district was particularly impacted. To begin with, people of this district were witness to the cross-movement of both Hindu-Sikh and Muslim refugees. While a large number of Hindu and Sikh refugees who were leaving West Pakistan and were going towards Indian Punjab passed through the route of Sialkot–Jammu, Muslim refugees who were leaving Indian Punjab for Pakistan also passed through Jammu towards Sialkot in Pakistan. Explaining the phenomenon, Bose notes that,

> Because of its location, after Partition the Jammu region became a transit point for the huge number of refugees in both directions—traumatised, terrorised Hindus and Sikhs fleeing to India from Pakistani Punjab and the NWFP, and the traumatised, terrorised Muslims fleeing to Pakistan from

> Indian Punjab—both sides with harrowing experience of slaughter and atrocities (Bose 2003: 40–41).

While many of those passing through Jammu went ahead, many remained here for a longer time. Many Hindu and Sikh families had relatives in the region and they stayed on as refugees and were located in various parts of the region, apart from Jammu city.

The sudden movement of people and influx of refugees initially did not impact the local people. As Somnath remembers, the first response of people in the Arnia belt was that of sympathy for the refugees who had fled Pakistan and a sense of responsibility towards those who had taken shelter in their villages. He narrates: 'At first we were not affected by violence. The clashes that were taking place at that time were between Sikhs and Muslims. Sikhs would come as refugees to our village and we would feed them. That is all. Otherwise, we were not disturbed.'

The influx of refugees and the stories of their traumatic experience gradually generated an environment of tension in this district, which ultimately resulted in tension at the local level and communal killings all over the region. By the time the dust had settled, the state had witnessed massive communal violence, mostly on the side of Jammu region. A large number of Muslims from Jammu, Kathua and Udhampur were either massacred or migrated across the border (Bose 2003: 40–41). Meanwhile, the state had been divided and the areas now under the control of Pakistan, Muzaffarabad, Bagh, Rawalakot, Kotli, Mirpur and Bhimber, were divested of their Hindu and Sikh population, with many of them being killed or forced to migrate to Jammu city.

The situation in the newly developed Jammu–Sialkot border meanwhile had become very tense after October–November 1947. Following the tribal raids, there was a warlike situation and, besides the incursions on the border, there was a free-for-all kind of situation. Apart from the battle being fought between Indian and Pakistani forces, there were attacks by organised civilian groups from both sides of the border. A cycle of violence started which was motivated by communal rage and revenge.

People in the area under this study were caught up in this situation. Being closest to the border, the Arnia belt had to face such violence. Though violence reached Arnia village, some distance away from the zero line, there were many other villages inhabited by Muslims and Hindus that bore the utmost brunt of this violence. As informed by the respondents, among the Hindu-dominated villages which were intensely affected by the communal violence were—Allah, Pindi Charkan and Kathar. They also refer to nine villages that were mostly populated by Muslims in this belt and were affected by communal violence. Referring to the mayhem that took place at that time, Somnath of Allah village stated: 'It was first Navratra. I remember it distinctly when our village was attacked. The whole village was burnt. Almost all the houses were destroyed. A few women were also kidnapped.' He said a total of 350 people were killed in Allah. A mention of the ongoing violence in this belt has been made in Maharaja Hari Singh's correspondence with Sardar Patel:

> On the Kathua-Sialkot border attacks have been intensified. Everyday there is one raid after another. A number of villages have been burnt, women abducted and there have been killings also. The result has been that all the border villages have been vacated and we have about 70,000 to 80,000 refugees in the city of Jammu...
>
> Letter from Maharaja Hari Singh to Sardar Patel, Home Minister of Government of India, 31 January 1948, cited in Aggarwal and Aggarwal (1995: 86–87).

Since it took some time for order to be restored and protection to be provided to the people, the affected villages were evacuated and people fled to safer villages. Prem Pandit of Pindi Charkan Kalan recalled:

> In 1947 we had to flee from the village. It must be the month of October; there were continuous attacks by Pakistanis. They came in hordes and burnt our houses and killed people in our and other villages. Around 100 people were killed in this village. The weapons were not guns but things available at home—swords, axes, knives and other sharp-edged things.

On the whole, it was a very chaotic situation. With no single authority available either to explain the situation or to provide assistance, people were left on their own. Ram Rattan stated: 'We did not know what was happening. We were just stuck with the situation. While many from our villages were killed, many others fled. We left our fields unattended and shifted to Jammu and stayed there in a government hospital. Muslims of the village also fled.'

There was a spontaneity and suddenness about the violence, as Ram Rattan stated:

> When the attack took place, we were not prepared for it. Everything was going on in a normal manner. All the members of the family were busy in their respective routines. That is why the sudden attack created so much confusion that members of my family were separated. While other members of the family could unite immediately, though with some difficulty, one of my sisters was found only after eight days. Every day my parents would go to identify the dead bodies and try to find her among the dead.

For an area which had a history of mixed living with not much acrimony among communities, the situation turned so uncertain that communication between the communities was totally broken. With hatred and suspicion reigning in the minds of people, they were fully destabilised. Ram Rattan described the sense of insecurity among people at that time thus:

> My uncle who fled from the village did not know where, in which direction, he was moving. Running all the time, he reached a village near Bishnah but dared not come out of the bushes. For days together he was hiding in the fields, trying to escape the attention of the Muslims there. He used to eat *hirham*—a kind of plant—and take water from the river. So scared he was.

The intensity of violence was so high that people of both the communities were killed in large numbers. The nine villages dominated by Muslims, called *Naunama*, were deserted thereafter as the Muslims fled from there. However, the cycle of violence did not end with the killings and displacements on both sides, but continued. There were revenge killings later on, as Ram Rattan said:

> The Muslims who were affected by violence fled from the nearby villages and went to the side of Pakistan. But they came back with Pakistanis and attacked us. Brigadier Ghulam Baksh of J&K Rifles was sent to protect us. But he joined forces with Pakistanis and started a killing spree.

It took a lot of time for the people to rehabilitate themselves. Since there were several retaliatory attacks, the villages around the border were burnt a number of times and people did not dare to return to stay there. Beli Ram, a resident of Allah, which was severely affected by violence, informed:

> Our family came back in 1952–1953. Since the whole of the village was burnt, there were not many places to live. Hence, a few houses were constructed. Not only our village but many other villages were also burnt. Dwalian (Barhi and Choti), Chak Gran, Khoju Chak, Gulab Singh Pura—all these villages were burnt.

Even when they returned after a few years, the villages around the newly formed IB were not free from disturbances.

Since it was an almost open border, the movement to and fro was unrestricted. Organised gangs from both sides would look for an opportunity to attack the other side, either for the purpose of looting or retaliation. We were informed by Arun, the senior school teacher, about the situation:

> There was uncertainty all the time. *Jatthe* (organised groups of people) used to come from Charba in Pakistan and would burn down the villages. A number of times a number of villages were burnt. So frequently were these villages burnt that many people chose not to go back there. These villages continue to remain uninhabited till this time.

These uninhabited villages are officially known in the revenue records as *bechirag* villages—literally meaning villages in which no lamp is lit or, more specifically, 'deserted villages'. These *bechirag* or deserted villages represent the psyche of fear that was linked with the Partition and post-Partition-related violence.

Safety was the major concern when people fled. While many fled to Jammu, many others went to Punjab on the Indian side. Many even went to Punjab on the side of Pakistan. Bodh Raj, an elderly respondent from the village Charwan, stayed as long as 10 years in an adjoining village on the Pakistani side and then came back. Explaining the reasons for his return to the Indian side after 10 years, he stated:

> From being part of a Hindu-dominated society, we were now part of a Muslim-dominated society. Though no one compelled us to change religion, yet some Hindus volunteered to be Muslims. We remained as we were. But there emerged issues related to marriage. The Muslims would not give their daughters in marriage to us, so we decided to cross over to the Indian side.

As per information provided by Bodh Raj, the border remained porous for a long time. He talked of a person whose family went towards Pakistan in 1965. 'While he came back after some time, his sister did not. He goes to meet her once in a while. Since long, she has become Muslim.'[10]

In this whole situation of violence, women became the target of sexual violence and abduction on both sides. As per Ram Rattan, at least three or four women were abducted from Allah. This was the same story in the whole of the Arnia belt. After a few years, women who were abducted were exchanged across the border. Some women returned but some chose not to go back to their families.[11]

One respondent in Devipur told us that his maternal uncle had killed his wife and daughter, fearing the loss of their 'honour'. Similar stories were narrated in Allah. Ram Rattan narrated a situation when the locality in which his family was living was caught up in hostile attack:

> Our locality was surrounded by the attackers. All the people of the locality, around 150 men, women and children, took shelter on the roof of one house. At one point in time it seemed that they would be captured, and it was decided that the women would be killed so that they do not get into the hands of the attackers. Each woman was given a rupee as a ritual preparing them to be killed. Many women started crying. But meanwhile the army came and we were saved.

The 1947 violence changed the demographic structure of the area. The Arnia belt, which used to have a mixed Hindu–Muslim population, came now to be comprised mainly of Hindus. Arun told us that after 1947, there were only three houses of Muslims in Arnia village. They also shifted to Jammu city later on. A mosque and a Muslim shrine located in the centre of this town, however, tells the tale of the significant presence of Muslims here in the pre-1947 period. This fact is corroborated by Master Chander. There were lots of Muslims in this area, he notes.

> The locality where the middle school is situated now, was the locality of Muslims. However, most of them were from a very poor background. With the exception of one Muslim family which was landowning and was producing and selling rice, others were poor and did not own land. They were mostly craftsmen and labourers—*dhobi*, *teli*, etc. There were a few Muslim fakirs (Sufi ascetics) who were dependent on the offering of Peer Baba. There were a few government employees and a few Gujjars.

The shrine of Muslim Peer Wali Shah Kamal Dana is even now a prominent part of Arnia town. The history of the shrine is traced back to the Dogra period. The familiar story associated with the shrine goes like this: During the period of Maharaja Gulab Singh, a fort was being constructed in this area. A Sufi saint came here from Baghdad and started working here as a labourer. But his Sufi stature and the miracles that he performed made him famous. The legend states that though he used to carry a basket full of construction material on his head, it did not touch his head but rather floated in the air (in the words of a respondent, '*Tokri unke sar se sawa hath upar rahti thee*'). Hearing about his fame, the Maharaja came to see the miracles and the saint asked the king to start a practice of offering *prasad* and *chaddar* in the shrine.[12] There is a belief in Arnia that the discontinuation of this practice during Maharaja Hari Singh's time led to the end of Dogra rule. Many respondents reiterated their faith in this shrine. They believe, the shrine has been protecting itself and the town of Arnia through periods of turbulence. They also referred to an incident that took place in 1947 when an unsuccessful attempt was made to demolish the shrine. The suspect was mysteriously hit by a bullet and died instantly. As the belief goes, Arnia village was saved from the violence of 1947 mainly because of this shrine. While there were ghastly cases of violence in the adjoining villages, in Arnia, this was the only case of killing. There are other stories of the shrine protecting the people during the 1965 war. As per the respondents, the Pakistani forces could not cross the river to reach Arnia and 'were blinded'.

The faith of the people of Arnia in the shrine is very strong and they continue to revere it. Every Thursday there is a big festival in the shrine and many people visit it. While both the devotees and the caretakers are Hindu, they lead the life of Sufis. Every year during a particular monsoon day, an *urs*[13] is organised, which is attended by a large number of people, both locals and from from other places.

While referring to the demographic change in the Arnia belt, it is important not only to mention the killing and exodus of a large number of Muslims from this area to Pakistan, but also to the influx of Hindu refugees from Pakistan-occupied Kashmir and West Pakistan. Like other border areas which were depleted of their Muslim population, the Arnia belt also became a place of refuge for 1947 refugees – including the West Pakistan and the Chhamb refugees.[14] The West Pakistan refugees migrated from the Pakistani side of Punjab.[15] Referring to them, Ved Bhasin notes:

> Several people crossed over to Jammu from Pakistan, large number of them especially from Sialkote and adjoining areas ...There were few families, mostly rural people who crossed over and settled in border areas of Jammu ... That time (in 1947), their number was 60,000 to 70,000 but now (in 2023) their number has gone up to 2 lakhs (Dey and Sengupta 2010: 123).

Bordered Life

For a long time, the borders drawn remained porous. This was true not only of the Ceasefire Line but also of the IB. People now settled in villages like Allah and Devigarh had to live the new reality of being 'on the border'. Living on the border meant living with uncertainties of a new kind. Despite the security forces manning the border, there were a lot of unmanned gaps from which people could move across, especially along the rivers Basentar and Aik. For the villages close to the IB, this meant severe insecurity. As stated by Prem Pandit of Pindi Charkan village: 'When we started living here after the Partition, conditions were quite hazardous and we were quite vulnerable. Our cattle would be taken away. We would keep watch by turns.'

Incidentally, this was the practice in most of the villages near the border. Every village would have a team of people keeping vigil at night to ward off looters who would come from across the border and take away valuables, mostly the cattle. However, the cross-border theft was not a one-sided affair. The looters from the Indian side would also go across the border to fetch cattle from the other side. Our respondents in Arnia often referred to a well-known character named 'Charna Kumhar', who had made this his profession. In a very organised manner, he would cross the border and loot cattle from the Pakistani side, which were then brought to the Indian side and sold to people. Somnath from village Allah linked these cattle-related thefts to the poverty of people living on the border: 'With not many opportunities of finding a livelihood, some people, especially those who did not own any land, would find this an easy option to make some money.'

Besides the looters, smugglers also made use of the porous border. Like many other borders, this border also became a route for international drug and other kinds of trafficking. Our respondents had many stories to tell about the ways in which the smuggling would be done. Apart from the smuggling of cattle from both sides, there was also smuggling of gold and liquor. A respondent narrated a story of smuggling taking place with the aid of donkeys. Liquor would be hidden on donkeys, under cover of transporting mud and sand to be dumped on the border, with gold brought back from the other side in a similar fashion. With the passage of time, the smuggling of charas and heroin also started and soon flourished.

It was in 2003 that the border was fenced. Before that time, it was not completely sealed and there were many possibilities of crossing it. Earlier, it was quite difficult to trace the border at many points and hence many people would inadvertently cross it. Since straying of cattle was a usual phenomenon, there were regular flag meetings between the Pakistani Rangers and the BSF to facilitate the exchange of such strayed animals. Referring to this phenomenon, Prem Pandit recounted:

> Though there was a demarcated border between India and Pakistan, it was not possible to follow it all the time. For human beings, there was some idea of 'our land' and 'their land' and they were taught so by their governments, politicians and leaders. But for animals, no such training was possible. They followed their instincts, which did not tell them the difference between 'our land' and 'their land'.

Prem Pandit also informed us that for the cattle, certain rivulets were marked as free spaces by both sides as common areas where cattle could drink water. 'There was this Dhamala Nala where animals from either side could drink water. Water is a common need and hence under an agreement, a time was fixed for when animals from each side could be brought by their owners to drink water.'

But it was not only the animals that strayed to the other side of the border; even human beings accidentally often crossed the borders. We came across many personal stories of people straying to the other side. Arun, the school teacher, informed us that when he was a teenager and a student of class XI, he was to attend a marriage in Jabbowal, but by mistake he strayed to the Pakistani side:

> There was no sign of the border. No fencing or anything. I was on my motorbike and I did not come around any barricade. I saw a board in Hindi stating 'Savdhan, aage Pakistan hai' but I did not pay any attention to it, because I always thought that there would be some barrier. There was no way I could

> know that I had already crossed the border. It was the same terrain, the same kind of fields, the same kinds of houses. I could hear music being played somewhere, but that was also familiar. These were the same songs that we used to play—the Punjabi songs of Mohd Sadiq and Ranjeet Kour. When I approached a house and asked about the way to Mr Prakash's house where I had to go for the wedding, I was asked by an old woman who I was and where I had come from. I told her that I had come from Arnia and wanted to go to Jabbowal, she told me that I had strayed into Pakistan. I was stunned. It took me some time to collect my wits and then I rode back to my village very fast. So scared was I that I did not dare to go to the wedding. It was after four days that I could inform even my parents that I had gone by mistake to Pakistan.

A villager in Devipur told us a similar story about an old woman who had strayed to the other side and when it was discovered that she had come from the Indian side, the villagers on the Pakistani side asked her to remain quiet about it and not tell anyone where she had come from. It was only during the evening that she was guided along the River Aik, from where she could reach her village. Ram Rattan narrated his own experience:

> I was in school, must be a student of class V. I remember going across the border a number of times along with other school friends. We would just go across and bring the sugarcane and melons from there. We would go out of curiosity to see what Pakistan is like. I remember feeling bad seeing the sorry state of people there. There were mostly kuchha houses, though the land was very fertile.

All these stories reflect similar empathy among people on both sides of the border. Anticipating the trouble that the people would face if they were 'officially' detected to have crossed the border, those on the other side helped them quietly, without any fuss, to return to their own side. These stories also highlight that despite borders being drawn and mutual communication being discontinued, there was a continuity of lifestyle, language and culture.

Militarisation of Civilian Areas

Borders are no ordinary areas and cannot be compared to other spaces where the civilian population lives in a normal manner. Seen from the perspective of the state, these are the 'strategic points' which need to be 'secured' at all costs. 'Securitisation' being the priority vis-à-vis these areas, the people become secondary and their lives are bound by such prioritisation of the state. In any case, the people on the border bear the brunt of the hostility of the other country and are not considered when this 'other' state strikes. In the fight over and on 'territory', people become the major casualty.

But the irony of the border residents is that they not only face the consequence of 'enemy' action, but also that of their own state. The militarisation of the areas has had a number of ramifications for the local residents. Apart from constraints of various kinds, particularly the freedom of mobility and their areas being declared 'out of bounds', there are other implications of the process of securitisation and militarisation. Of these implications, one of the most important relates to the usage of the land that people own. There are various situations in which people are alienated from their own land, for example, enemy shelling, or the planting of landmines by their own army. There may be other 'security' reasons for which the land belonging to many may be under the control of the armed forces. As the State Development Report generated by the Planning Commission in 2003 notes, 'According to the available reports, about 70,000 acres in Jammu and Kashmir is being occupied by the army, which has land mines in 25,000 acres of land. The remaining land is being utilised by the army for other defence related purposes' (Government of India

2003). Though much of the mined land in the Arnia belt has been de-mined and reclaimed by the people, there is still the issue of land coming under fencing and people not being able to undertake normal cultivation, as discussed below.

The whole process of militarisation, however, takes many forms and affects the lives of people in a variety of ways. Importantly, the army presence often invokes a sense of security in the people as their location on the hostile border makes them feel vulnerable. Hence, they generally take the presence of the army for granted. Their lives are interwoven in many ways with the armed forces, more specifically due to the fact that the 'belt forces'[16] form a major source of occupation for the people here. Like many other areas of the 'Duggar belt',[17] the villages in the Arnia belt have a very old tradition of serving in the armed and other forces and almost every family has a member serving in one of the forces—whether it is the army, BSF, CRPF, or even the local police force. As Ram Rattan informed, 'There is a large number of people who serve the forces, at least 30 to 40 per cent of the total employed are in one or the other kind of "forces".'

The tradition of serving the armed forces is an old one for the Dogra belt, both for the elites and the masses, dating back to much before the Partition. Dogras were part of the Frontier Force and later, the Dogra regiment was formed in 1887. The Dogra battalions became important constituents of the Indian armed forces. While the elites[18] joined the forces in the commanding positions, the other classes joined in the lower positions. Even now, most of those who are part of the army join at the lowest ranks. Despite their lack of education, a large number of people are accommodated in the army. The 'Dogra certificate', a document which is a privilege of the people of the Dogra belt, provides an additional incentive because it places them in a beneficial position when it comes to army employment. 'Soldiering', therefore, is an important aspect of Dogra life and can be seen to be linked to the lives of the people beyond the occupational and livelihood level.

It is also integrated with the social and cultural aspects of their lives (KT News Service 2015). In many of the Dogri folk songs, the male hero is depicted as a soldier and his long absences from the family form the recurrent theme of these songs. *Bhalla Sipahiya Dogrya*, one of the most popular Dogri songs, for instance, eulogises the 'Dogra soldier', *Chann Marha Chariya*, another popular Dogri song, talks about the moon being witness to the distance between the Dogra soldier in the service of the king and his beloved left back at home.

Identification with the armed forces, therefore, is very strong in the entire border belt in Jammu, including Arnia. In fact, a visit to the villages clearly reflects this sense of identification through a number of monuments and memorials to the 'martyrs'. Since many people are in the forces, there are a large number of 'martyrs' who have been killed during the various wars. Other than the wars, many people have been killed during the period of militancy. Being part of the CRPF and BSF, a large number of people belonging to these areas have been involved in the counter-insurgency operations and have been killed by the militants. Besides this, there were a few casualties during the Kargil War. The armed forces therefore invoke intense emotions in the people.

Since the lives of the people here are economically, socially and culturally linked to the armed forces, their presence does not invoke a negative response. But such identification with the army notwithstanding, one also finds a certain reaction to the constraints imposed by the militarisation of their areas. They express their resentment at the restriction on the freedom of movement, about the overarching authority of the army during the hostilities and its intervention in their lives. Many of our respondents talked about their movements being restricted by the army. 'During any tension at the border, we are not allowed to move around in a normal manner. That time, we feel alien in our own place. We need permission to do our daily chores,' stated Satpal. Another respondent resentfully pointed to a high school in Treva which had a hall that served as an underground ammunition store during the tension at the border. Gopal Das stated:

> Army has its own priorities and goals during the times when things are not normal at the border. They view things from the perspective of security only. Then all kinds of restrictions are placed on people, which makes the normal life of people difficult. There would be a lot of restriction on movement. I am a teacher but I would not be allowed inside my own school. To enter it, it would require the permission from the army. But not only for this, for everything we would require permission. We would not be allowed to move freely, visit our fields and at night would be asked not to put on the lights.

Shelling and Firing

Continuous tensions on the border impact the quality of life for the people residing close to it. Analysing the border situation, Surinder Singh Oberoi notes that 'the people along the border live under a state of siege' (Oberoi 1998: 12) This feeling of siege was expressed by Somnath, a respondent in Allah:

> It has not been easy living near the border. There are too many problems, not merely the problems of facing the enemy on the other side of the border, but the problems of day-to-day kind. Actually, one does not know what is going to happen. Everything may seem to be normal and suddenly something abnormal might happen.

Echoing this feeling, another respondent, Surinder stated, 'When there is firing, life stops. Crops remain unattended. Life becomes endangered. Being inside the locked room is also not safe as the firing and shelling reaches the interiors of our homes.' The feeling of living under constant danger is more specifically expressed by most of the residents of those villages which are on the zero line. To quote Raj Kumar:

> *Goli ghar pahunchati hai* (gunfire reaches inside homes), it can happen any time, even now when we are talking. Anything can trigger this process anytime. A mere suspicion of someone crossing the border can lead to the escalation of tension and an exchange of fire can take place. The people on the border become hostage to this situation.

During our visit to the villages touching the border, we could feel that every house has a story to tell—a story of facing a bullet or someone being injured during sudden firing. Many of them had personal cases to talk about. One respondent stated that his brother-in-law was injured in firing while sitting in his room. He died a few days later. Another respondent (Mangtu Ram) stated that his son was similarly injured within his home, though he survived the attack. Sevak Ram told us how there was an explosion inside his house when he and his grandson were taking care of the cattle. Talking about Treva, Raja Ram informed that during the shelling in 2000, there were 19 explosions in the village and two people (one man and one woman) were killed.

In Allah and Devipur, we could see that the houses did not have windows facing the border. This clearly reflected the vulnerability of the villages there. The borders in J&K have not been quiet even during peacetime. Since 1948 when the ceasefire was declared after the first war between India and Pakistan, there have been numerous violations and frequent cases of firing and shelling.

The situation improved drastically after 2003 when as a result of the Indo–Pakistan peace process, a formal ceasefire agreement was put into place. It was agreed to have ceasefire on the IB, LoC and Actual Ground Position Line (AGPL). This ceasefire came into effect from midnight of 25 November 2003 (Chakravarty 2017). The effect of ceasefire was clearly felt in this belt. The tension that had prevailed here since the onset of militancy was greatly eased. Earlier, shelling and firing accompanied the process of infiltration and whenever a major attempt was made by the militants to cross the border, the Pakistani rangers would start firing. The silence on the border helped the border residents to return to their economic activities. And especially after 2006 (after the area was fully de-mined), they could reap the benefits of peace through their agricultural produces, especially the Basmati rice.

However, as time passed, the pressure on the border started increasing and the number of ceasefire violations went up. In the Arnia and adjoining R. S. Pura belts, there have been many ceasefire violations, starting from 2010. Throughout the summer of 2010 and 2012, there were frequent ceasefire violations in this area. The area came under heavy firing and shelling in August 2014 when around 3,000 people had to be evacuated from these belts. An explosion in Jora farm led to two members of a family being killed and a number of persons injured (*CNN-IBN* 2014). The area experienced high-intensity shelling during September 2017, May 2018 and January 2019 as well. The firing and shelling were so intense in 2018 that around 100 villages in the Arnia belt had to be evacuated. Arnia town was particularly affected and people had to be shifted to other places. As per the people of the town, the shelling was unprecedented and reminded them of the 1971 war. This was one of the worst situations faced by the people since 1971 (PTI 2018).

Displacements

All through our field visits, we were confronted with the major issue of displacement. Displacement has been the normal story of people living around the border, who have faced multiple displacements. All the major wars between India and Pakistan resulted in tensions on the border, which forced the residents to flee to safer places.

The story of the displacement of people here started in 1947 and continues till now. As narrated above, the Partition itself resulted in displacement. The next major displacement of people took place during the 1965 Indo–Pakistan war. All the villages around the border, including Arnia, were severely affected and people had to be evacuated. After the ceasefire in 2003, however, the people who had left their villages returned, and so did those who were dislocated from the Chhamb area and had settled in many parts of this belt, particularly in Devigarh. Devigarh fomed a part of the land which had been left vacant after the migration of Muslims from this belt in 1947. At some point, this vacant land was converted into a farm which was unsuccessfully run by a society. Thereafter, in the 1960s, the refugees from Chhamb or Bhimber who were dislocated in 1947 or in 1965 were allotted land here. However, they were not given ownership rights and the land continues to belong to the state. These people are called allottees—who are allowed land but do not enjoy the '*malikana*' or the ownership rights.[19]

After 1965, it was in 1971, in the wake of the India–Pakistan war, that the people of this belt had to evacuate their villages. Talking about the situation in Allah during the 1971 war, Ram Rattan recalled how the village encountered such heavy shelling and firing that people were forced to move out, and soon, the whole village was deserted. This was the same story for other villages in this belt.

During this time also, many people originally hailing from Chhamb were relocated to this belt. This was a major relocation as India gave up its claim on Chhamb and gave it away to Pakistan. People belonging to 28 villages had to give up their lands and relocate themselves on lands allotted to them by the state. Among other places, the vacant land in the Arnia belt was chosen to accommodate many of these people. Such was the nature of migration that a number of villages were vacated and the villagers relocated to a new place. We were shown a government school in Arnia which was relocated from Deva Batala in Chhamb. Now running from Arnia, it has the same name and the same staff as it had in Deva Batala.

About the Chhamb refugees of 1971, Prashant Sood (1998) notes,

> Unlike the other 1.50 lakh persons inhabiting about 380 villages that were uprooted by the 1971 war, Chhamb residents could not return home as most of their land, estimated at 37,000 acres, where Pakistan had always enjoyed a strategic advantage, was given by India under the Line of Control delineation of 1972 in lieu of advantageous positions elsewhere... [They] were put up in refugee camps ... till their rehabilitation for which the Chhamb Displaced Persons Rehabilitation Authority (CDPRA) was set up. Against the 20 villages in which these 17,400 persons stayed in the Chhamb niabat ..., the CDPRA in its rehabilitation award of 1976 scattered them over 129 *bastis* (localities) in seven *tehsils* in border areas of Jammu and Kathua districts.

Although there was no war in 1986, the people in this belt were forced to leave their villages for safer places. This was when tensions had increased between the two countries and forces on both sides were engaged in military exercises on the border. Again during the Kargil conflict, the borders became tense and the people had to evacuate. During this conflict, the areas close to the border started coming under fire and the people started moving out. They camped in school buildings in various places. As per the government figures, around 18,252 families, comprising 83,804 persons, migrated from border areas to safer places after May 1999. Of these, only 2,625 families were provided tents and other facilities, while the rest made their own arrangements. Apart from the dislocation, there was also loss of life. Around 12 persons were killed and 37 were wounded.[20]

The next major migration took place in 2002. This was the time of Operation Parakram when Indian forces were mobilised on the LoC and IB, following the terrorist attack on the Parliament. At that time, there was a massive evacuation of people from the LoC and the IB.[21] As per a news item published in *Daily Excelsior*, around 16,000 people 'deserted their houses in 12 forward villages of Arnia and Ramgarh sector following shelling by Pakistan army leading to the killing of a civilian' (as quoted in Verma 2011). This report stated that thousands of people had shifted from six villages closest to the border in Arnia sector. These included the villages of Nilowal, Sei Khurd, Sei Kalan, Kaku De Kothe, Treva and Pindi Charkan. A civilian, Bachan Lal, was killed in the Arnia–RS Pura sector while preparing to migrate. This triggered migrations of people from other villages to safer places. In the month of June 2002, Arnia came under heavy Pakistani fire. Mortars reached the town of Arnia and its suburbs and this triggered fresh migration (*The Tribune* 2002). This situation continued for months and even in late July, there were reports of Pakistani troops opening fire on various border outposts, including those in Arnia sector.

The impact of war or warlike conditions or even the border tensions during peace time has led to frequent displacements of the people in the whole belt. Many people in the belt, including Prem Pandit of Pindi Charkan and Raja Ram of Treva village, stated that they had migrated as many as 12 times since 1947. Master Chander of Arnia thus stated:

> During all these years, whenever there were warlike conditions—we would be living by our suitcases—suitcases were packed for leaving anytime. We would be prepared to leave and carry the suitcase along with some rice and wheat flour and *gur* (jaggery). Generally the pattern was like this—when we would get some indication of some tension on the border, women and children would leave. Men would remain in the village during the day time but by the evening, the men

> would also leave. And then there would be a time when the men also had to migrate.

Prem Pandit described how the migration disrupted their normal life and made them dependent on the state dole. Referring to his displacement in 2002, he said:

> We were moved to a camp which was located in a government school in Bishnah. We had to stay there for three months. To begin with, we were fed by the people of Bishnah. They would collect food from each house and provide it to us. But later on, government started giving us ration and some cash compensation, which amounted to Rs 400 per head, up to a maximum of Rs 1,600. It was the bare minimum and we could just about survive on that.

The continuous vulnerability of the border villages and the frequent dislocations in villages like Devigarh, Pindi Charkan and Allah have long-term implications for the villages. Prem Pandit of Pindi Charkan says the continued tension on the border and their impact make the lives of people near the border very uncertain. It is because of this reason that those people who can afford it shift out of these villages permanently. That is also why one does not find many educated and prosperous people in these villages. Those who are educated and employed and those who have improved their economic status have moved out and settled elsewhere. According to him, 'Due to displacements, many people from my village have constructed houses in Jammu, many have shifted to nearby towns of Bishnah, Sarore, Bari Brahmna. On the whole, I can say that around 30 per cent people have shifted away.' A similar narrative comes from Devigarh. Being at the edge, this village remains vulnerable to firing and shelling, whether during wartime or peacetime. Since the search for settlement and certainty continues to elude people, many of them have been preferring to move out of the village.

Mines Endangering Human Life

Among the biggest hazards to life that the border residents face is the process of laying landmines. Almost each war has led to laying landmines in the border areas, which has resulted in not only the displacement of people and loss of their livelihood, but also a loss of life and limb.[22] The respondents in the Arnia belt informed us that their villages were landmined a number of times during the wars, and even otherwise. As Raja Ram of Treva stated:

> We have faced incidents of mines being laid a number of times. In 1987, there was some tension, maybe some false alarm, but even then our area was mined. It was after six months that the area was de-mined. This was despite the fact that there was no war going on. But certainly during the war, the mining is inevitable, like in 1965 and 1971 when our areas were mined. In 1971, our side of the border was peaceful, but even then our area was mined and people had to flee from their villages. This also happened during the Kargil war in 1999. One of the largest mining operations, however, was undertaken after the terror attack on Parliament in 2001.[23]

Though the logic behind laying mines was to restrict the process of infiltration, it impacted the lives of people in the areas where such mines were laid. The villages and agricultural lands were converted into minefields, which became 'forbidden zones' for the people who were forced to move out of these places.[24]

The most problematic part of mining for the people of the border villages was the fact that it impacted on their agricultural activities. For a long period after the areas were mined, the fields were out of bounds. There were large agricultural areas where no cultivation could take place. Giving a graphic report of this situation, Jamwal (2002) noted,

> Walk anywhere along the 1,000 kilometre stretch of the international border and the line of control, and one would find the villages at the fringes abandoned and empty. They are almost out of bounds and a visit could well be 'at your own risk' with signboards on the paved pathways or roads leading to these villages saying 'danger'. A major reason is the extensive mining operations that began in the fag end of 2001.

Our respondents informed us that the whole area was mined and remained like that for four years. 'Our land remained mined for four years and we did not have any access to it,' stated Raja Ram of Treva. 'It created a lot of inconvenience to us. We could not move freely in our village. The whole place was mined. We did not even have a place to go for latrine. Then two latrines were constructed with the help of the army,' stated Prem Pandit about Pindi Charkan.

While some areas remained mined for four years, there were others which remained mined for six years. Some areas in this belt were mined prior to the Parliament attack, during the Kargil war in 1999. These areas were de-mined in 2006. It was after a long period therefore that the people could access their land. This directly impacted the livelihood of those people whose cultivable land was mined. To quote Raja Ram,

> As the tensions started on the border, we had to leave the village and go to safer places. We stayed in a camp, which was located in a government school for girls in Bishnah, for three months. After we came back, life was not normal for us. The whole place was mined and we did not have access to our lands. Agriculture is our main source of occupation and livelihood and we could not pursue that. It was after four years that the area was de-mined. But by that time the land had become infertile. There were weeds all around and due to the lack of irrigation, the land had dried. Though the government had cleared the fields and prepared for cultivation, there remained the impact of the land not being used for four years.

Another respondent, Babu Ram stated,

> For years together we were dependent on government's dole for our survival. This is ironic since we are the owners of such a good quality of land. But instead of living on our own hard work and our land, we were living on the money and ration being paid by the government.

The dole consisted of a ration of 9 kgs of flour and 2 kgs of rice per person and Rs 1,600 per month per family.[25]

However, as per many respondents, the compensation did not justify the loss that the people had undergone because of mining. For them, it was too meagre. As one respondent, Shiv Kumar stated,

> Compensation is not enough and does not compensate what we actually lose when we do not have our land under our control. Money that is given is not enough. It is a fertile area and we produce rice which has huge demand in the market. Basmati grown here is famous all over the world. We get only Rs 50,000 as compensation. This is not equal to the value of Basmati that we would have produced. For all the long years when our areas were mined, we were telling the government that we do not want compensation, we want our areas to be vacated.

Once the fields are mined, it is not easy for the people to reclaim their land. People are allowed to go back only after senior officers of the army have certified that the area is de-mined. However, even for the areas that are certified to have been cleared of mines, there remains the threat of live mines. There are a number of reported cases of deaths and injuries due to the live mines that have remained undetected. The process of demining itself is full of hazards and leads to injuries and casualties. *Landmine Action* has reported that 73 people were killed and 216 injured in the demining operation that started in June 2002 in Rajasthan, Punjab and J&K (Landmine Action 2005: 83).

Our respondents also reported a number of mine-related accidents. In every village that we visited, we were told stories of people being injured, maimed or killed by the accidental explosion of undetected landmines in the fields. They remarked that the frequency of cattle being caught by the mines was very high and they had to suffer huge losses because of that. Raj Kumar told us about the death of a villager in Arnia in 2003 when he accidentally walked over a landmine. He also mentioned another case of injury to another man the same year when he was taking his cattle back towards his home. Sevak Ram told us about Devigarh, 'Daya Ram lost his leg when he went to feed the cattle. He slipped and his leg accidentally touched the mine and he lost his leg. Similarly, a few more people lost their legs.' He further informed us that two landmines were recovered in the village in 2011. These were removed but left psychological impacts on the people.

Fencing

One of the issues confronted by the people living close to the border is that of fencing.[26] Fencing is a part of the 'multi-tier security structure' set up by the army during the last two decades or so (Mahapatra 2011: 10).[27] The IB on the side of Jammu, being porous, was used by militants in the early 1990s to cross over from Pakistan. This period therefore, 'saw an influx of militants, who used the Jammu route in order to circumvent patrols along the Line of Control up north in the Kashmir Valley'[28] (Patnaik 2005). The decision to construct the fence was to counter the process of infiltration.[29]

Swami (2001) explains the need for fencing thus:

> It is not hard to see why the new fence is so important to India, while being a real threat to Pakistan. For one, both National

> Highway 1 and the Pathankot-Jammu rail line are only a few kilometres from the border. With the fence in place, the kind of sabotage enterprises and terrorist attacks that have been taking place regularly since 1994 would become extremely difficult to carry out. Pakistan would also find it difficult to push espionage operatives across the border, while Indian intelligence would have no difficulty in identifying them. Also significantly, the fence would make an important symbolic point. India argues that the southern frontier in Jammu and Kashmir is a border, because it has remained unchanged ever since the accession of the state. Pakistan accepted this position until the rise of insurgency in the late 1980s. It now describes the border as a 'working boundary'.

Given the fact that the influx of militant infiltration had generated a sense of insecurity, the erection of the fence helped create a sense of security in the Arnia belt. However, it also led to problems for the people. The intensity of shelling and firing increased during the period when the fence was being erected. 'All through the period that the fence was being erected, the border did not remain silent. There was far greater frequency of firing by the Pakistani Rangers as compared to the earlier period,' informed Manmohan. Because of the intensity of the fire from across the border, the fence could not be constructed at the zero line, but had to be located much inside the border. As per a report of the Ministry of Home Affairs, '... due to heavy fire from across the border, in a stretch ... IPB fence was erected at a distance, varying from 400 meters to 1.5 Km away from the IB' (Government of India n.d.).[30]

With fencing around 400 m to 1.5 kms inside the Indian territory, a substantial part of the agricultural land has come under fencing. Most of this land, especially in the Arnia belt, is very fertile and was being cultivated by the villagers. However, this land has now become restricted due to the fence. Though there are gates built along the fence to allow people access to their land, it constrains their agricultural activities. Normal farming, therefore, is not possible. The opening of gates is as per the scheduled timing and it is only during this time that farmers are allowed to access their land and participate in agrarian activities. Most of our respondents whose land came under fencing reported that the time allotted to people was not sufficient, and this impacted their overall level of productivity. As one respondent, Brijraj stated:

> We do not get sufficient time for our activities. Every day we have to wait for the gate to open and then it takes us at least one hour to reach our land. And before we know, it is time to close the gate and we are forced to shortcut the whole process. I need to stop work one hour before the gate closes so that I can get back to the gate and that does not leave me much time.

Another respondent, Bhushan Kumar stated:

> We have lost the pleasure of being in the field for longer time. Sometimes we are in the middle of watering the crop or harvesting and we have to leave it, since we have to follow the rules. I used to be in my field before sunrise and remain there till it would become dark. But that is not possible anymore.

As per many respondents, the fencing had a deeper impact on the way they controlled their land and pursued their agricultural activities. This feeling was expressed by Bhushan Kumar in the following manner:

> It has changed our relation with our land. Earlier we would not be bothered about the time. It was our field and we could enter it at any point in time. We did not need to take anyone's permission. But now we need to have formal permission. I cannot take the liberty of going to my field when I feel like.

The farming, as most of the respondents stated in this belt, has traditionally been 'family farming' with all the adult members of the family, including the women, participating in it. But with the land coming under fencing, this has been affected. A respondent, Brijraj, stated,

> Our farming activity has been quite restricted, not only because of the shorter duration of time I get to spend on my field but also that I don't have the support of my family. Now I cannot take my wife along for farming activities. I do not feel that it is safe for her.[31]

Apart from this, there are many other issues related to the land being fenced. Of these, an important one concerns compensation not being paid in time. Also, not everyone is entitled to compensation. To quote Somnath,

> Most of the land under fencing is the state land where people do not have the land right and the land is just allotted. Hence people do not get compensation for that. Compensation is given only to those who have ownership right (*malikana*) on land.

State and People on the Borders

Acknowledging the special needs of the people living close to the border and the fact that they need to be supported by the state,[32] a special programme was initiated in 1986. Known as the Border Area Development Programme (BADP), it caters to the people living in the states bordering Pakistan, including J&K, Punjab, Gujarat and Rajasthan.[33] A 100 per cent centrally sponsored scheme, the BADP in J&K has been intervening in border areas in matters related to education, health, roads, bridges, water supply, etc.[34] However, despite such state intervention, the people in the border areas, especially in those areas on the zero line, feel neglected. A general feeling remains that whatever the advantages of these schemes, these are accrued by the areas which are closer to the towns, or which have been urbanised over the period.[35] This point was emphasised by Gopal Das while explaining the lack of development in Devigarh village. He informed us about the pathetic condition of this village as compared to Arnia and other better-off villages. He told us about the meagre infrastructure; there is only one middle school, and no higher secondary school. The lack of educational facilities means that people cannot be educated beyond a point. There is no graduate in the village and Das is the only one who succeeded in completing his education through the Indira Gandhi National Open University (IGNOU). No government bus plies up to this point; there are private Matadors (vans), which also have a very low frequency. People walk for 1.5 kms to reach Sai, which has better facilities. The supply of drinking water and electricity is also not sufficient.

The sense of neglect is deep-rooted in the villages around the border, and due to the lack of attention of the government officials or even the politicians, it gets expressed, at times, in a non-conventional manner. In 2011, the people of Jabbowal organised a unique protest that caught the attention of the media and government. To make the point that they are not being looked after in their own country and are not able to enjoy their basic rights as citizens, they made an attempt to cross the border. This was a symbolic protest and was foiled by the BSF (*Early Times* 2011). In a similar instance of protest, the villagers in Devigarh also sought to highlight their plight by making a symbolic attempt to cross the border. Sevak Ram told us about an incident where the government had taken the decision to give the land they were cultivating given to the 1971 refugees. The villagers protested and crossed the border and went towards the Pakistani side, and camped there for around two weeks. The whole village participated in this protest. They were persuaded to return only after the intervention of Babu Parmanand, a prominent politician of Jammu region.

Land and State Policy

There are various issues related to ownership of land. Not everyone who cultivates the land owns it. There are two kinds of relationship with the land—those who own the land and have the ownership right (*malikana*), and those in whose name land is allotted, but they do not have the ownership rights. As we have been discussing, the Arnia belt, like many other places in Jammu, Samba and Kathua districts, hosts many people who have migrated from Pakistan-controlled Kashmir or from West Pakistan at different points in time. Many of these displaced people were settled in the border areas, especially in the erstwhile Muslim-dominated areas which were lying vacant after 1947. They were 'allotted' land to cultivate, but were not given occupancy rights since the state took the position that the land so vacated belongs to the original owners who are living in the area now controlled by Pakistan. Since that area is still officially claimed as a part of J&K, the original owners area were also considered citizens of this erstwhile state. Hence, the right of malikana remained with these original owners. Many of the refugees have also been given state-owned land but, as Gupta notes, even the 'rights on the land allotted to the Chhamb displaced have stringent conditions that if the land allotted is acquired back by the Government, they would not get any compensation' (Gupta 2005).

As Somnath tells us, in Arnia belt there are many refugees from West Pakistan who were not State Subjects. To quote him:

> Every village has around 10–20 per cent of people who are refugees from West Pak. Disturbed by the chaos of 1947, many people from Punjab took refuge in this belt. This area was close to Sialkot and hence became a place of refuge for those dislocated from Pakistan. Moreover, many of them had relatives here and due to their support they restarted their lives here.

However, not being the original residents of the state, they were not entitled to be considered State Subjects or permanent residents of the state. As per the law of the state as it was applied until the recent abrogation of Article 370 and 35A, only those people were to be treated as permanent residents of the state who were either State Subjects of Class I or Class II before 14 May 1954, or having lawfully acquired immovable property in the state, were ordinary residents in the state for not less than 10 years prior to the date.[36] Since the West Pakistan refugees did not fall in either of the two categories, they were not entitled to the Permanent Resident Certificate with which a number of privileges were attached. Of these, the most important privileges included the right to state employment, the right to own land within the state, and the right to vote and be elected in the state's political institutions. The West Pakistan refugees, denied these privileges, therefore could not own the land, even if they have been cultivating it for years.

However, there were not only the West Pakistan refugees but also many of the refugees from Pakistan-controlled Jammu and Kashmir (or POJK refugees, as they are officially termed), who were allotted land but were not given the right of ownership. For these refugees, the settlement of their claims to land left behind in Pakistan-controlled Jammu and Kashmir has not been finalised for the simple reason that the Government of India claims the whole of POJK as part of India, and therefore the refugees from that area are not seen at par with refugees from Pakistan. They have been given some token compensation in the form of agricultural land for the rural refugees and a residential plot for the urban refugees. In case the agricultural land or residential plot is part of state property, then they have ownership rights. However, if the land or plot is part of the evacuee property, then they do not have ownership rights. Since the evacuee property belongs to those people who have migrated to the POJK, the claims of the evacuees to the property are protected by the state.

The refugees who are allowed land on evacuee property have been feeling aggrieved. Their lack of ownership of the land entailed its own kind of problems. Not having the right of ownership, they are beset with insecurity that the land they are cultivating may be taken away from them. This has been more so in the context of the political position taken by the governments in the erstwhile state, particularly those held by the National Conference. This party from the beginning appeared keen to 'resettle' the people who crossed the border to the Pakistani side during 1947, 1965 or later. During the chief ministership of Sheikh Abdullah in 1982, the state assembly passed the Jammu and Kashmir Resettlement Act.[37] As per this Act, residents of J&K who had migrated to Pakistan-controlled Jammu and Kashmir (as well as their descendants) were permitted to settle down in J&K and claim the property which they owned before their migration.[38] However, the Act could not be implemented since it was sent to the President of India, who referred it to the Supreme Court. However, the Supreme Court did not take any decision on it and returned it without any remarks. In 2002, the Act was challenged in the Supreme Court, which issued a stay order on it.

The passage of this Act created a lot of apprehension among those people holding evacuee property. Despite the assurance given by the state that the Act did not affect the status of evacuee property holders, the apprehensions remained. As per a statement issued by the government in 2005, the Act only dealt with issuing permits to citizens of undivided J&K to return to the state and settle here, and there was no specific provision in it for dealing with issues related to the ownership of property now known as 'evacuee property'. It sought to assure the evacuee property holders that the 'interests of displaced persons, now in possession of the evacuee property, were fully protected under the law and there should be no apprehension on that account' (*Rediff.com* 2005). Many of our respondents referred to one particular case of a migrant who had returned and had made a claim on the land in this belt. Many of them felt that while the state had shown its intent to protect and preserve the rights of the people who have left the state, it had done nothing to protect the rights of the people who have migrated to this part of the state. That is why they objected to the idea of opening the borders and allowing people from Pakistan-controlled Jammu and Kashmir to settle in this part. They clearly saw the loss of their rights in such a settlement, since no alternative policy had been simultaneously devised for them.[39]

The changes that have taken place since August 2019 have altered the situation for many, particularly the West Pakistan refugees. With the modifications in Article 370 and with Article 35A becoming redundant, the land-related laws are no longer linked with the Permanent Resident Certificate. A new domicile policy has been put in place for J&K, which is now a Union Territory. As per this domicile policy, the West Pakistan refugees, being the domiciles here, have been given rights at par with the other residents of the state, and now have equal rights to hold the land and also be treated as the owners of the land. However, the problem still remains for them and the POJK refugees, in the case of evacuee land. Since evacuee land is still treated as being under the ownership of the original landowner who is now a resident of POJK, the holder of this land cannot have the right to ownership of the land.

Conclusions

Elisa Patnaik, who studied the response of people living close to the border, noted that the response is not as aggressive as in the areas where people have not directly confronted the wars. 'Antagonism towards Pakistan is more palpable in New Delhi and the Indian hinterland than it is in these frontier communities of Jammu, among villagers who have been on the receiving end of various aggressions…', she notes. As far as these people are concerned, 'most harbour little ill will towards Pakistan, even though it is they who have faced the brunt of cross-border firing and militant infiltration' (Patnaik 2005).

The comment is very interesting in view of the ground situation. As we have seen in this study, the people on the border have been severely affected by the creation of Pakistan as they had to bear the brunt of Partition-related violence. They have been further forced to face the hostilities between the two countries through shelling, mining and repeated displacements. They also have reason to be aggrieved by the situation of militancy as they have lost their close relatives in counter-insurgency operations in the last three decades. Being part of the Jammu belt which has the largest number of family members employed in the security forces, they have seen much loss of life of their closed ones, whether as part of the army, CRPF, BSF, or other security or paramilitary forces. In this situation, hostility towards Pakistan is expected. The resentment is certainly there, but it is not as intense as may be expected. In fact, if one talks to the people in the border area, one sees a very strong peace constituency here. People on the whole are very favourable to the idea of building bridges with Pakistan and having normal relations with it. There are a number of factors which explain this peace constituency.

Of these, the first most important factor can be termed as a 'vested interest' in peace. Living on the border and facing its vagaries for the last seven decades, they understand the human cost of conflict. Being the constant victims of this conflict, they would like to see its end. Having experienced ceasefire in effective ways in the 2003–2010 period, they understand what they have been missing when it comes to normal development.

People here nostalgically talk about the pre-Partition era when they were closely connected with Sialkot and their economic life was linked with it as well. Even after being cut off from the other side for so many years, they continue to refer to their cultural linkages. We would like to reiterate what Arun, who had strayed accidentally into Pakistan, says about cultural continuity and the lack of difference at the level of the people:

> When I had accidentally strayed on that side, I was not able to distinguish between the two places as different. The woman who guided me back to our side of the border spoke the same language as mine. What confused me most thinking that I was in my own land was the 'music' that was being played there. It was the same music that we hear, the same singers, the same songs....

It is in this context that one would tend to agree with Patnaik (2005) that 'after so many years in the crossfire, Jammu's border residents would still be the first to wave the flag of peace to their next-door neighbours on the Pakistani side'.

Notes

1. Zero line is the last point on the border—the actual point where the territory of one country ends and that of the other country across the border starts. This point is quite different from the point where the fence is located. Though 'fence' also signifies the border, there may be a lot of distance (in some cases running into miles) between the fence and the real end point of the border. It is the real end point that is called the zero line.

2. Sainis, who have been recently recognised by the Central government as OBCs, are mainly involved in agricultural activities and are mostly settled along the International Border in Jammu region. In addition, there are a few Mahajans and Jats also. There are only two families of Rajputs.

3. Of the total population of around 9,057, there are 3,859 Scheduled Castes (Census of India 2011).

4. By the Big Landed Estate Abolition Act of 1950, ceiling was imposed on landholding and a large part of land was acquired by the state and redistributed among the landless cultivators. Since the Dalits were the largest cultivating class in Jammu region, they thereby became the landowners.

5. However, rather than being a homogenous group, the SCs are internally divided into various sub-castes like Mahashas, Meghs, Batwal and Ramdasis. The largest of these castes are the Mahashas.

6. Sulekha, who was working as a teacher in the Higher Secondary school, informed me that a number of male students belonging to the poor families were working in the fields as well.

7. Names of all the respondents cited in this book have been changed to protect their identity.

8. Referring to the vibrancy of Sialkot city, Khalid Hasan mentioned the hotels and cafes and a department store, Gollam Kadir and Sons, the biggest in northern India where the Maharaja of Kashmir used to shop (personal communication).

9. To quote Rakesh Rocky (2004), 'the 14 kilometer road between RS Pura and Sialkot was also a major trade link before 1947 .... At that time sugarcane used to come from Sialkot in trains and buses ....'

10. There were also the stories of some men being left behind. Ram Rattan talks of a family where one brother was left on the Pakistani side of the border: He is now a practising Muslim. He came recently to meet them, but due to the religious differences, he maintained a distance and would not eat with them.

11. Although a large number of women were abducted in 1947, there was no narrative around the abduction of women for a long time. On the whole, families and society maintained a silence around the loss of these women. It was with the opening of the LoC in 2005, when large numbers of people travelled from across the LoC, that some stories emerged. A number of women who were left behind in POJK and had converted from Hinduism/Sikhism to Islam made efforts to get in touch with their families on the Indian side. For a few stories of this kind, refer to Jamwal and Shuchismita (2012: 95–104).

12. Prasad is a devotional offering in the form of some eatables distributed to the devotees in a shrine. Chaddar is a long cloth that covers the grave of the Sufi saint. Many devotees who visit the shrine offer it as a mark of respect to the saint.

13. An urs marks the death anniversary of a Sufi saint, which is celebrated as a wedding, a mystical union with the divine.

14. The Chhamb refugees were those who were displaced not only during 1947 but also during the 1965 war. Around 8,100 families were displaced from Chhamb in the 1965 war, and a large number of them (around 3,500 families) were resettled in the districts of Jammu and Kathua.

15. Due to their origin in Punjab, the West Pakistan refugees were not treated on par with the POJK and Chhamb refugees. These other refugees being part of the undivided princely State of J&K, were privileged as the permanent residents of the state and given all those rights enjoyed by the other residents. The West Pakistan refugees, on the other hand, were denied various rights, including the right to state employment and ownership of land.

16. Belt forces include the police force, Border Security Force, CRPF, and the Indian Army.

17. Duggar belt is the largest part of Jammu region—mainly the plains adjacent to Punjab as well as the hilly areas of Jammu region comprised of Dogri-speaking people. Referring to areas of Jammu region excluding Poonch-Rajouri and Doda-Kishtwar districts, it can also be termed as the 'Dogra belt'.

18. Elites were the socially influential, upper-caste, well-to-do people of the region who not only controlled much of the land but also the state employment. Their elite status also emanated from their association with the Dogra ruler.

19. One gets a glimpse of the kind of problems that the displaced people had to face in Devigarh from the story of Sevak Ram, who was displaced from Chhamb in 1947. After being temporarily relocated in different places, he was allotted land in Devigarh in the 1960s. He claimed that he belonged to a big land-owning family in Chhamb but was reduced to the status of a labourer after his displacement. The land that he was allotted was of very low quality. Not only was it barren and difficult to cultivate but it was also inhabited by wild animals. Further, being right on the border, it was open to cattle thieves from across the border.

20. This information was provided by the Minister of State for Home, Mushtaq Ahmad Lone, in the J&K Assembly. According to him, an assistance package comprising free ration, kerosene, tents, water and electricity was provided by the state (Ahmad 2000).

21. To quote Jamwal, 'over 1 lakh families were uprooted along the International Border (IB) and the LOC. The areas in a mad frenzy were being forcibly evacuated, though shelling and heavy mortar firing had forced several people in these villages to flee. What added to the woes was the largest ever mine laying operation along the IB and the LOC...' (Jamwal 2008: 246–247).

22. As per the Landmine Monitor Report (2003: 588), India is not a signatory of the Mine Ban Treaty. Landmines here are used actually as a very crucial defence strategy. As Mahapatra (2011: 8) notes,

> During the time of actual Indo-Pak hostilities in 1965 and 1971 mines were planted all along the border, in cultivated land and pastures, around infrastructure and even houses, to obstruct movement from across the border. In late 1980s with the rise of militant movement in the Indian state of J&K heavy mining in border areas was undertaken purportedly to check cross-border infiltration, and to stop all kinds of support and patronage from across the border.

23. Although there is no official acknowledgement of the laying of mines, there have been studies which have reported that almost all the villages on the border in the Jammu region were mined. To quote Mahapatra,

> Indian army took under its control a total of 70,100 acres of land in Jammu, Kathua, Rajori and Poonch districts after deployment of forces .... As per the unofficial claims, more than 25,000 acres of land in the state came under minefields by the plantation of Anti-Personal Mines (APMs) and Anti-tank Mines (ATMs) with a density of 1,000 sq miles per sq. kms (Mahapatra 2011: 8).

24. Writing about this period, in a report of the Mahanirban Calcutta Research Group (MCRG), Jamwal notes that 'much of the migration this time took place, not just due to the shelling and firing exchange between the two troops on both the sides but more so, because of the heavy landmines emplaced by the Indian and Pakistani troops in their respective territories' (Jamwal 2004).

25. There are thus huge implications of agricultural land being used for laying mines for four years. Despite owning the land, people were forced to be dependent on the dole from the state. The state was committed to provide compensation, but there were a number

of administrative issues in getting the compensation as well. Further, there was the problem of reworking the land once it was de-mined. Not cultivated for years together, it required extra effort to make it cultivable. Referring to these issues, Sevak Ram stated:

> After the Kargil war, the border was mined. There was no crop for six years. Only in 2006, mines were cleared. Till that time, we could not pursue agricultural activities. Of course, we were given compensation. But compensation does not come immediately. It takes years to get compensation and to get it we have to face all kinds of hurdles. Compensation comes through tehsildar who was asking for 50 per cent share to release that money. Some people bargained, but I refused to pay the tehsildar. It was after the intervention of a political activist that I could get the full money.

26. The fence forms a 'wall' which is comprised of 'twelve-foot-high fences of barbed wire, set about twenty feet apart' (Hagerty 1998: 148). It is equipped with electric wire that runs throughout its length. To prevent infiltrators from sneaking into the Indian side, there are numerous watch towers and searchlights.

27. Apart from fencing, this security structure is comprised of the ditch-cum-bandh system (DCB). Before the process of fencing was undertaken, a ditch was dug some distance away from the zero line of the border and a *bandh* (wall) was erected there. While the ditch served the purpose of sheltering the forces during shelling and firing from across the border, the bandh worked as a 'barrier to prevent the rival forces from watching the activities of their troops' (Mahapatra 2011: 10). The pressure on the border during the period of militancy resulted in the decision to further fortify the border and create an electrified fence.

28. Patnaik (2005) notes, 'Suddenly, the villagers began to notice discarded Pakistani biscuit-wrappers and cigarette packs in their fields.' The militants at that time chose the route from Jammu to cross over to India from Pakistan since there was a very strict vigil on the LoC.

29. It was in the year 2000 that the decision to construct the fence and set up floodlights along the IB in Jammu was taken by the Government of India. By March 2006, BSF was able to fence 186 kms of IB and had illuminated 176.04 kms of the IB (Verma 2011).

30. As per a press release of the Ministry of Urban Development

and Poverty Alleviation, for the border that runs along Rajasthan, Punjab, J&K and Gujarat, CPWD had in 2003, 'already completed the work of border fencing in Punjab and Rajasthan sectors for a length of 1500 km (Ministry of Urban Development & Poverty Alleviation 2003).

31. Sumona Dasgupta has focused on the impact that the fencing has had on women cultivators in the Suchetgarh Border area. She refers to the challenges that women face while negotiating mines in the field, or difficulties in the field during cross-fire, as well as the 'everyday insecurities' of the 'gate pass system' (Dasgupta 2012).

32. To quote a report of the Planning Commission of India,

> people living in these [border] areas continue to suffer from various problems .... People have long been the victims of hostility between the two countries as a result of frequent shelling along the Line of Control (LoC) and International Border, which has inflicted miseries on the poor, downtrodden inhabitants. On the other, lack of employment opportunities other than in the government sector and improper functioning of the sectors of the state governments have also contributed to an increase in the problems of the border areas. Consequently, literacy rates still remain quite low, there is little improvement in infrastructure—schools, hospitals, paved roads, electric powers and piped drinking water are almost non-existent, especially in remote border villages... (Government of India 2003).

33. Of the two objectives of this programme, one relates to ensuring a balanced development of border areas through 'adequate provisions of infrastructural facilities' and the second relates to 'promotion of a sense of security amongst the local population' (Government of India 2003: 370).

34. It was introduced in the state during 1992–1993. Among the works undertaken via this programme are those related to schools (buildings, additional classrooms, toilets, hostels, playfields), health (public health centre [PHC] buildings, MOD quarters, sub-centres, dental units, operation theatres), rural development (community centres, link roads, lanes/drains, bunkers, latrines, sarais, etc.), power (construction of sub-stations, electrifying villages), Public Health Engineering (upgradation of water supply and sanitation, construction of dug wells, installation of hand pumps), road and

building, agriculture, food and supplies, irrigation, animal husbandry, horticulture, etc.

35. This point has been acknowledged in the report of the Planning Commission itself, which notes, 'Most of the developmental activities has taken place in urban areas, where the index of Social development (which includes indicators like literacy, health care, access to other social services, etc) may rank moderately high' (Government of India 2003: 370).

36. Originally, the term State Subject was defined by a notification of Maharaja Hari Singh in 1927. As per this notification, the term State Subject meant and included:

> Class I: All persons born and residing within the State before the commencement of the reign of His Highness the late Maharaja Ghulab Singh Sahib Bahadur, and also persons who settled therein before the commencement of samvat year 1942 [Vikram Samvat is the form of calendar used in J&K during the time of Dogra rule], and have since been permanently residing therein.
>
> Class II: All persons other than those belonging to Class I who settled within the State before the close of samvat year 1968, and have since permanently resided and acquired immovable property therein.
>
> Class III: All persons, other than those belonging to Classes I and II permanently residing within the State, who have acquired under a rayatnama any immovable property therein or who may hereafter acquire such property under an ijazatnama and may execute a rayatnama after ten years' continuous residence therein.
>
> Class IV: Companies which have been registered as such within the State and which, being companies in which the Government are financially interested or as to the economic benefit to the State or to the financial stability of which the Government are satisfied, have by a special order of His Highness been declared to be State Subjects.

After defining the term State Subjects, the notification further provided that a) In matters of grants of the State scholarships, State lands for agricultural and house building purposes and recruitment to State service, State subjects of Class I ashould receive preference over other classes and those of Class II, over Class III, subject, however, to the order dated 31st January, 1927 of his Highness the Maharaja Bahadur regarding employment of hereditary State Subjects in government service. Notification 1-L/84 dated 20-04-1927 (LSS 2017). (Available at chrome-extension://efaidnbmnnnibpcajpcglclefindmkaj/https://

ceojk.nic.in/PDF/Extracts%20from%20the%20Constitution%20of%20Jammu%20and%20Kashmir.pdf [accessed April 2024]).

37. Titled The Jammu and Kashmir Grant of Permit for Resettlement in (or Permanent Return to) the State Act, 1982, the Act provided for an application for permit 'for resettlement in the State of any person who, before the fourteenth day of May, 1954 was a State Subject of Class I or of Class II and who has migrated after the first day of March, 1947 to the territory now included in Pakistan may be made by the person himself or by his relative, who is a permanent resident of the State, to the competent authority in the prescribed Form.' The Act also provided that such an application would be followed by an enquiry by the State government that the person desirous of resettlement in or permanent return to the State has a bona fide intention for such resettlement in or permanent return to the State, and 'was a State subject of Class I or Class II before the fourteenth day of May, 1954 and had migrated to the territory now included in Pakistan after the first day of March, 1947 or is a descendant, wife or widow of such State subject as the case may be'. Following such satisfaction of the government, the person could be given the permit for resettlement in or permanent return to the State (Available at https://www.indiacode.nic.in/bitstream/123456789/5552/1/grant_of_permit_for_resettlement_act.pdf [accessed December 2023]).

38. The law was made in view of Section 6{1}(2), which reads:

> Any person who, before the fourteenth day of May, 1954, was a State Subject of Class I or of Class II and who having migrated after the first day of March 1947, to the territory now included in Pakistan, returns to the State under a permit for resettlement in the State or for permanent return issued by or under the authority of any law made by the State Legislature shall on such return be a permanent resident of the State.

39. Ved Bhasin, acknowledging the apprehensions of holders of evacuee property, argues that 'one of the alternatives that could be drawn up is that this [evacuee] property should be given to the people who are staying there and owners should be provided with alternative ... [property] as and when they return' (Dey and Sengupta 2010: 124). However, no serious thought on the issue has been offered by the state government.

References

Aggarwal, J. C. and S. P. Aggarwal. 1995. *Modern History of Jammu and Kashmir*, Vol. I. New Delhi: Concept Publishing.

Ahmad, Mukhtar. 2000. 'J&K Border Shelling Forces Thousands to Migrate'. Available at https://www.rediff.com/news/2000/oct/13mukh.htm (accessed February 2024).

Bhasin, Yash. 2012. 'Jammu & Sialkot: The Tale of Two Cities'. *The Kashmir Times,* 27 November. Available at http://www.kashmirtimes.in/newsdet.aspx?q=19648 (accessed December 2023).

Bose, Sumantra. 2003. *Kashmir: Roots of Conflict, Paths to Peace.* New Delhi: Sage Publications.

Chakravarty, I. 2017. 'As guns boom on the Line of Control, the 2003 ceasefire agreement must not be forgotten'. Scroll.in, 1 June. Available at https://scroll.in/article/839282/as-guns-boom-on-the-line-of-control-the-2003-ceasefire-agreement-must-not-be-forgotten (accessed February 2024).

CNN-IBN. 2014. 'Army, BSF responding effectively to ceasefire violations by Pakistan: Defence Minister', 23 August. Available at https://www.news18.com/news/politics/jaitley-sot-5-709427.html (accessed December 2023).

Chattha, Ilyas Ahmad. 2009. 'Partition and its Aftermath: Violence, Migration and the Role of Refugees in the Socio-Economic Development of Gujranwala and Sialkot Cities, 1947–1961', PhD Thesis. School of Humanities, Centre of Imperial and Post-Colonial Studies, University of Southampton.

Dasgupta, Sumona. 2012. 'Borderlands and Borderlines: Renegotiating Boundaries in Jammu and Kashmir'. *Journal of Borderland Studies* 27. Available at https://www.tandfonline.com/doi/abs/10.1080/08865655.2012.687210 (accessed February 2024).

Dey, Ishita and Sucharita Sengupta. 2010. 'An Interview with Ved Bhasin on Forced Migration in Jammu and Kashmir'. *Refugee Watch* 36, December.

Early Times. 2011. 'Border crossing bid for basic facilities: "grass is surely not green on the other side...!"', 22 July. Available at https://www.earlytimes.in/newsdet.aspx?q=77024 (accessed February 2024).

Government of India. 2003. *State Development Report: Jammu and Kashmir.* New Delhi: Planning Commission. Available at http://164.100.161.239/plans/stateplan/index.php?state=sdr_jandk.htm (accessed February 2024).

———. n.d. 'Fencing and Flood Lighting of Borders'. New Delhi: Ministry of Home Affairs. Available at https://pib.gov.in/newsite/PrintRelease.aspx?relid=68240 (accessed February 2024).

Gupta, Virender. 2005. 'Refugees in J&K—A Hapless Lot', *The Daily Excelsior*, 11 September.

Hagerty, Devin T. 1998. *The Consequences of Nuclear Proliferation: Lessons from South Asia.* Massachusets: MIT Press.

Jamwal, Anuradha Bhasin. 2002. 'Walking into the Deathtrap'. '*Newsline*, 5 February. Available at http://www.newslinemagazine.com/2002/02/walking-into-the-death-trap (accessed December 2023).

———. 2004. 'Auditing the Mainstream Media: The Case of Jammu & Kashmir'. In Samir Kumar Das (ed.), *Three Case Studies: Media Coverage on Forced Displacement in Contemporary India.* Kolkata: Mahanirban Calcutta Research Group. Available at http://www.mcrg.ac.in/mediareport2.htm (accessed December 2023).

———. 2008. 'Homeless and Divided in Jammu and Kashmir'. In Sibaji Pratim Basu (ed.), *The Fleeing People of South Asia: Selections from Refugee Watch*, 244–248. New Delhi: Anthem Press.

Jamwal, Anuradha Bhasin and Shuchismita. 2012. 'Women's Voices in Jammu and Kashmir' *Journal of Borderlands Studies* 27(1): 95–104.

KT News Service. 2015. 'Jitendra Bats for Dogra Certificate for Jammu Youth', 9 July. Available at http://www.kashmirtimes.in/newsdet.aspx?q=44731 (accessed February 2024).

Landmine Action. 2005. 'Explosive Remnants of War and Mines Other than Anti-personal Mines: Global Survey 2003–2004'. London. Available at https://article36.org/wp-content/uploads/2008/10/global-impact-survey.pdf (accessed February 2024).

Landmine Monitor. 2003. 'Towards a Mine-free World, Executive Summary'. Available at http://www.the-monitor.org/media/1704629/lm2003execsum-nomaps.pdf (accessed February 2024).

LSS (Lok Sabha Secretariat). 2017. 'Article 35A of the Constitution: An Overview'. Reference Note: No. 43/RN/Ref/October/2017. Available at https://loksabhadocs.nic.in/Refinput/New_Reference_Notes/English/Article 35A of the Constitution – An overview.pdf (accessed February 2024).

Mahapatra, Debidatta Aurobinda. 2011. 'Positioning of People in the Contested Borders of Kashmir', CIBR, Working Paper 21. Available at http://www.humiliationstudies.org/documents/MahapatraContestedBordersKashmir.pdf (accessed December 2023).

Martinez, Oscar J. 1994. *Border People: Life and Society in the US–Mexico Borderlands.*Tucson: University of Arizona Press.

Mezzadra , Sandro and Brett Neilson. 2020. 'Foreword'. In Anthony Cooper and Soren Tinning (eds), *Debating and Defining Borders: Philosophical and Theoretical Perspectives*. London and New York: Routledge.

Ministry of Urban Development & Poverty Alleviation. 2003. 'Border Fencing Work Along India-Pakistan And India-Bangladesh Border In Progress', PIB, 4 June. Available at https://archive.pib.gov.in/archive/releases98/lyr2003/rjun2003/04062003/r040620034.html (accessed December 2023).

Nail, Thomas. 2016. *Theory of the Border*. New York: Oxford University Press

Newman, David. 2007. 'The Lines that Continue to Separate Us: Borders in Our "Borderless" World'. In Johan Schimanski and Stephen Wolfe, *Border Poetics De-Limited*, 27–57. Hannover: Wehrhahn.

Oberoi, Surinder Singh. 1998. 'Kashmir: Caught in the Crossfire'. *Bulletin of the Atomic Scientists* 54(5), September.

Patnaik, Elisa. 2005. 'Jammu's Borderlanders'. *Himal*, November. Available at https://www.himalmag.com/jammus-borderlanders-2/ (accessed February 2024).

PIB. 2021. Joint Statement, Ministry of Defence, 25 February. Available at https://pib.gov.in/PressReleasePage.aspx?PRID=1700682 (accessed February 2024).

PTI. 2018, 'Arnia town, nearly 100 villages deserted as thousands flee Pakistan shelling'. *The Economic Times*, 23 May. Available athttps://economictimes.indiatimes.com/news/defence/40000-

border-residents-in-jammu-and-kashmir-migrate-amid-warlike-situation/articleshow/64283201.cms (accessed December 2023).

Puri, Balraj. n. d. 'Refugee Problem in Jammu and Kashmir', *Kashmir Newz*. Available at http://www.kashmirnewz.com/a0002.html.

Rediff.com. 2005. 'Kashmir Resettlement Act under Review: J&K', 3 May. Available at http://www.rediff.com/news/2005/may/03jk.htm (accessed February 2024).

Rocky, Rakesh. 2004. 'Jammu-Sialkot: Residents of Border Town Hope to See Floodgates Open'. *Express India*, 7 December.

Scott, James Wesley. 2012. 'European Politics of Borders, Border Symbolism and Cross-Border Cooperation'. In Thomas M. Wilson and Hastings Donnan (eds), *A Companion to Border Studies*. West Sussex, UK: Wiley-Blackwell.

Sharma, Arteev. 2012. '20 Yrs on, Govt Sets Deadline for Compensation to Farmers'. *The Tribune*, 6 April. Available at http://www.tribuneindia.com/2012/20120407/j&k.htm#2 (accessed December 2023).

Sood, Prashant. 1998. 'Once Landlords, Chhamb Refugees Now Work as Labourers'. *The Indian Express*, 14 July.

Swami, Praveen. 2001. 'Border Barrier'. *Frontline*, 15–28 September. Available at https://frontline.thehindu.com/other/article30251978.ece (accessed February 2024).

The Tribune. 2002. 'Three killed in Pak firing', 9 June. Available at https://www.tribuneindia.com/2002/20020609/main3.htm (accessed February 2024).

Vaughan-Williams, Nick. 2009. *Border Politics: The Limits of Sovereign Power*. Edinburgh: Edinburgh University Press.

Verma, Mohinder. 2011. '2/3rd Length of Border Bund along IB Demolished, Remaining in Next Phase'. *Daily Excelsior*, 19 December.

Wilson, Thomas M. and Hastings Donnan. 1998. 'Nation, State, Identity at International Borders'. In Thomas M. Wilson and Hastings Donnan (eds), *Border Identities: Nation and State and International Frontiers*. New York: Cambridge University Press.

———. 2012. 'Borders and Border Studies'. In Thomas M. Wilson and Hastings Donnan (eds), *A Companion to Border Studies*. Hoboken: Wiley-Blackwell.

IV

So Close, Yet Far Apart

Borders and Divided Families in Rajouri and Poonch

Mohita Bhatia

Introduction

> *These borders and fences are dividing our hearts, souls, relations, emotions. Our lives have been partitioned. These lines symbolise sorrow, pain and our incomplete lives. Whose national interest do they serve? Wars, national enmity, borders have not served our interest ... we still live in the hope that one day these lines will be erased.*
>
> Rahim Malik, a retired government officer

Malik belongs to the border district of Poonch in the Jammu and Kashmir (J&K).[1] Like many others in the border areas, he belongs to a family that has been divided by the *de facto* India–Pakistan border known as the Line of Control (LoC). He desires to meet his two elder brothers, uncle, aunt and cousins, who had crossed over the LoC in 1965 and could not return due to security reasons. Malik fondly remembers his brothers, and remarks that he 'hopes to meet them at least once before he dies'.

In various parts of India, including Delhi, Punjab, West Bengal and Rajasthan, one might come across families that have been separated from their kin as a result of the Partition of the Indian subcontinent. Border areas are particular spaces that are overwhelmingly marked by the phenomenon of divided families. This is especially true of the border areas of Jammu and Kashmir (J&K), the erstwhile state and now the

Union Territory, that not only bore the brunt of the India–Pakistan Partition, but also witnessed internal division due to indigenous rebellion, tribal invasion and consequently, an unresolved border fuzzily conceptualised as the LoC (as distinct from the IB, or the International Border). An armed rebellion against the Dogra monarch which coincided with the invasion of tribals from North-Western Frontier Provinces resulted in the division of the state. Those involved in rebellion were militarily trained local Muslims, who had participated in the Second World War on the side of the British. After the war, these soldiers were demobilised and could not be absorbed within Dogra forces. Unemployed and disgruntled, these militarily capable Muslims of Poonch rebelled against the Maharaja and joined the tribal invaders in seizing large parts of Poonch. It was this chaotic situation which compelled the Maharaja to finally accede to India in October 1947 and seek military help. The India–Pakistan war that took place soon after ended with the division of the state between Jammu and Kashmir on the Indian side, and the areas of Jammu and Kashmir now under the control of Pakistan. It was at this time that the temporary boundary between the two parts of J&K, later named as LoC was drawn (Lamb 1997; Samaddar 2004).[2]

With both the nations staking a claim over the state, as explained thus far, the LoC continues to remain provisional, yet strictly guarded, and is often analogised to the erstwhile Berlin Wall in Germany. On the Indian side of Jammu and Kashmir, a large part of the LoC, which is densely populated, adjoins the Poonch and Rajouri districts of the Jammu region.[3] The impermanence of the LoC has proven to be both a boon and a burden for the people of the border districts. The prolonged conflict that has engulfed the border regions owing to the non-fixity of the LoC, has produced disastrous repercussions for its inhabitants. While the Partition might be a closed or semi-closed chapter for many other parts of India, such as West Bengal or Punjab, it remains an ongoing and incessant phenomenon in Rajouri and Poonch—two densely populated border districts of Jammu. Events starting from the tribal invasion and leading up to multiple India–Pakistan wars in the post-1947 period and later, the Kashmiri insurgency, have produced several waves of movement back and forth across the LoC. As a result, 'divided families' is a common and widespread occurrence in these twin border districts. While the provisionality attached to the LoC provided opportunities for the people of these regions to sneak in and out of the border areas and move to the other side in search of better economic prospects or safe refuge, movement across the LoC was not always free, voluntary or devoid of surveillance troubles. Heightened militancy in the late 1980s and later, the fencing of the LoC, made it more stringent and heavily guarded. De facto yet heavily guarded borders have left a large number of divided families in despair. While some might be living only a few miles apart, they can hardly, if ever, meet each other. It is common to come across stories of elderly members of such families passing away without being able to meet their loved ones. Some hope, however, was generated with the opening of the Poonch–Rawalakot bus service in 2005.[4] It provided opportunities for many people to trace their family members on the other side and visit each other, even while bureaucratic hassles, delays and tight surveillance proved to be some of the major impediments of this process.

Divided families and their cultural and political lives are linked to the 'bordering practices'—constructing, challenging, as well as reinforcing borders and border-related activities. Although constructing borders and boundaries has largely been a state-oriented, top-down project in South Asia, many bordering practices and performances as well as the changes that they undergo entail the close engagement and participation of the divided families. Their memories, imaginations, narratives, jargons, everyday practices and politics become part of the popular and widely used 'border-terminologies', and often influence and compel the state to modify or reconstruct border-related practices. Demanding a shift in stringent India–Pakistan border policies through various measures—making borders porous, facilitating the cross-border movement of people—their discourse has offered at times a dialogic opportunity towards minimising the intensity of the ongoing conflict. This study will explore the lives of the divided families as well as the possibility that their politics offers to resolve the prolonged conflict over the state. Till now, most studies on conflict resolution have looked at the Kashmir region, and tried to explore the negotiatory possibilities between Indian and Kashmiri nationalisms. The present study (conducted between 2014–2015, and later in 2018 to incorporate updates) will instead focus on the Poonch and Rajouri border areas of Jammu in an endeavour to bring out the alternative politics of conflict resolution. Before focusing specifically on the divided families in these districts, it would be pertinent to look briefly into the debates on borders and bordering processes.

Recent scholarship on borders, particularly work on biopolitics in border studies, has enriched and broadened our understanding of the subject. No longer to be viewed just as lines drawn along the national periphery, borders have become more diverse and diffused, existing in various forms (overt and covert) and serving different purposes. There could be socio-cultural borders, political borders, regional borders, local or global borders. Mass policing and surveillance at airports, of refugees and mobile populations, or everyday forms of policing and control at various social spaces, where these techniques might not be conspicuously visible, also point to the notion of borders that go beyond their strict territorial conceptualisation. Moreover, as Chris Rumford has pointed out, borders may appear more concrete and visible to some than to others. He, for instance, highlights the 'different experiences of the border for the businessman, the academic travelling to a conference, and the itinerant agricultural or unskilled worker' (Rumford 2008: 41). As mentioned earlier, Étienne Balibar has propagated the notion, 'borders are everywhere', to suggest the dispersed, multi-layered and polyvalent nature of borders as against the canonical approach towards borders as mere territorial divisions. Balibar forcefully argues that 'the idea that the borders are concentrated in particular places and along well-defined lines is one that should be associated with the nation-state's bordering preferences, rather than being features of borders per se' (Balibar 2002: 84). This, however, does not imply, as he argues, that borders are fading away. In fact, borders are being multiplied and dispersed throughout the body social.

Contemporary theories of diffused, multi-layer borders have added new vigour to border studies, indicating a shift away from state-oriented studies towards studies of spatially mobile populations, cultural politics, gated communities, overlapping local and global trans-boundaries, discriminatory border practices, and so on. We have discussed earlier how rather than fixed outer edges, borders are becoming more complex and hybrid, and pervading everyday lives. Despite their inhibiting and bounding propensities, borders are being questioned and reshaped. The responses of divided families can be analysed using these newer perspectives to understand the ways in which they have contested the territorial notion of borders as absolute and impermeable. The fluid and multi-layered identities of the members of the divided families as well as their novel ways of interpreting boundaries have influenced to some extent the state's narrative on borders in recent years. Despite border hostilities, these spaces are now also simultaneously viewed as sites from where peace can be negotiated.

While the terminology in vogue—'borders are everywhere' and a 'shift away from territorial borderlines'—has changed the way we think about 'borders', an overemphasis on such arguments/ideas may be misleading. In South Asia, 'borders are everywhere', but these are exceptionally limiting and robust in particular territorial locations, especially around the edges of the nations. Borders, in their classical territorial sense, remain relevant, given the ever-increasing process of militarisation and escalating geopolitical tensions in the continent. Borders, in various forms, do extend to interiors as well, yet the coercive impact of national borders on the lives of residents living in strategically peripheral regions is quite distinct, and to an extent totalising, compared to those experiencing 'internal borders'. To reiterate, I argue that the 'borders are everywhere' rhetoric should not be used to underplay or render redundant the role of national borders that use exceptionally strong measures to control and monitor the everyday lives of people inhabiting those particular areas. The ways in which residents living on the national peripheries negotiate with the bordering practices is quite different from the manner in which people in the mainland deal with various types of internal and diffused borders.

Given the conflict that has engulfed the state, the border locations of the Rajouri and Poonch districts in J&K are of specific importance. While various parts of the state have witnessed conflict in different forms, these border districts have been particularly and directly vulnerable to a series of unending turmoils—tribal invasion, wars, Partition horrors, militarisation, frequent shelling and mining, and multiple displacements. These bordering processes have resulted in the disruption of the normal lives of people in these regions.

To locate divided families in their geographical and socio-cultural contexts in Rajouri and Poonch, the following section will offer a brief general description of the border areas. This study will combine a territorial approach with non-territorial, diffused and interpretational conceptions of borders. It seeks to understand how borders and their meanings have changed over time and are contextualised by the divided families in ways that contradict the state's understanding of borders.

Living with Fences

Much has been reported about the conflict politics of Kashmir Valley. Border districts of Jammu have not found much space in the narrative of conflict, despite the fact that there has been an almost continuous volatility at these borders. Of the 740 km-long LoC that divides Jammu and Kashmir on the Indian side and POJK, a 240 km-long stretch adjoins the Rajouri and Poonch districts of Jammu. Since the LoC is the major route for armed militants to infiltrate over to the Indian side, the area has come under strict systems of surveillance. The fencing project of the LoC that was started in 2003 has covered the entire periphery of the two districts with a concrete three-tiered barbed wiring. As one travels across the hilly panorama of these regions, one comes across scenes of continuous fencing, security barriers and military posts every few kilometres, keeping a watch on each and every movement.

Since the fencing is done 2 to 5 kms inside the *de facto* border, there is a gap between the fencing and the LoC. Consequently, a few villages are wedged between the fence and the LoC. In the Nowshera belt, an entry point to Rajouri, my research assistant, two of my local acquaintances and I visited some of the villages—Janghar, Makri, Laam and Bhawani—situated between the fence and the LoC. A large self-contained army post guards these villages. Security personnel are constantly on high alert and keep an eye out for any suspicious movement in and around them. To visit the villages that lie behind the fencing, we had to submit our identity cards and seek permission to enter at this security point. After the inspection of our IDs and detailed inquiries, we were given a warm welcome, offered tea, and granted permission to visit the villages. Since the local Muslims who accompanied us are familiar with the security personnel here, the process was relatively easy.

Our vehicle thus crossed the elaborately marked fencing, and we headed uphill. We were aware of being observed by the border guards at all times. To our surprise, a few locals and village headmen were already aware of our visit—some of them welcomed us, while others inquired about the purpose of our visit and did not want us to stay long. Right across the villages, we could clearly see parts of POJK—houses, agricultural land and security check-posts on the other side of the LoC. The two sides appeared so close, yet so far; merged, yet inaccessible; intimate, yet hostile.

Witness to frequent incidents of cross-border firing and some cases of infiltration, the villagers are highly suspicious of 'outsiders'. Sandwiched between the fence and the LoC, and encircled by posts of the Indian Army and other surveillance authorities, their lives are spatially confined. Though they are free to move in and out of the fencing gate and access the interiors of the Rajouri district and beyond, their everyday lives are perfused with structures of security and scrutiny. Considering their fear of Pakistani military aggression and infiltration, their suspicion of 'outsiders' seems natural. Yet, it would be incorrect to argue that all structures of security are forcibly imposed by the state. While enforcement is an inevitable part of the bordering process, people living in these villages do participate in these procedures. While being critical of the wars, escalating India–Pakistan tensions and the military apparatus at large, they often justify the presence of the Army and cooperate with the security personnel by providing them with relevant information. Many villagers believe that 'the Army is necessary to check Pakistani aggression and infiltration'. The Army, thus, is viewed as a protector.

Several villagers claimed that the army has, in fact, maintained good relations with the locals, thus allowing for some sort of collaboration between the two. Many schools and medical centres here are run by the army, for instance. In case of medical emergencies in remote regions, it provides vehicles to take patients to hospitals that are often located far away. This, however, does not take away from the villagers' discomfort linked to security and bordering practices. If they happen to be out of their fenced area late at night, for example, they have to take official permission. Their absence from the village for a long time is noted and family members are interrogated in such circumstances. 'I understand that these restrictions are for our protection .... Otherwise, in these tense circumstances, infiltrators might cause havoc. But it affects our lives. We feel as if we are living inside a cage,' said Umar, a young Muslim vendor from Rajouri. Others informed us that at times, frequent firing and shelling lead to temporary displacement of families directly affected by the warlike situation. Members of the divided families lamented that despite living so close to the border, they cannot visit relatives on the other side—some have kin living just across the LoC, approximately 5–6 kms away, yet visiting each other is impossible. Impermeable borders and strict visa regulations act as impediments to cross-border movement. A middle-aged Rajput Muslim, Hamid, who had once visited relatives across the LoC, surmised,

> Living next to the border is not good. These boundaries keep reminding us of our near ones whom we can never visit again. The air they breathe also reaches us ... we can feel each other. But it will hardly be possible to meet, see each other's faces, talk face-to-face.

The districts of Poonch and Rajouri also have several villages that lie close to the border but are not sandwiched between the fencing and the LoC. The fence here lies between the village and the LoC. Yet these settlements are vulnerable to excessive militarisation and cross-border hostilities. Instances of people crossing over to the other side illegally, or at times, inadvertently, and not being able to return due to the vast security cover are many. Such narratives prevail even when one ventures away from the border regions, towards mainland Rajouri and Poonch. Though illegal cross-border migrations have been taking place since 1947–1948, I was informed that many of the recent crossings from the Indian to the Pakistani side had taken place during the militancy period in the 1990s. Although very few Muslim youth were directly involved with the insurgent movement in the border areas of Jammu, threats by the insurgents as well as the stringent security environment led to many such migrations. These cross-border movements have more or less come to a halt since the LoC was fenced in 2003 (Chowdhary 2012). Fencing was undertaken to cleanse these areas of insurgents and construct an almost impermeable security cover in order to curb any possible infiltration. Despite its provisional status, post-2003, the LoC acts more or less as a concrete wall.

This concreteness of the LoC, however, does not imply that borders have been static. Notwithstanding the tight vigilance, people and goods have been moving to and fro across the borders. This movement has been haphazard and risk-prone. While many people attempting to cross the LoC were successful in their attempts, many others have faced arrests, harassment and have even lost their lives in the process. Some people who managed to move to the other side could not return due to the fear of security at the borders. Despite these complex cross-border mobilities, for many, borders symbolised a closure. In particular, for many members of the divided families, the LoC represented a concrete, impermeable wall that had permanently severed their links with their kindred.

It may be pertinent to mention here that different eras illustrate divergent stories of crossing over. Narratives from some phases implied hassle-free movements, while other phases characterised by India–Pakistan tensions implied a tightening of boundaries and risk-prone crossings. Although cross-border mobility was curtailed to a large extent in the post-2003 phase, politics emerging from the border areas during this period engaged the nation-state and persuaded it to acknowledge a new vocabulary, which included phrases like 'porous borders' or 'making borders irrelevant'. This popular political terminology ran parallel to the concreteness of the border and pushed the Indian and Pakistani governments to facilitate people-to-people movement across the LoC. The following section describes the complex and changing patterns of mobility across the LoC, and how these movements have come to define and shape the lives of divided families. Their topographical location and spatial mobilities have also shaped their relationship with the notions of nation and nationalism. Just like the changing nature of borders, the lives of divided families and their engagements with the idea of 'nation' and 'nationalism' have also been a changing, non-static reality.

Multiple Displacements and Divided Families: A Chronological Account

Notwithstanding its vigilant and spatially confining tendencies, the conflicts and tensions produced at the borders have often propelled the movement of people in and out of the defined and demarcated territorial boundaries. Post the accession period of 1947–1948, both the Indian and Pakistani states have been trying to restrict mobility and dissociate from the ethnic and cultural ties that the two parts share. Yet, their respective claims on J&K as a whole, and the consequent volatile situations at the borders, have triggered a series of displacements. Chaos, uncertainties and violence that accompanied these unplanned displacements resulted in the separation of many family members who found themselves on different sides of the border. These movements, though messy, defy the regulatory border processes and state-oriented efforts to sever links between the two sides of the LoC.

While there is no clear and well-defined pattern of movements across the LoC, three main waves of displacement can be identified in the context of the Rajouri and Poonch districts—the tribal invasion of 1947 and migration of Hindus towards Jammu and Kashmir on the Indian side; the India–Pakistan war of 1947–1948 and displacement of Muslims towards POJK (and for some, a return to the Indian side); the India–Pakistan war of 1965 and displacement of Muslims towards POJK (again, for some, a return to Jammu and Kashmir on the Indian side).

Tribal Invasion and Displacement of Hindus in 1947–1948

During times of Partition, the tribal invasion by Pathan Muslim tribesmen from the North-West Frontier Province of Pakistan led to the first wave of displacement and Partition of the state. These tribesmen infiltrated various parts of the state, creating a situation of communal violence, massacre and unrest (Schofield 2003: 47). The killings of Hindus in these areas resulted in their displacement. Hindus from the Mirpur, Kotli and Muzaffarabad areas (now in POJK) migrated to regions such as Rajouri and Poonch (now in the Indian side of Jammu and Kashmir), and many others moved further south to other parts of the state with a higher Hindu population. Amidst the invasion as well as Partition-related violence that had gripped the entire subcontinent; many women and men were left behind on the 'wrong' side of the border, while others managed to migrate and reach safer places. A large number of Hindu families living in Rajouri and Poonch are refugees, originally from the Mirpur and Kotli areas in POJK. These Hindus still refer to themselves as refugees, or as 'Mirpuris' and 'Kotliwalas'. Some of their relatives, who could not migrate from these regions, later converted to Islam and are now residents of POJK. This kinship across religions provides a distinctive socio-political outlook to these divided families. Despite reiterating and often selectively exaggerating the Partition narrative of Hindu killings, for many Hindu refugees in Rajouri and Poonch cross-religious familial linkages made it possible to relate to and bond with the Muslims around them who have also suffered displacement and atrocities. Many of my Hindu respondents talked about the communally charged fallout of Partition that also led to a number of Muslim killings in parts of the state. Some of them accused the political elites of drawing boundaries for their own vested interests and inciting communal divisions. In Rajouri, Hira Mani, an elderly Hindu who owned a grocery store (and who is originally from Kotli in POJK), alleged,

> This is a game of political elites. I remember those horrible times .... Neither I nor my Muslim neighbour in Kotli knew what was going to happen. We became victims of the situation. Some Hindus and Muslims participated in the communal violence. But most of us were completely confused and vulnerable. We were longing for normalcy, longing for the violence to be over.

Nevertheless, the memories, Partition stories and political narratives espoused by the divided families are too complex to be classified within any singular category such as 'secular', 'bigoted', 'liberal' or 'communal'. These intricate memories of Partition violence and massacres during the tribal invasion still define to some extent the political vocabulary of Hindus in border areas. Thus, on certain occasions, space is created for religious and nationalist politics among some Hindu groups. However, their proximity to border processes may also moderate their political stands. They often articulate their awareness of the dangers inherent in the ultra-nationalist jingoism which endorses the idea of making borders permanent and rigid. The cross-border linkages of Hindus, not only with their Muslim relatives but with other Muslims who come from across the LoC to visit their ancestral lands or meet their kinsfolk, also tones down their inflexible political stances.

The 1947–1948 War and Displacement of Muslims

Another wave of displacement and migrations in the border regions was that of Muslims, which also took place in 1947–

1948. Invasion by the tribesmen compelled the monarch of the state, Maharaja Hari Singh, to accede to India and seek military help in October 1948 (Bose 2003: 33–37). The India–Pakistan war that ensued led to the Partition of the state. The advance of the Indian Army to the Rajouri and Poonch caused panic among the Muslims of these areas. There was a widespread fear that the Indian Army would avenge Hindu killings and take action against the Muslim community on the suspicion that some of them might have provided cover to the tribesmen. This led many Muslims to flee to the other side of the border, albeit a large number of them returned after a few years when the situation appeared relatively normal (Gupta 2007). Some, however, chose not to come back, or were left behind amidst uncertainty and chaos.

The 1965 War and Displacement of Muslims

After 1947–1948, yet another wave of Muslim displacement took place during the 1965 India–Pakistan war. Infiltration of armed men known as Razakars from POJK at several places in Jammu and Kashmir on the Indian side, including the border areas, resulted in the 1965 war (Chakravorty 1992). The process of clearing the border areas of infiltrators resulted in a large-scale migration of Muslims across the border (Bose 2003: 148). In comparison to 1947–1948, this time a relatively larger number of Muslims took refuge in Pakistan (Chowdhary 2012). While some of them returned after a gap of a few years, others remained there, thus resulting in the phenomenon of divided families.

Despite the presence of surveillance mechanisms, borders were relatively porous in the 1947–1965 period. These cross-border flows defied the nationalist logic of absolute loyalty to one supreme nation, as Muslims developed cultural, familial and emotional ties with areas across the border. In many instances, the question of nationalist loyalty took a backseat and was superseded by more important issues related to economic interests, personal survival and security, as well as ethnic, cultural and familial affiliations. For many families divided by borders, 'imagining a nation' was not a seamless process. Rather than a celebratory or eulogistic practice, their national sense of belonging was marked by fractures, loss and incompleteness. The 1965 war was followed by the gradual tightening of the LoC, attempting to bring cross-border movements to an end. Yet, the 1971 India–Pakistan war as well as the insurgency phase of the 1990s witnessed incidents of migrations across the LoC. While the post-2003 era witnessed the fencing of the LoC, it also opened up some legal, political and dialogic avenues for restricted cross-border movements. These messy, haphazard flows and the changing nature of the LoC have impacted the divided families as well as enabled them to interact with the nation-state's notion of borders and national identity in specific ways.

Divided Families, Mobilities and National Imagination

Partition scholarship has controverted the official reading that describes 1947 as a moment of jubilation, accomplishment and completion—a moment when the long-cherished aspiration of statehood was achieved and neatly concluded. These studies point out the tragedies and irresolvable contradictions that were not just inherent to, but also succeeded the event of Partition. Critiquing the official histories, Vazira Zamindar (2008: 4) remarks:

> Most histories of the region as a whole end at this 'moment of arrival,' as nationalism achieves its celebrated goal of statehood, or thereafter sever into studies of distinct nation-states, as if in this 'moment of rupture' 'India,' 'Pakistan,' and their borders simply emerge fully formed.

Highlighting the genocidal violence, unprecedented displacements and disillusionment of the refugees, she points to perplexing questions that puzzled people at the moment of Partition. 'Where, indeed, is India? Where is Pakistan? Who is an Indian? Who is a Pakistani?' (ibid.: 2)—these questions reflect the ambiguities faced by people who do not fit into the apparently 'neat', officially assumed cartographic categories.

While questions related to national status or 'to which nation does one belong' were (relatively) resolved over time for many who were displaced during Partition, for those living near the LoC, these issues remained open-ended and contested for a longer period. Even for the inhabitants of other somewhat porous border areas in West Bengal and Rajasthan, the question of 'national status' or 'citizenship' continued to be ambiguous in the post-Partition period. However, what made the LoC distinct from these international borders was its provisional, disputed and unsettled character, adding further intricacies to the 'national' question. The *de facto* nature of the LoC as well as the frequent India–Pakistan military skirmishes and their sheer intensity necessitated the constant movement of people in these areas, often leaving behind their lands, homes and property for short or long spans. Many of those who were separated from their families—left behind in chaos and violence or forced to be on the move to seek safe refuge—were uncertain about the ideas of 'nation' and 'national belonging' for a long time: How many times would they have to move? To which nation will they eventually belong? Where is home? Where exactly do borders begin and end? Will they ever be reunited with their separated kin? Would they be forced to snap ties with their extended families residing on the other side of the boundary? How do they reconcile with these divisions and demarcations that are in conflict with their aspirations? These apprehensions remained somewhat unresolved till 1965, and beyond, as cross-border flows were witnessed most in the first couple of decades after the accession in 1947.

A large number of the Muslim respondents in Rajouri and Poonch recounted their experiences of shuttling back and forth across the LoC, unsure of where their journey would end, or to which 'nationality' they would finally belong. Narrating his experience, Anwar Alam, an 82-year-old sarpanch from Gulpur village in Poonch, says:

> In 1947–1948, I was a young boy. [But] I do remember some of the moments. At that time my family had no idea if we were Indian or Pakistani. We knew that we belonged to the Karmara village in Poonch. When we heard stories about the Indian Army ... that it was advancing towards the border areas, my family left everything in our village. With other Muslims who were fleeing India, we went to a small village in Pakistan. We stayed there for some time and then moved to other places in the country ... in search of better shelter, livelihood. But Pakistan was in bad shape and we did not get much help from the government. It was difficult to survive, and we had our lands back in Poonch. Many of my family members and relatives were separated from each other in this struggle for survival. After seven years, we returned to Poonch in 1954. Some of my relatives are still in Pakistan. One of my sisters is also there, married off to a relative. She must be very old now (sighs) ... I migrated to Pakistan again in 1965. This time I came back after three years but many of my other relatives who went along with me did not return ... including my brother. He came to visit me a few years ago. Our meeting was happy yet full of despair. We could not stop crying. Tears wouldn't stop flowing.

In Poonch, a middle-aged Rajput Muslim, Sajid Khan, offers a similar account of his family's temporary migration across the LoC in 1948:

> My father with his entire family was displaced in 1948. We were told that the Indian Army is arriving and we would be safer on the other side in Pakistan ... Lines were drawn and my father was unsure of the consequences. There was news

> of blood, violence and horror. Those were difficult times. My family went to the Pakistan side and stayed there for eight years. We were taken care of by fellow Muslims ... my father would always tell us stories about their goodwill. Some of my relatives, my brother-in-law, my sister, my uncles, my mother's sister and her family ... they are all in Pakistan, across the border. They never came back as they got some land there. They run a very good business and are very prosperous. But my father came back. He did not find a good source of livelihood and faced many hardships. He was very attached to his land back home ... We went to Pakistan to meet our families. Who knows if we will ever be able to meet again? The visa system is not easy ... I wish it was easy to move here and there, so that I could take my father there again. He talks very fondly of the places he lived in.

Another elderly gentleman, Arif Hassan, a resident of Rajouri, says

> I went to Pakistan in 1948, then came back after some years. I went again in 1965 and returned after four years. I was wandering, *kabhi border ke is paar, kabhi us paar* (sometimes on this side and sometimes on that side of the border). I was unsure.... I have family both in India and Pakistan [in POJK]. I wish both the regions could be united. At least one should be allowed to move freely between the two regions. *Par ye tar aisa hone nahin deti* (but this fence/border doesn't let it happen).

These accounts from the LoC do not altogether refute but problematise the homogenised and institutionalised meaning of 'nation' and 'national imagination'. In 1947–1948, these respondents had a vague idea about the formation of India and Pakistan as two separate entities. The complex patterns of geographical mobility that they experienced questioned the idea of 'imagined communities' as homogeneous in space and time. The experiences of the respondents above add heterogeneity to the concept of 'national imagination', implying that not only may people at the margins imagine 'nation' differently than those at the centre or in the mainland, but also that their national sense of belonging may be viewed as a 'process' that shifts with time. People and families divided by borders were engaged in a process of imagining a nation that was fraught with contradictions and uncertainties. But more significantly, this process was dynamic rather than static—whereby it was only over time that their national sense of belonging became a relatively settled idea, albeit still marked by dilemmas and fluidities.

While territorial uncertainties complicated and delayed the imagination of belonging to a national entity, the families that were divided in the process further extended and loosened the definition of 'imagination'—a sense of belonging that is based not just on territorial demarcations, but one that often transcends these geographical boundaries to form more fluid affiliations based on cultural, religious and familial factors. Thus, even after 1965, when territorial borders were further reified and people developed an awareness of 'national identity', this sense of 'belonging' was not straightforward and unambiguous. Cross-LoC family and religious affiliations often enabled the members of the divided families to prioritise fluid and multiple identity markers, expressing an emotional association with regions on both sides of the LoC. This does not imply a complete rejection of the idea of a 'nation', since a majority of my respondents did refer to themselves as 'Indians', one of their many identities. Nevertheless, this did not erase their attachment to the other nation on the basis of religion, family networks, cultural symbols and various other socio-political factors. The narratives of the respondents above—representing affiliation and attachment to areas across the LoC—suggest a counter-narrative to the 'nation' that eludes its absolute hegemony.

What emerges clearly from these accounts is that economic opportunities, better quality of life, and attachment to land and security issues were the decisive factors that shaped people's national preference. Though a large majority of the inhabitants of the LoC areas did not get to choose their nationalities, whatever agency or preference they had in carving their own national destiny was determined by these pecuniary issues rather than any linear association with 'India' or 'Pakistan'. Even the formation of Pakistan as a 'Muslim nation'—and by implication, the notion that Muslim refugees could 'naturally' become its citizens—was only a theoretical idea. Pragmatically, the Pakistani state was neither prepared nor willing to accommodate all Muslim refugees as citizens. While many refugees managed to take temporary refuge in areas across the LoC or even settle there permanently, the prevailing confusion and lack of government response accentuated the disorientation of displaced Muslims. 'Nation' and 'national imagination' thus remained nebulous concepts for a long time.

These concepts were comparatively less vague for Hindus who had been displaced from POJK in 1947–1948. Their association with the 'Indian nation' and 'Indian nationalism' has been less problematic. Yet, their unresolved refugee status, memories of 'home' and ancestral villages back in POJK, as well as their association with their now Muslim relatives still living in Pakistan, creates a counter-space for interrogating the rigid and ultra-nationalist readings of 'nation'. On the issue of India–Pakistan wars and hostilities at the border, a middle-aged Hindu, Satnam, was critical of the aggressive nationalism: 'Those of us who live in border areas, we have to face repercussions.' Satnam belongs to a refugee family and has been able to visit his relatives in Mirpur a couple of times. During a conversation on India–Pakistan relations and their competitive aggression, he mentioned that he wants to be left alone: 'When India talks about war, I pray it doesn't touch Mirpur in Pakistan.'

Sharing a border identity, many Hindu and Muslim inhabitants of the areas around the LoC do form alternative national narratives that place the emphasis on intertwining inter-border relationships. One of the spaces where the symbolic as well as discursive expression of this narrative is conspicuous is the point near Chakan-da-Bagh in Poonch.

It is here that the fortnightly bus service connecting the two sides of Jammu and Kashmir commences and terminates. A complex mix of emotions—jubilation, sorrow, mourning, sobbing and even fainting—dominates this location, where separated families and friends meet and part. It is hard to illustrate the odd screams, awkward silences, excitement and disturbing farewells that characterise the unexpected union of families. Here, the divided families create an alternative symbolic space—a space that mocks borders and underlines cross-religious, cross-national and cross-LoC ties. Categories of borders, nations and religions are at least momentarily nullified as people of both sides meet and separate. The discourse that unfurls from here propels the Indian and Pakistani nation-states towards an alternative paradigm of porous borders and accommodative nationalisms.

Complex Conflict, Personal Suffering and Political Meaning

Notwithstanding the space for interrogation generated by these counter-narratives, territorial borders and violent conflict remain a reality for the inhabitants of Rajouri and Poonch. These areas got caught up in a complex situation during the 1990s when militancy and separatism overtook the Kashmir Valley. While the separatist movement did not gain momentum in the Muslim-majority parts of Jammu, such as Rajouri and Poonch, these areas along the LoC have been inevitably caught up in the vicious cycle of the conflict (Bose 2003). A large number of my respondents expressed their vulnerability as they stated that they have been involuntarily trapped in the complex 'India–Pakistan–Kashmir' conflict. Border areas have suffered the direct and most brutal implications of the conflict, whether in the form of Partition, excessive militarisation, wars, everyday shelling, displacements, separation of families or extension of

Kashmiri insurgency. In all its dimensions and shades, conflict has produced armed aggression and turbulence on the borders, with grave repercussions for the divided families. Yet, the personal suffering of these families has not been an integral part of conflict studies, which tend to focus mainly on the India–Pakistan or India–Kashmir dimensions of the dispute.

It is extremely important to focus on these individual, personal stories that are not only the narratives of pain and trauma, but also offer possibilities for reconciliation. While Indian and Pakistani nationalisms on the one hand, and Kashmiri identity politics on the other, often assume mutually exclusive positions, the stories and discourses of the divided families offer a dialogic space. The sufferings of the divided families constantly emphasise the need to go beyond the national rhetoric and fallacious jingoism that has separated members of the same familial, ethnic and cultural stock. By bringing a humane angle to the otherwise strategic and nationalist facets of the conflict, the divided families make a case for blurring the borders and bringing two parts of the state closer. Their stories of despair and their 'national imaginations' offer alternative ways to understand and resolve the conflict.

Sharing many characteristics, the collective accounts of the divided families offer a political vocabulary for contestation as well as reconciliation. Yet each individual account is significant, each personal story of suffering is different from the other. The personal needs to be woven together with the collective, so that individual stories do not get obscured in the collective political discourse.

The personal and the political are enmeshed in the story of the 80-year-old respondent from Poonch, Ahmad Hussain. His life evokes a broader political message:

> We migrated (to POJK) in 1965. ... All of us—my wife, my sons and daughters, and me. There, we had to start life anew. We came back in 1968, but I could not get my eldest son to come along with us ... He had been keeping wrong company.

We persuaded him to come back, but he refused. He was young and immature. One of our relatives promised to take care of him. We had to return, as there was no source of income in Pakistan. We used to live in camps, and I had to struggle a lot to put clothes on the backd of my family. My younger daughter used to cry as we lived in horrible conditions ... After many years, my eldest son started missing the family. We could not talk to him. There was no India–Pakistan phone facility and the situation became worse after the 1971 war. The authorities in India would not have responded positively if they got to know that we have connections on the other side. So we did not talk about him. But once we got a letter from an acquaintance in Pakistan, stating that our son misses the family. We were helpless. What could we do? Our fate was sealed by borders. The security issues made it impossible for him to return. Now he is settled there (in POJK) ... *Ye lakeeren, ye taren sirf taren nahin hain, inmein rishte bhi ruke hue hain* (These lines, these fences are not just fences per se, they are also barriers for relationships).

These borders also snatched away my second son later... It must have been about 15 years ago, during the time of militancy. He accidentally crossed the border. He was taking care of some grazing animals ... [Hussain was hesitant to talk about this incident in detail]. He also could not return. We fear that if he returns, the security forces here would harass him on the suspicion that he is a militant who had gone to the other side for training. That is why he can't come back. When we went to Pakistan a few years back, we met him. We could stay only for a month, that too by extending our visa. In such a short time we could not gauge how he feels in Pakistan. But his mother misses him. When we were leaving, mother and son clung to each other. They cried ... That was years ago. We are still trying to cope with the reality ... *1947 khatam ho gaya, par humare liye to abhi tak khatam nahin hua* (1947 has ended, but for us it continues). Till these borders are there, till the India–Pakistan enmity prevails, there can be no peace in our lives. We don't want fences to be removed completely. We know that in these circumstances, fences cannot be removed.

> Fences are there for our safety as well. But people should be allowed to visit each other.

When Ahmad Hussain narrates his story, one can closely relate to the agony that he and his family have been undergoing. His voice is relevant here to establish how conflict has destabilised many individual lives and families in the border areas. The term 'divided families', then, does not remain just a term for scholarly analysis, but denotes many such personal tragedies that continue to define people's lives.

These personal accounts also serve a political purpose—of describing the conflict in ways that go beyond our normative understanding, which is limited to the ongoing 'Kashmir dispute'. Conflict politics that is otherwise multi-dimensional and multi-layered has somehow come to be focused on Kashmir. However, what gets obscured by this Kashmir-centric meta-narrative, and is brought out in the personal narratives above, is the form that the conflict assumes in the context of borders. At the borders, the conflict does not arise out of the demands for 'self-determination' as in Kashmir. Rather, as mentioned above, there the conflict is an extension of the stressful India–Pakistan and India–Kashmir relationship—one that is thrust upon its inhabitants perforce, be they the border-related refugees, the people living amidst the volatility of borders, or the divided families. The stories of divided families highlight the consequences of this prolonged, enforced dispute, which have remained unacknowledged in the mainstream understanding and discourse on the conflict. In his personal account, Hussain brings the Partition and 'borders' within the framework of conflict. It is interesting that he redefines Partition as an ongoing phenomenon, specific to the LoC areas, when he remarks, '*1947 khatam ho gaya, but humare liye to abhi tak khatam nahin hua*' (1947 has ended, but for us it continues). Unlike in many other parts of the country, here in the border areas, the Partition is not history for the inhabitants. Elsewhere in the State of J&K,

too, the Partition has not been a continuing, everyday reality. But the strategic and provisional nature of the LoC has turned these areas into an unstable war zone, causing an unending series of disruptions in the lives of the locals, including multiple dislocations. While the effect of Partition diffuses as it enters the mainland, the most direct and everyday consequences are experienced in this geographical realm.

Hussain vividly weaves the personal and the political. On the one hand, he goes beyond the personal to offer wider socio-political perspectives on conflict, borders and the Partition. On the other, he adds a personal, subjective, emotive tone to these analytical categories. Borders and boundaries thus acquire a humane character, emphasising the need for pacification and reconciliation. This is reflected in Hussain's statement, *'Ye lakeeren, ye taren sirf taren nahin hain, inmein rishte bhi ruke hue hain'* (These lines and fences are not merely fences, but also barriers to relationships). Such sentiments are widespread among divided families, and their narratives also assume a political form and urge the nation-state to redefine national and strategic priorities.

Another account that may be mentioned here is that of a retired Sikh schoolteacher in Poonch, Jaspal Singh. Singh's family originally belonged to the Mirpur area in POJK. Though he does not remember the 1947–1948 violence that led his family to migrate to the Indian side, he says he has always had clear memories of his brother, who was left behind on the other side:

> I do not remember anything about the Partition violence. But I felt a chill down my spine whenever my father and mother described their condition during that time—how they managed to escape, and how there were bloodthirsty people and massacres all around. On their way [to India], in a refugee camp, my elder brother went missing. They never found him. They had to move ahead with the *kafila* (caravan), as it was dangerous to stay there any longer ... I

> do not remember anything, I was very young, but I had some memories of my brother. Then, around 1965, some Muslims of our village were able to trace my brother. They had fled to the Pakistan side in 1965. You must know all that happened during that time... Meanwhile, we received news that my brother had become a Sheikh (Muslim). But we were excited that he is alive. How does it matter whether he is Sikh, Hindu or Muslim? *Khoon to ek hi hai na* (the blood is same) ... We knew we wouldn't be able to meet him; we were resigned to our fate. *Ye lakeeren jo khich gayi hain bhaiyon aur parivaron ke beech mien* (After all, these lines have been drawn between brothers and families).
>
> But then by god's grace, he [my brother] came to see us. After so many years... so many years have passed by. My parents are no more. And they missed the cross-border bus service. By the time it was started, they were dead. Earlier, the situation was very strict...I could not recognise my brother, though he had sent his photo some time ago. We were speechless. *Madamji*, I can't describe those emotional moments. My brother had become a devout Muslim. He would offer *namaaz*. I made it comfortable for him. I took him to mosques around here ... It was not a pleasant experience when he was leaving us. I am also trying to get a visa. Let us see ... If only borders were open, many families could visit each other in times of joy and sorrow.

In yet another instance, when an elderly Atif Beig, a renowned community leader in his town in the Rajouri district, was recounting his story, he pointed to the constructed nature of religion, nations and borders. Beig told me that in the various moments of turmoil—1947–1948, 1965 and 1971—many of his family members had been moving back and forth across the LoC. Consequently, many of his immediate and extended family members now reside across the LoC, including his father and two of his sisters. Beig told me that his father stayed on in Pakistan to look after his sisters. Besides, after a point in time, sometime in the 1970s, he said it was not safe for him to return due to the strained India–Pakistan relations, although he visited Beig thrice after 2005. Beig's mother had died long ago when they had moved to Pakistan in 1947–1948. Beig also spent some years across the LoC, but returned to India with his brothers and relatives in 1954. He remarks:

> We thought that my entire family would return to India. There was uncertainty, violence all around…issue of livelihood, and other problems. There was India, there was Pakistan, and we were trapped in between. Some Muslims thought areas across the border would be safer for them. Some wanted to stay in India. This went on till 1965. People went from one place to another…*Mein samajhta hoon ki siyasatdanon ne Hinduon aur Musalmano ko laraya, aur phir Hindustan aur Pakistan banaya* (I think that the political elite made Hindus and Muslims fight with each other, and then they created India and Pakistan). We are still bearing the brunt of these divisions…*Kabhi humein Hindu aur Musalmano mein baant dete hain aur kabhi humare beech mein border bana dete hain. Aur kabhi humare hi parivaar ke logon ko alag alag kar dete hain* (Sometimes we are divided into Hindus and Muslims, sometimes we are divided by borders. Sometimes families are split apart).
>
> Now India and Pakistan are two separate countries. Like any other country, they should allow people to meet each other [travelling] from India to Pakistan and from Pakistan to India. Let the fences be there. Fences need not be completely erased. Otherwise bad elements from Pakistan will keep entering our areas and our lives will be in danger….But let people freely go and meet their families. *Mein samajhta hoon ki ye diwaren khari kari ja sakti hain to tori bhi ja sakti hain* (I believe that if these walls can be erected, they can be brought down as well). *Par humare liye koi nahin sochta, na Hindustan na Pakistan ki hakumat. Ye Kashmiri leader bhi sirf apni baat karte hain. Jab zaroorat hoti hai humein apne saath milana chahte hain; varna humein neecha samajhte hain* (But no one thinks about us, neither the Indian nor the Pakistani state. These Kashmiri leaders also speak for themselves. When

they need to, they include us in their discourse; otherwise, they consider us inferior).

The stories of both Singh and Beig do not begin and conclude with 1947–1948, but cover a long span of time—a lifetime. While Singh was separated from his brother and other extended family members, Beig lived a major part of his life away from his father, sisters and other relatives. The creation of India and Pakistan as two nation-states did not provide any spatial or emotional permanence to the respondents and their families. Uncertainty, shifting of boundaries as well as religion in some cases marked the lives of divided families. In this context, the lived experiences of separation and unpredictability of both the respondents have enabled them to view religion, boundaries and nations not as static categories with single, fixed meanings, but as 'processes' that are politically constructed and refashioned over time. Despite his strong Sikh identity, Singh warmly accepts the Islamic identity of his brother. Although religion does not lose its significance for either Singh or his brother, it becomes a loose, negotiable and interactive category rather than a rigid one. Another interesting insight that Singh offers is that despite viewing his personal tragedy as a matter of 'fate', he clearly refuses to consider borders as natural and eternal. Like many other respondents, he defines a border as a *lakeer* (or line) that has been sketched in the temporal and geographical realms. The border, for him, is a line that led to personal tragedy, and the only resolution to his suffering and that of other divided families is to blur that 'line'. Underlying this political message is the reference to the political elites who actively engage in the construction and reshaping of borders.

By commenting on the role of the political elite in labelling and freezing the categories of Hindus and Muslims, as well as in creating the two nations, Beig draws attention to such processes of construction. Although he may not be well-versed in the nuances of colonial or post-colonial history, his own experiences enable him to understand the complex and messy ways in which the categories of borders and nations are defined. His lived insights have much to offer to the academic and political understanding of the processes of 'categorisation', 'labelling' and 'construction' of the seemingly rigid notions of nations, boundaries and religion. Nevertheless, these notions do not become unreal or irrelevant. Despite the element of construction or redesigning inherent in them, these are corporeal realities that are part of people's everyday lives. Beig recognises and even justifies the tangible existence of fences. Fences have come to be reinforced in consent with the people of border areas, who believe in the underlying rationale of 'security' to some extent. While acknowledging the relevance of fences, the stories of these respondents highlight the need for reconciliation and the softening of borders.

Like Ahmad Hussain's account, Atif Beig's narrative also points to the specificity and the localised nature of the conflict in the LoC areas, which is overlooked in the meta-narrative. On the one hand, he criticises the Indian and Pakistani nation-states for ignoring their problems, and on the other hand, he accuses the Kashmiri leadership of failing to represent their grievances. Many of my respondents pointed to the omission of the subject of divided families and other problems pertaining to the LoC areas in the broader Kashmiri political narrative. Since these respondents mainly define conflict in relation to borders and boundaries, it will be interesting to underscore how some of their aspirations and imaginations on the subject of borders are shaped by contemporary global events.

Imagining a Borderless World: An Alternative Vocabulary of Conflict

Global debates have increasingly entered the border areas not just through the media and the Internet, but also through the mobility of people within and outside India. Many people have been relocating to countries like Dubai or Saudi Arabia on a short-term or long-term basis in pursuit of better economic opportunities. Many Muslim residents of Rajouri and Poonch have their extended kin now settled in England or the United States of America. These linkages often expose the people of border regions to current affairs around the world. While conducting my fieldwork, I was intrigued by their awareness of Europe's territorial and economic integration processes. Since borders influence their mundane lives and divide many families, many of my respondents were exposed to the debate of Europe's 'borderless' world—the idea of people moving freely amongst the various European countries for tourism, work or other purposes without a visa. Many members of the divided families were fascinated by the idea that neighbouring countries need not engage in skirmishes to advance themselves; instead, mutual cooperation and removal of economic and territorial barriers is the way forward. Separated by fences, for them the idea of a 'borderless' world seems like a distant dream, yet a very practical model that could benefit their families as well as the two nation-states.

Among the other respondents, Haji Pervez Khan of Agrati village in Rajouri also expressed similar views. He has many of his close and distant relatives now living in POJK, England and Saudi Arabia. Khan himself lived and worked in Saudi Arabia from 1981 to 1985. He returned to Rajouri in 1985 and found a job with the Army supply corps. In one of our conversations, he stated:

> See, I feel there is a difference between people in Saudi Arabia and India. People there are more concerned about economic progress. Here, in India and Pakistan, people die fighting one another. Rather than economic progress, they spend more time fighting with each other; they spend time making enemies. Politicians here also earn their living by dividing people, drawing borders.... My relatives told us about the situation

> in Europe too. You must already know about Europe and the Berlin Wall…Germany was divided into two parts; the politicians had constructed the Wall. But there came a time when people became conscious. The Wall was brought down and the people were united…. Here, there is no such wall, only fences. Why can't we in India and Pakistan forget our problems and hostilities and become one and focus on our economic issues? If these two nations also follow this model, then people of the border zones can freely meet each other without any visa hassles…. However, this cannot happen just because I so desire. Politicians have their own interests in creating fences. Our thinking cannot be like that of the European nations….

Khan's views were also echoed by Gowhar Choudhary, a retired police officer in Rajouri. Choudhary's close maternal family relations are now settled across the border. His relatives have visited Choudhary twice in Rajouri, and he keeps in touch with them through Skype and email. Talking about the larger geo-political issues at hand, Gowhar Choudhary told me:

> I have heard about free movement of people in Europe. No boundaries, no fences, no wars. What we, the people of LoC, want is peace, and this can only happen if India and Pakistan open borders and start having friendly relations. They should learn from Europe. Peace and solution to Kashmir conflict can come through the opening of borders. Kashmiris say first listen to our grievances. India says first give us POJK. And Pakistan also says first give us Kashmir. None of the three parties understand that it is we the people of border areas who have been suffering since 1947. We have seen wars…. We have been uprooted from our homes. We face mines and shelling everyday…I feel that if borders are softened, all these issues will also eventually be resolved. Let the borders be guarded against infiltrators, but let people move freely without visa restrictions…. We want peace between the two countries. We do not have any problems living in India. We have more facilities—infrastructure, education and economic opportunities. Women have more freedom. *Bus raaste khol*

> *do ki shaadi ho ya koi maut ho to milne ja sake. Koi meeting point bana do* (All we want is the opening up of routes, so that we may get together to celebrate marriages and mourn deaths—a means to gather with our near and dear ones across the border).

The two conversations clearly highlight the alternative political vocabulary to resolving the prolonged conflict. It clearly shows that the 'Kashmir question' represents one dimension of the complex conflict politics. However, another dimension of the conflict is presented by the border Muslims. Their arguments are based on the blurring of borders and they want their perspective to be incorporated into the conflict discourse. An awareness of the European borders debate manifests the anguish as well as the hopes of the divided families, thus appealing to the Indian and Pakistani nation-states to match their nationalist impulses to changing global realities. This perspective calls for retaining the relevance of nation-states, yet making space for fluid, overlapping identities and accommodative nationalisms.

The vocabulary of a porous, borderless world is widely prevalent among the LoC residents. Representing people's voices, this vocabulary brings to the fore the plural realities of the erstwhile State of Jammu and Kashmir, and the diverse aspirations of various groups of people that need to be incorporated within the broader narrative of conflict. This process of redefining conflict also reflects a clear cut rejection of the separatist politics of self-determination. In fact, people in Rajouri and Poonch have a desire to shift away from the aggressive territorial and militaristic forms of nationalism towards a more people-centric and open-ended ideal. The popular terminology of fluid, overlapping and intertwining boundaries indicate this aspiration. The comments of various respondents underscore this alternative reading of conflict politics. For instance, Shaukat Aziz, a retired government servant in Poonch, remarked:

> When I went to meet my relatives on that side, I met some people who called Poonch 'makbooza Kashmir' (slave or occupied Kashmir). I did not like it...I told them, come to our side and you will realise that we enjoy a lot more freedom than you do.

On the issue of security and fencing the LoC, he said: '*Hum logon ko milne do, beshak beech mien taarein lagao, lekin milne to do, shakle to dekhne do ek dusre ki* (Put up fences if you so wish, but at least let us meet each other, see each other's faces).

Another elderly Muslim gentleman from Poonch, Fareed Khan, has many relatives settled in POJK. He also aired similar views: 'What we want is azadi from these *lakeeren* (lines) and *taaren* (fences). Make this (Jammu and Kashmir) a borderless zone. Let people move freely. We long to meet our sisters and brothers...hug each other, share joys and sorrows with each other.'

Humour, Competition and Class Divides

Despite the pervasiveness of uncertainty and conflict, people of border zones do not necessarily view themselves as victims. At times, many of my respondents exchanged jokes about their personal or collective tribulations, demonstrating their ability to cope well with their realities and to move on with their lives. In many conversations on the issue of divided families, sadness and grief were not the only prevailing sentiments. There were instances of a pragmatic humour towards relations on the other side of the border. The lives of these people are not just consumed by issues of conflict, but their quotidian activities are not very different from that of other villages and small towns elsewhere in India. Men and women talk about their local political issues and internal political factionalisms; they love to dress up and talk about fashion; they form social and cultural recreational groups; they engage in gossip and other day-to-day activities of life. The society of Poonch and Rajouri exhibits class inequities and other social, religious, political and ethnic cleavages. Their 'border identity' is obviously defined in relation to conflict, but also with regard to their cultures, politics and languages. The issues of conflict and divided families, however, seamlessly intertwine with their other mundane affairs. As in other routine activities, humour along with competition and jealousies finds a place in their narratives about conflict and divided families. One of my Muslim respondents, Tariq Ali, for instance, described his visit to POJK to attend the marriage of one of his male cousins with levity and wit:

> Their marriage ceremonies are in some ways very different from ours. My cousins carried guns around. After every few minutes, they would fire in the air. In India, we light firecrackers, there they just like blasting here and there... That was scary. I thought someone would die (laughs). All of them were enjoying, and I felt like running away.... Here, we follow law and order....

Tariq Ali's witty narration was accompanied by gestures. His family members were also sitting beside him, and were laughing and enjoying the conversation. Humour allowed Ali to make light of the grand narratives of nationhood. While the notion of national identities are taken too seriously and revered in such grand narratives, Ali used humour to bring out the absurdities in them. Humour also allowed him to negate political labelling or the necessity to strictly align with one nation or the other. Humour provides this flexible and subversive space that is otherwise absent in the realm of general socio-political discussions.

Along with emotions and affection, many of my respondents also showed feelings of jealousy or competitiveness towards their relations across the LoC. Nisar Chowdhary, a well-to-do businessman from Rajouri, and his wife, Shahida, for instance, strongly voiced their desire for a 'borderless' state. Since Chowdhary and his wife's relatives reside in POJK, they strongly argued for softening the boundaries, so that their divided families could meet with ease on important family occasions. However, both of them as well as their family members here also cracked jokes about their kin across the border. They expressed a sense of competitiveness towards them too. Chowdhary, for instance, remarked:

> I have been there [POJK] twice to meet my relatives. They try their best to make us feel comfortable. My relatives are very rich and Westernised. They speak good English (he jokes and mimics their put-on accents). But they do not know the real meaning of hospitality. They have a busy routine. They cannot spend much time with us, though they spend a lot of money on us and give us expensive gifts. What I am supposed to do with their money and gifts...dance with excitement? (His family giggles at his remarks.)

Shahida too humorously recounted her cousin's last visit, while the rest of her family broke into peals of laughter:

> When [cousin] Zaida came here last time, she told me that you come to Pakistan and I will hand over my kitchen to you. You do whatever you want, cook whatever you want. She told me that she won't be able to cook everyday as she is very busy. *Maine socha ki phir maine teri kitchen ko aag lagani hai?* (I wondered what the hell would I do with her kitchen then? Set it on fire?). I cook here all the time, why should I go and cook there as well?

Chowdhary's younger brother participated in the discussion as well:

> They have become very well-off...that is why, they think we are less than them. They also think our houses are not as big as theirs. We are not Westernised like them. They think that the

> Indian government doesn't provide good facilities. Therefore, whenever we have had a chance to visit them, we have taken 20–30 boxes of presents for them, so that they don't think that we are less wealthy.... When they came to India, we made all the comforts available to them, and again, showered them with presents. No matter how rich they are, they would not enjoy the kind of freedom we have. We know the condition of Pakistan....Unlike here, the law and order situation is bad. Here, education is better too. We live with all religions. And women have much more freedom....

Though the respondents above did express a sense of competition, the entire conversation was imbued with humour. Again, it could be argued that a discussion cloaked in humour offers space for expressing envy, competition and sarcasm. In a cheerful manner, Chowdhary and his family were able to joke about their extended family members, bringing out those dimensions of the 'divided family narratives' that may be considered 'trivial' otherwise—facets that would not usually be incorporated into accounts that focus exclusively on suffering. Yet these aspects make the narrative more dynamic by taking it beyond the 'war and conflict' framework. Chowdhary and his family spoke on various interesting issues, including ways in which relationships between divided families might be changing due to Westernisation and individualisation among some sections of the middle class. While Chowdhary is a prosperous businessman in Rajouri, he, along with his wife and brother, clearly identify a class gap between them and their prosperous, modern relatives in Pakistan.

It is important to note here that Muslims in the border districts may be critical of their situation—of being stuck in their bordered realities and yet, when competing with their Pakistani counterparts, they may boast of their 'Indian-ness'. In a part of the conversation quoted above, class competition gradually metamorphoses into nationalist competition. Chowdhary's younger brother tries to confront the issue of his relatives' class superiority by indulging in nationalist rhetoric, and by demonstrating how, in many ways, as Indians they are better-off than their Pakistani kin. Such dynamics also underscore the fluidities that are manifested by people who assume various national, trans-national and local identities.

Aziz Rahi, a Pahari Muslim who owns a school in Rajouri city, voiced another interesting opinion. He brought out the local issue of Gujjar versus Pahari politics. Paharis have been contesting the Scheduled Tribe (ST) status provided to Gujjars, which enables the latter to avail of reservations in government jobs and educational institutions. Gujjars are a nomadic Muslim group, even though many among them are now settled. Paharis, comprising of both Hindu and Muslim inhabitants in the Poonch and Rajouri districts, have been questioning the ST status provided to Gujjars. They argue that since their socio-economic situation is similar to that of Gujjars, similar political advantages should be extended to their community as well. Aziz Rahi said: 'Give us Paharis the status of ST at par with Gujjars and then do a referendum on Kashmir issue. We will all vote for India. But first give us that status.' His friends sitting next to him endorsed his statement and told me that the progress of their community depends on getting such a status, and this is their foremost political demand. The comments of Rahi and his friends are intriguing—for them and many other Pahari Muslims, it is neither the sovereignty of the Indian state nor the issue of self-determination that is contested, unlike Kashmiri Muslims. Their interest lies in competing for political and economic space within the mainstream Indian and local politics, as well as procuring benefits that would enable the development of their community. Incidentally, by the time this book will be published, this aspiration of Paharis to acquire the status of Scheduled Tribes has already been fulfilled. More recently, in early 2024, the Paharis have been given the status of ST that entitles them to a benefit of 10 per cent reservation in government jobs and other facilities (*The Hindu* 2024).

These interpretations of nationalism offer a complex depiction of the conflict that is generally rendered invisible. More importantly, it fractures the notion of Muslim homogeneity, in contrast to the generally projected view of a 'unified Muslim politics' in the State of Jammu and Kashmir. This is indicated, for example, by Shaukat Aziz's rejection of the term 'makbooza Kashmir' (slave or occupied Kashmir) used by his Pakistani relatives in relation to Poonch. Like many other Muslim residents of the border areas, he has a different standpoint. By opposing his Pakistani counterparts in this regard, Aziz, in fact, displays a desire to prove that Muslims on his side of the LoC enjoy more freedom.

The ways in which the Muslims of border areas engage in national imaginations as well as contestations is to an extent different not only from Muslims of Kashmir, but also from other mainland inhabitants of the erstwhile State of Jammu and Kashmir. This brings forth the argument that nationalism is not a singular, homogeneous idea in the experiential, spatial and temporal spaces. Various voices, imaginations and political perspectives offer a layered and heterogeneous reading of nationalism(s). Nation, thus, is imagined, reproduced and questioned in plural ways, and it is imperative to foreground these processes emerging from the most marginal domains. This chapter has argued for nuanced views on borders and nationalism, coming from the lived experiences and performances of border residents and divided families, and has demonstrated how an alternative perspective on the Kashmir conflict and possibilities of resolution emerges from the hitherto ignored border spaces.

Notes

1. Names of all respondents in this chapter have been changed to preserve their anonymity.

2. When the India–Pakistan war came to an end in January 1949 (and the LoC, initially known as the Ceasefire Line, was drawn), the Indian Army reclaimed Rajouri, parts of Poonch and many other parts of the state that had come under the control of invading forces. However, Mirpur, Kotli and Muzaffarabad came under Pakistan's control and so did the Haji Pir Pass connecting Uri and Poonch. Gilgit and Skardu also went to Pakistan (Chakravorty 1992).

3. Jammu and Kashmir, till very recently, comprised of the three main regions of Jammu, Kashmir and Ladakh, each with a distinct geographical and cultural character. However, in August 2019, as mentioned earlier, this state was reorganised into two Union Territories—the Union Territory of Jammu and Kashmir and the Union Territory of Ladakh.

4. Post 2002, a peace process was initiated by the then Prime Minister of India, Atal Bihari Vajpayee, which was reciprocated by the then President of Pakistan, Pervez Musharraf. An important outcome of this forward-looking India–Pakistan dialogue was the opening of the Uri–Muzaffarabad bus service in 2005 and the Poonch–Rawalakot bus service in 2006. In 2008, cross-LoC trade at these two points was also started (Razdan 2010).

References

Balibar, E. 2002. *Politics and the Other Scene*. London: Verso.

Bose, S. 2003. *Kashmir: Roots to Conflict, Paths to Peace*. London: Harvard University Press.

Chakravorty, B. C. 1992. *The History of the Indo-Pak War, 1965*. New Delhi: Ministry of Defence, Government of India .

Chatta, I. 2009. 'Terrible Fate: "Ethnic Cleansing" of Jammu Muslims in 1947.' *Pakistan Vision* 10(1): 117–140.

Chowdhary, R. (ed.). 2012. *Border and People: An Interface* (A Report). New Delhi: Centre for Dialogue and Reconciliation.

Gupta, S. 2007. *Reconciliation Across the Divide: Survey Research about Divided Families in the Border Districts of Jammu*. Centre for Dialogue and Reconciliation.

Lamb, A. 1997. *Incomplete Partition*. Hertfordshire: Roxford Books.

Mehta, K. 2005. *Kashmir 1947: A Survivor's Story*. New Delhi: Penguin.

Razdan, S. 2010. 'Cross-Line of Control Trade in Jammu and Kashmir State Through the Poonch-Rawalakot Route. Jammu and Kashmir: Trade Across the Line of Control'. Available at http://www.c-r.org/sites/default/files/JammuandKashmir_DiscussionPapers_201012_ENG.pdf (accessed December 2023).

Rumford, C. 2008. *Cosmopolitan Spaces: Europe, Globalization, Theory*. New York: Routledge.

Samaddar, R. 2004. *Politics of Dialogue: Living Under the Geopolitical Histories of War and Peace*. Aldershot, UK: Ashgate.

Saraf, A. N. 2007. *Rajouri Remembered* (Translated by Babli Moitra Saraf). Jammu, distributed by Amar Nath Saraf.

Schofield, V. 2003. *Kashmir in Conflict: India, Pakistan and the Unending War*. London: I.B.Tauris.

Snedden, C. 2013. 'The Forgotten Poonch Uprising of 1947'. *Seminar* 643.

The Hindu. 2024. 'Rajya Sabha clears Bills to add Paharis, Valmikis to ST, SC lists in J&K', 9 February. Available at https://www.thehindu.com/news/national/other-states/rajya-sabha-clears-bills-to-add-paharis-valmikis-to-st-sc-lists-in-jk/article67830152.ece (accessed July 2024).

Zamindar, V. 2008. *The Long Partition and the Making of Modern South Asia: Refugees, Boundaries, Histories*. New Delhi: Penguin.

V

Contested Borders

Divided Families in the Kargil Region

Seema Shekhawat

Introduction

A cursory look at the global scenario makes it easy to argue that the impact of bordering, de-bordering and re-bordering on the lives of people living along the borders is colossal. This chapter argues that an intense engagement with the borderlands in the erstwhile State of Jammu and Kashmir, which has received far less attention than it requires, would bring the contested landscape to the centre of the discourse. The attention would also provide insights into the further conceptualisation of borders, borderlands and borderlanders. The chapter focuses on an otherwise neglected aspect of border life in the region—the division of families. A large number of families living in the princely State of Jammu and Kashmir were divided due to an abrupt creation of borders in the region following the first India–Pakistan war in the late 1940s. Though people living all along the newly created border suffered due to the forced division of their families, this chapter will primarily focus on those living in the Kargil sub-region in the Ladakh district of the erstwhile Indian State of Jammu and Kashmir. I am using the term 'erstwhile State' because following the reorganisation of this state on 5 August 2019, Ladakh region was separated from Jammu and Kashmir (J&K) and both Ladakh and Jammu and Kashmir were reorganised as separate Union Territories (UTs).

The chapter argues that the divided families have been enduring the trauma of separation persistently. They also have been confronting the consequences of hostilities between India and Pakistan on an almost daily basis. Having acquired different 'nationalities', these people have to bear the burden of belligerent borders in the most horrific manner. Their only hope for reunification lies in the softening of the borders drawn following the Indo–Pak wars to facilitate, even if temporarily, reunion with loved ones. The chapter largely draws from my qualitative fieldwork in the border villages of the Kargil district, carried out over a decade from 2005–2015.

Theorising Borders

Borders constitute a central element of modern states regardless of interesting debates on a borderless world gaining ground. Borders continue to be an intrinsic part of states, as critical geographical edges (Kalir and Sur 2013). Often regarded as a 'given territorial fact, a static, unchanging feature' of the modern state system (Kilot and Newman 2000: 9), and 'domains of contested power... (to) negotiate relations of subordination and control' (Wilson and Donnan 1998: 10), it may be sufficient to argue that borders are accorded the utmost attention by states. For Johnson and Graybill (2010: 2), 'National borders represent the territorial embodiment of a bundle of ideas that modern states have propagated and enforced. They tell us that ... these nations have sovereign powers over particular territory ...' This intrinsic yet complicated linkage of state, territory and sovereignty has knotted several states into a 'territorial trap' (Agnew 1994), as is also evident in the erstwhile Indian State of Jammu and Kashmir.

The post-Cold War border discourse is remarkable. A significant literature exists on borders with scholars researching physical, political, socio-cultural, and even philosophical aspects of bordering, de-bordering and re-bordering. The theoretical orientation alongside impressive empirical research has paved the way towards border studies emerging as an important area of interdisciplinary academic attention. The scholars are busy in elucidating borders and their multifaceted interlinkages with the concepts and issues of state, territoriality, sovereignty, security and human life (see, for instance, Agnew 1994; Anderson 1996; Baud and Van Schendel 1997; Donnan and Wilson 1999; Diener and Hagen 2010; Kumar-Rajaram and Grundy-Warr 2007; Newman 2006; Newman and Passi 1998; Van Houtum et al. 2005; Wastl-Walter 2011; Wilson and Donnan 1998; Zartman 2010).

Conspicuously, the border discourse has witnessed a shift from the traditional statist focus. The discourse has broadened to include not only the land but also the people located on or near these traditional markers of state sovereignty. Kilot and Newman (2000: 13) explain this changed scenario: 'From an almost exclusive focus on the physical nature and demarcation of the territorial lines, the study of boundaries has become multidimensional, focusing on different scales of boundaries....' From being considered as merely geographical lines, borders have come to be recognised as 'central to understanding political life', to raise 'questions concerning citizenship, identity, political loyalty, exclusion, inclusion and of the ends of the state' (Anderson 1996: 1).

Amidst the vast existing scholarship on borders, South Asia has recently claimed its position, though reluctantly (Cons 2013; Gellner 2013; Jones 2009, 2012; Middleton 2013; Shewly 2013; Van Schendel 2001, 2005). In the erstwhile princely State of Jammu and Kashmir, a region with contested borders, lying at 'the world's only nuclear trijunction,' with boundary claims from India, Pakistan and China (Baghela and Nüsser 2015: 24), borders have received comparatively less attention. Interestingly, there is somewhat plentiful scholarship available on inter-state (see, for instance, Blinkenberg 1998;

Brines 1968; Dasgupta 2002; Gupta 1960; Gupta 1966; Jackson 1975; Jha 1996; Paul 2005) and intra-state (Behera 2006; Bose 1997; Ganguly 1997; Puri 1993; Widmalm 2002) dimensions of the Kashmir conflict. Nonetheless, the contested border remains a marginal issue for most of these studies. Only lately have there been some attempts to document the lives of borderlanders in this contested region (Aggarwal 2004; Aggarwal and Bhan 2009; Mahapatra 2011, 2013; Shekhawat 2006; Shekhawat and Mahapatra 2006, 2009).

Contested Border and Distressed People

A unique situation confronted the princely State of Jammu and Kashmir, following the Partition of the Indian subcontinent. Being located at the geographical margins of the newly created sovereign states of India and Pakistan, this land became a source of constant conflict between the two countries. Both the states claimed the princely State of Jammu and Kashmir. The ruler of the princely state, however, signed an Instrument of Accession with India on 26 October 1947, following an internal revolt against the monarch and evident support for the revolt from the newly created Pakistan. The two geographical neighbours fought a war in 1947–1948. The United Nations-mediated ceasefire led to the division of the region. The region was divided with a major part remaining with India and a sizeable chunk under the control of Pakistan. India and Pakistan fought again in 1965 and 1971. The ceasefire that followed each war led to minor redrawing of the borders between the two parts of J&K.

The history of the region under scrutiny, Kargil, needs to be explored as well to understand the complexity of the scenario. Prior to 1948, Baltistan was part of the Ladakh province of the State of Jammu and Kashmir. The province was dismembered during the 1947–1948 war as Baltistan district went under Pakistani control while the remaining two districts of Ladakh—Kargil and Leh—became part of the Indian state.

There is a context of specificity to the demography of this area as well. The Shia sect of Islam, much like in the adjacent Gilgit-Baltistan region of Pakistan-controlled Jammu and Kashmir, dominates the Kargil district. These people have distinct religious practices, different from the rest of the Sunni-dominated region of Kashmir. For thousands of years till the Partition of India, people used the Kargil–Skardu road as a main route linking the Ladakh region with Central Asia. The wars of 1965 and 1971 led not only to border readjustments, leading to border villages being claimed and reclaimed by India and Pakistan, but also to the closure of the intra-Jammu and Kashmir roads, including the Kargil–Skardu road. This closure of major roads brought about multiple adverse consequences for the people living in these far-flung areas.

Of the about 3,323-kms land border that India and Pakistan share, about one-third (1,225 kms) passes through the erstwhile princely State of J&K. Of this, 210 kms is the International Border (IB), about 150 kms is the Actual Ground Position Line (AGPL) and about 800 kms is the Line of Control (LoC), an agreed yet contested border drawn and redrawn following the three wars between geographical neighbours. Jammu and Kashmir, hence, has been majorly divided between India and Pakistan along a *de facto* border, known as the LoC. The LoC—an arbitrarily drawn, provisional and contested border—encompasses far more complexities than an internationally settled border. Borders 'materialize, rematerialize, and dematerialize in different contexts, at different scales, and at different times' in complex ways, as has been evident in Jammu and Kashmir (Megoran 2012: 477). The Partition of the erstwhile princely State of J&K and the creation of the border was hasty. It was forced upon the people of a region that remained unified till the late 1940s. Aggarwal (2004: 1) describes the J&K border as, 'Drawn and redrawn by battles and treaties, the line is identifiable by traces of blood, bullets, watchtowers, and ghost settlements left from recurring wars between India and Pakistan.' The borders in this contested region have a sore past, a hurting present and an indeterminate future. Mahapatra (2015: 173) notes,

> The partition of Kashmir ... did not happen within the confines of a smooth political framework; rather, the region was torn asunder due to the conflict between India and Pakistan which escalated into war, separating the people, destroying their integrated identity and eventually paving the way for one of the most intractable territorial conflicts in the world.

Martinez's (1994: 2) description of alienated borderlands as having 'extremely unfavourable conditions', including 'warfare, political disputes, intense nationalism, ideological animosity, religious enmity, cultural dissimilarity and ethnic rivalry' and 'militarization and establishment of rigid controls...', pertinently labels the geographical margins of the erstwhile State of J&K. The heavy security apparatus, in terms of observation towers, permanent deployment of the security forces, landmines, electrified fencing and frequent firing and shelling are all near permanent features of this contested borderland. Ambiguity along the border profiles the life adjoining it. Placed at the vanguard of the complicated and intense contestation between the two neighbouring rival states, borderlanders here suffer on a nearly everyday basis (Mahapatra 2011, 2013). These people confront innumerable challenges originating from the disputed landscape they are trapped in. They negotiate their survival almost everyday amidst a life-threatening condition.

Some areas of the borderland resemble military cantonments even when life goes on (though with difficulty) near them. Border residents are under strict security surveillance with highly restricted entry. Their mobility is constantly constrained. The border areas remain underdeveloped since border security is prioritised over human security. Owing to the geographical marginality of this region, some of the border villages are even non-existent for the civil administration, even though there may have been heavy military presence. While these regions are important for the security apparatus, their remoteness and sparse population position many of these villages as invisible for the civil administration. Gupta (2013: 59–60) notes,

> it is not surprising that border villages like Lato and Badgam are invisible on maps of the region ... the inhabitants of these areas are ... effectively excluded from the geo-body of the nation, as alluded to in the rhetorical statement from Lato about the civil administration not even knowing the village belongs to India.

The research suggests that officials of the civil administration have not visited some of the border villages in the Kargil region even once. Mahapatra (2016: 6) argues:

> Some of the border residents claimed that their villages have not been visited by officials of civil administration even once. For instance, during my visit to the village Hunderman Brok, situated on a hill top in the Kargil region, in May 2007, the residents informed me that they have never been visited by any political leader or civil administrator since the village came to the Indian side after the 1971 war. In order to reach this village, one has to trek for about four hours without any carved path in difficult mountain terrains.

Basic amenities of life, such as communication, transportation, electricity, primary education and health services, and drinking water supply, remain out of the reach of a significant number of people in these remote villages located in a contested region.

Division of Families

The everyday struggle of the border residents coupled with the division of their families stemming from the division of the erstwhile princely state, have understandably brought immense difficulties and sufferings for these people (Shekhawat and Mahapatra 2009). The ceasefire line, which abruptly created the LoC, cut through not only valleys and mountains but also through villages and houses, leading to the division of thousands of families along the newly created border. No reliable statistics exist to ascertain how many families were divided following the abrupt creation of the LoC. The pangs of separation are, however, scattered across the dividing line, suggesting that the number must run into tens of thousands. In almost all the border villages one can hear the tragic narratives of separation due to abrupt border drawing.

These divided families depict an unusual yet tragic condition of an almost permanent division of a community between two neighbouring states—a division based on no particular principle or rationale other than the fact that the line of separation represented the respective state's control on the day of ceasefire in 1947–1948, 1965 and 1971. The families in the Kargil region, unlike in other regions of Kashmir, got divided repetitively, in 1948, in 1965 and again in 1971. People in Gilgit-Baltistan were, for one or the other reason, cut off from the Indian part of Ladakh after the ceasefire and border redrawing. At Hunderman village on the Indian side, almost every household has a relative living in Brolmo village of Gilgit-Baltistan. More than seven decades have passed but these divided families are still separated. Many of the members passed away without seeing each other, while many others continue to live with a hope of reunion. These people do not tire of talking about their familial bonds with the people in Gilgit-Baltistan. Notably, the division was not only of the villages and families, but also of the shared history, culture, economy and stories. The divided families in the border villages in Kargil district are separated from their kith and kin by a distance of merely a few kilometres. It is, however, impossible to cover this distance due to the heavily guarded border. Tragically, they live so near, yet are so far from each other.

The Kargil borderland is a landscape of 'emotions, fears and memories' (Johnson et al. 2011: 62). The spur-of-the-moment creation of the border and consequential separation brought gigantic sufferings for the border residents—wife separated from husband, children from parents, and siblings from each other. The division of families resulted in wide-ranging sufferings, extending from the social and cultural to the economic and the emotional. Farad from Badgam village has been in a state of shock after being separated from her husband. Her village came to the Indian side after the 1971 war and her husband, away for marketing, was stranded on the other side of the border. Gul Mohammad of Badgam village has been waiting to meet his son, who was stranded on the other side of the border that was redrawn after the 1965 war. The occasional letters exchanged between the separated relatives often take a long time to reach their destination. Divided families learn of even the death of their loved ones after several weeks, as letters take more than a month to reach the other side of the LoC. In Shah's case, there has been no exchange of letters since the late 1980s. Shah's wife died longing to see their son. Shah sent a letter to his son when his wife died, but there has been no response. The agonised father noted with regret that his son may not know about his mother's death in the early 1990s. This humanitarian dimension of the J&K conflict was superseded by the political and security dimensions for a long time. The divided families suffered in silence as geo-strategic security considerations in New Delhi and Islamabad dominated the scenario, with the humane consideration for border residents remaining neglected.

For many border residents, the pain of separation from their loved ones runs so deep that it is even difficult to discuss it without becoming overwhelmed with emotions. In many cases, people have been unable to bear the trauma, which affected their mental and physical health and consequently, their life span. 'My mother died very early. She was only 38. She could not accept the separation from my father. My mother wanted to see my father at least one more time, but

I could not fulfill her wish. Even today I feel so helpless and emotional,' said a respondent. Another respondent mourned,

> My mother lost her psychological balance as soon as she comprehended that she may not be able to meet my father and my brother again. They both went for marketing in Skardu. They could not come back due to the abrupt border creation. We are since then Indians and they are Pakistanis. My mother is now near insane. She just keeps calling my father and brother, as if they are still here and will respond to her calls. Now, she does not recognise anyone, not even me.

Bisma from Hunderman recounted the tragic story of her parents. Her father could not even attend the funeral of her mother despite living only a few kilometres away, across the border in Brolmo village where he was stranded after border creation. Fatima was stranded in 1971 in Badgam, a village that came to India, while her family lived in Skardu, now with Pakistan. Nasiba tried to cross the border many times without success. Later, she married a resident of Badgam. Her family could not celebrate with her. She is now settled in the place she was stranded in with a husband and three children, but a part of her heart seems to be missing. She still longs to see her parents and siblings in Skardu. Zahara's father had gone to visit his ailing sister in Skardu. He also got stranded and never returned. 'My mother died longing to see my father, who could not return even after she died. I do not know if my father is still alive. The LoC is not line of control, it is a line of catastrophe and devastation,' said Zahara. Jahan Bi had a similar experience. Her husband went to Brolmo village and never returned due to the division. Hameeda has lost hope of seeing her husband again in this lifetime. She said,

> I know my husband is there on the other side of the border, but I do not think I would be able to see him again. Not in this world, but I would meet him in the other world. Hopefully there would be no borders in the other world to separate us.

Ayesha from Brolmo was married in Hunderman. She has not met her parents and siblings for decades. Tearfully, she narrated, 'We are separated merely by a few kilometers, but to be able to go to my maternal village to see my family is a seemingly unachievable dream.' Sasha, who was married in Kirkit Khunda village close to the LoC in 1947, had a similar story to tell. She has not been able to meet her family as they live in a village which is now on the Pakistan side of J&K.

There are thousands of such unheard stories of separation in the border areas of Kargil. Mehreen became emotional while talking about her parents, who were separated:

> My mother and I got separated from my father when I was about eight years old. He got stranded in Skardu, in Pakistan as he went there for a relative's marriage. My mother did not remarry and raised me all alone. It has been a very traumatic experience. Due to the support of my grandfather, we did not face economic problems. But, the division of our family is a trauma that we relive every single day.

Her mother died waiting for her father to return. Mehreen continued, 'If the Kargil–Skardu road was open, my parents could have reunited at least for a while. After knowing the news of my mother's death, my father was heartbroken. He died after two months in Skardu. Our tragedy is beyond explanation. I am speechless.'

Afroza narrated her separation from her husband with tears rolling down:

> When the border was redrawn in 1971 following the ceasefire, I saw from the window that my husband was returning from Skardu with grocery. Look at our tragedy... he was not allowed to return to our village since the village was now in India and he was standing in the part which was with Pakistan. We both could see each other but could not hear each other. My husband had no choice but to go back to Skardu. Decades have passed

> since then. We got divorced and I remarried for the sake of my three children. But, my heart still bleeds. My children's father is no more with them. He is alive, but he is not with us.

Some people have no confirmed news about their separated family members. Myara's husband had gone to Skardu to buy groceries and never returned. In the early 2000s, she received unconfirmed news of her husband's death, but there has been no way to know the truth. Sabina said:

> Since the news is not confirmed, I do not know if I should mourn or continue to hope for our reunion. I am leading a life of a half-widow, but somewhere in my heart for all these years, I had hoped for reunion. This news has broken my heart. I am trying to save money to send my son to Pakistan to verify the news.

Notably, in a traditional and patriarchal society, separation from one's husband has both economic and socio-emotional implications. Sabina, just like many other women, has been struggling since separation, not only emotionally but also economically.

Sher Khan had no information about his wife, who went to visit her friend in Skardu before the first war was fought by India and Pakistan. He remarried after waiting for his wife for about five years. He said, 'I tried very hard to get any information about her. I do not even know if she is alive. I remarried and now have five children. But, I miss her, badly. I can never forget her. I never wanted to be separated from her.' Gazala lost her sanity after being separated from her husband, who was in Skardu when the border was drawn in the late 1980s. She only recognises the photograph of her husband, whose whereabouts remain unknown. Bushra is inconsolable, remembering the old days. 'My husband is missing since decades. There is unconfirmed news that he is still in Skardu.

I just want to know if he is alive. My wait has been very long. I am not even sure if this wait will be over one day.'

Most borderlanders have restrained themselves from crossing the border to meet their relatives due to the rigidity and militarisation of the border. However, there are many instances of temporary reunions through 'illegal' means. Desperate people have devised several strategies to reunite, through 'illegally' crossing the dividing line, or meeting after applying for a visa and going through circuitous routes to reach their destinations, or meeting in a third country. Dua of Kirkit-Badgam village met her separated husband, who lives in Skardu, after 50 years in a Karachi hotel room, where she had an overnight stay on her way to Hajj. The reunion, planned by her children, was a dream come true. To quote her,

> I did not talk to my husband. I just kept crying throughout the night. He looked like a stranger after 50 years of separation, but my heart knew that he was my man. My fellow passengers tried to console me, but I could not help it. I knew that the reunion is short and this kept bothering me throughout the night. My husband had brought two dresses for me. I wear only those two dresses now. When it was time for him to leave, I fainted. I do not know when he left, but he told the people accompanying me to assure me that we would meet again. I know this is not going to happen.

The Hajj congregation has become a major news provider and even a meeting point for the divided families, and thus provides an opportunity for both Indian and Pakistani border residents to share news about their relatives. Nusrat was able to meet her separated brothers during Hajj: 'It was a dream come true. However, since then we have no contact. I do not even know where they reside currently.' These reunion strategies are not only expensive, but also temporary and sparse.

The distance, economic factors and the prevailing hostile political environment has ensured that most divided families continue to suffer.

Borders Opening

The partial opening of the border, hailed as 'historic', 'a step towards bridging the divide in Kashmir' and 'mother of all confidence building measures' between India and Pakistan, was announced in February 2005 (for details, see Mahapatra 2005). An agreement was signed between the two geographical neighbours to start an intra-Kashmir bus service (that is, between the two divided parts of the erstwhile princely State of J&K), between Srinagar and Muzaffarabad. The first bus ran in April 2005. Then Indian Prime Minister Manmohan Singh said, 'The Caravan of Peace is now on its way, no one can stop it' (*Aljazeera* 2005). In June 2006, another intra-Kashmir route, Poonch-Rawalakot, was opened. Through these opened roads, a temporary reunion of some of the divided families was facilitated.

Newman (2003: 277) notes:

> If there is anything that belies notions of a deterritorialized and borderless world more, it is the fact that boundaries ... continue to demarcate the territories within which we are compartmentalised, determine with whom we interact and affiliate, and the extent to which we are free to move from one space to another.

The limited cross-border bus service started in 2005 allowed many members of the divided families in these two regions to meet their relatives. However, the facility accorded to the border remained confined to only J&K regions, with many other intra-Kashmir roads, including Kargil–Skardu, remaining closed. Some of these traditional routes were part of the Silk Road (for details, see Kaw 2009; Mahapatra 2008, 2009). The distance between Skardu and Kargil is about 170 kms, and the road is in workable condition. However, the road remains closed. At present, the divided families living in Kargil have to travel hundreds of miles via the Wagah route in Punjab or use the opened roads to meet their families. If the Kargil–Skardu road is opened, it will help them to reach their relatives within a few hours. The reopening of this road could lead to tourism, give an economic boost to, trade and help build confidence between the two arch rivals. From the perspective of this chapter, the humanitarian aspect of reopening the Kargil–Skardu road is the prominent one, since it could put an end to the long wait of divided families and help them reunite, albeit not permanently.

The narratives of separation and the longing for reunion in Kargil is the same as that associated with the Srinagar–Muzaffarabad road and the Poonch–Rawalakot road. Nonetheless, amidst the political euphoria accompanying the peace process and bus diplomacy, the voices of divided families in Kargil remain unheard.[1] Their equally emotional stories continue to be part of only the local discourse. They remain invisible on the vast political landscape. The people of Kargil long to see the Kargil–Skardu road open. Grief and sorrow marked their faces as they repeatedly urged everyone visiting them to open the road. There is a growing resentment among the people of Kargil region because the peace dividends of the India–Pakistan engagement has failed to benefit them in any way. Aslam noted, 'The people of Kashmir valley (Srinagar–Muzaffarabad road) and Jammu region (Poonch–Rawalakot road) reunited with their divided families but our tragedy is to remain hostage to the hostility between India and Pakistan. We are the most unfortunate ones.'

Shama said,

> I have already packed my bags to travel via Kargil–Skardu road to meet my uncle and cousins. I am waiting for the road to open so that we can reunite with our loved ones. We have to travel by air or via Wagah border to Lahore, which takes weeks of travel and is very expensive. Kargil–Skardu road will be cost-effective for us. Please tell the government to open this road.

Zoya from Hunderman village said, 'No one can ever forget his place of birth. I have spent my childhood in Skardu. My memories are still fresh though I am old now. I am desperate to see that place again.' Ifra said:

> I am afraid my wish to see my husband would remain unsatisfied. I do not know why India and Pakistan cannot work together to open this road. The old people like me will soon die, leaving behind a tearful legacy of peace and love, which can be used to foster peace and brotherhood between the people. Please let us meet our loved ones.

Sara said her last wish is to see her son, who lives in Gilgit-Baltistan: 'I wish I live till I can see my son and grandchildren. The opening of the roads in other parts of the region has raised my hopes. I would not be able to die peacefully if I do not see them,' she said. The yearning for reunion is acute, but when that will happen, if at all, remains shrouded in the mystery of the future.

Conclusion

The erection of the near-impermeable border, since 1949, has had immense adverse consequences for the border residents of the erstwhile princely State of J&K, particularly because it abruptly divided and separated many families. The borderland became extremely hostile and there was virtually no cross-border interaction for nearly 60 years. The J&K border has palpably evolved. The serpentine border that was lying inert and submerged under a dominant state security apparatus and discourse regained life and movement with the partial border opening in 2005. As we have discussed, the opening has facilitated the reunion of many divided families, even though on a temporary basis. However, this facility was available only in the J&K regions and was not extended to Ladakh region. Though there has been a constant demand to open the Kargil–Skardu road, no such decision has been taken till now. With this route remaining closed, the divided families in Kargil continue to wait for even temporary reunions with their separated family members.

The further evolution of borderlands, in terms of the opening of other roads, including the Kargil–Skardu one, is contingent upon relations between India and Pakistan, which is characterised by enduring rivalry. It is because of the hostility and aggression between the two countries that the two routes already opened (the Srinagar–Muzaffarabad road and the Poonch–Rawalakot road) have often witnessed suspension of the bus service. Since the reorganisation of the state in August 2019, the bus service has been withdrawn for the moment, which has has implications for the opening of new routes. Till the relations between the two countries are normalised and the already opened routes are made functional once more, it is difficult to imagine that any effort will be made to open new routes. The demand of the divided families in Kargil to open the Kargil–Skardu road is therefore unlikely to be fulfilled in the near future.

My research suggests that the borderlanders have kept alive their hope for an open border even in these difficult circumstances. It may be an extravagant indulgence to predict the course of the borderlands of J&K and Ladakh and conclude that the Kargil–Skardu road will be opened along with other closed intra-Kashmir roads, and people will be able to freely move in an undivided J&K (and Ladakh). And yet, this hope is sustaining the divided families in this part of the world. However, keeping in view the prevailing scenario, it seems to be a long wait for the divided families; the future of their quest for reunification with their dear ones remains uncertain.

Notes

1. This is despite the fact that the M. K. Rasgotra-headed Working Group Report, titled 'Strengthening Relations across the Line of Control', recommended the opening of various routes (other than the ones where the cross-LoC bus service was started). These suggested routes were Kargil–Skardu, Jammu–Sialkot, Turtuk–Khapulu, Chhamb–Jorian to Mirpur, Gurez–Astoor–Gilgit, Titval–Chilhan and Jangar (Nowshera). See *Report of the Working Group* (2007).

References

Aggarwal, R. 2004. *Beyond Lines of Control: Performance and Politics on the Disputed Borders of Ladakh, India*. Durham: Duke University Press.

Aggarwal, R. and M. Bhan. 2009. '"Disarming violence": Development, Democracy, and Security on the Borders of India'. *Journal of Asian Studies* 68(2): 519–542.

Agnew, J. 1994. 'The Territorial Trap: The Geographic Assumptions of International Relations Theory'. *Review of International Political Economy* 1(1): 53–80.

Al Jazeera. 2005. 'Landmark Kashmir bus service begins', 7 April. Available at https://www.aljazeera.com/news/2005/4/7/landmark-kashmir-bus-service-begins (accessed February 2024).

Anderson, M. 1996. *Frontiers: Territory and State Formation in the Modern World*. Oxford: Polity.

Baghela, Ravi and Marcus Nüsser. 2015. 'Securing the Heights: The Vertical Dimension of the Siachen Conflict between India and Pakistan in the Eastern Karakoram'. *Political Geography* 48: 24–36.

Baud, M. and W. Van Schendel. 1997. 'Toward a Comparative History of Borderlands'. *Journal of World History* 8(2): 211–242.

Behera, Navnita Chadha. 2006. *Demystifying Kashmir*. Washington, D.C.: Brookings Institution Press.

Blinkenberg, Lars. 1998. *India–Pakistan: The History of Unresolved Conflicts*. Odense: Odense University Press.

Bose, Sumantra. 1997. *The Challenge in Kashmir: Democracy, Self-determination and a Just Peace*. London: Sage.

Brines, Russell. 1968. *The Indo-Pakistani Conflict*. New York: Pall Mall Press.

Cons, J. 2013. 'Narrating Boundaries: Framing and Contesting Suffering, Community, and Belonging in Enclaves along the India-Bangladesh Border'. *Political Geography* 35: 37–46.

Dasgupta, C. 2002. *War and Diplomacy in Kashmir, 1947–48*. New Delhi: Sage.

Diener, Alexander C. and Joshua Hagen. 2010. *Borderlines and Borderlands: Political Oddities at the Edge of the Nation-State*. Lanham: Rowman & Littlefield Publishers.

Donnan, H. and T. Wilson (eds). 1999. *Borders: Frontiers of Identity, Nation and State*. New York: Bloomsbury Academic.

Ganguly, Sumit. 1997. *The Crisis in Kashmir: Portents of War, Hopes of Peace*. Cambridge: Cambridge University Press.

Gellner, D. (ed.). 2013. *Borderland Lives in Northern South Asia*. Durham: Duke University Press.

Gupta, Jyoti Bhushan Das. 1960. *India–Pakistan Relations, 1947–1955*. Amsterdam: Djambatan.

Gupta, Sisir. 1966. *Kashmir: A Study in India–Pakistan Relations*. Bombay: Asia Publishing House.

Jackson, Robert. 1975. *South Asian Crisis: India–Pakistan–Bangladesh*. London: Chatto and Windus.

Jha, Prem Shankar. 1996. *Kashmir, 1947: Rival Versions of History*. New Delhi: Oxford University Press.

Johnson, Benjamin H. and Andrew R. Graybill (eds). 2010. *Bridging National Borders in North America: Transnational and Comparative Histories*. Durham: Duke University Press.

Johnson, C., Reece Jones, Anssi Paasi, Louise Amoore, Alison Mountz, Mark Salter and Chris Rumford. 2011. 'Interventions on Rethinking "The Border" in Border Studies'. *Political Geography* 30: 61–69.

Jones, R. 2009. 'Geopolitical Boundary Narratives, The Global War on Terror and Border Fencing in India'. *Transactions of the Institute of British Geographers* 34: 290–304.

Jones, R. 2012. *Border Walls: Security and the War on Terror in the United States, India and Israel*. New York: Zed Books.

Kalir, B. and M. Sur (eds). 2013. *Transnational Flows and Permissive Polities: Ethnographies of Human Mobilities in Asia*. Amsterdam: IIAS Publications.

Kaw, Mushtaq A. 2009. 'Restoring India's Silk Route Links with South and Central Asia across Kashmir: Challenges and Opportunities'. *The China and Eurasia Forum Quarterly* 7(2): 59–74.

Kilot, Nurit and David Newman. 2000. 'Introduction'. In Nurit Kilot and David Newman (ed.), *Geopolitics at the End of the Twentieth Century: The Changing World Political Map*. London: Frank Cass.

Kumar-Rajaram, P. and C. Grundy-Warr (eds). 2007. *Borderscapes: Hidden Geographies and Politics at Territory's Edge*. Minneapolis: University of Minnesota Press.

Mahapatra, Debidatta Aurobinda. 2005. 'Bus Running for Reconciliation?' *Mainstream* 63(20): 27–29.

———. 2008. *Central Eurasia: Geopolitics, Compulsions and Connections, Factoring India*. New Delhi: Lancers Books.

———. 2009. 'Silk Route in Kashmir'. *Central Eurasian Studies Review* 8(1): 13–15.

———. 2011. 'Positioning the People in the Contested Borders of Kashmir,' Working Paper. Centre for International Border Studies Research, Queen's University, Belfast, UK.

———. 2013. *Making Kashmir Borderless*. New Delhi: RCSS Colombo and Manohar Publishers.

———. 2015. 'Negotiating Space in the Conflict Zone of Kashmir: The Borderlanders' Perspective'. In Martin Sökefeld (ed.), *Spaces of Conflict in Everyday Life Perspectives across Asia*, 163–186. Bielefeld: Transcript Verlag.

———. 2016. 'From Alienation to Co-existence and Beyond: Examining the Evolution of the Borderland in Kashmir.' *Journal of Borderlands Studies* 33(1): 141–155.

Martinez, Oscar J. 1994. *Border People: Life and Society in the US–Mexico Borderlands*. Tucson: University of Arizona Press.

Megoran, N. 2012. 'Rethinking the Study of International Boundaries: A Biography of the Kyrgyzstan–Uzbekistan Boundary'. *Annals of the Association of American Geographers* 102(2): 464–481.

Middleton, C. 2013. 'States of Difference: Refiguring Ethnicity and its "Crisis" at India's Borders'. *Political Geography* 35: 14–24.

Newman, D. 2003. 'Boundary Geopolitics: Towards a Theory of Territorial Lines?' In E. Berg and H. van Houtum (eds), *Routing Borders Between Territories, Discourses and Practices*, 277–291. Aldershot: Ashgate.

———. 2006. 'Borders and Bordering: Towards an Interdisciplinary Dialogue'. *European Journal of Social Theory* 9(2): 171–186.

Newman, D. and A. Paasi. 1998. 'Fences and Neighbours in the Postmodern World: Boundary Narratives in Political Geography'. *Progress in Human Geography* 22(2): 186–206.

Paul, T. V. (ed.). 2005. *The India–Pakistan Conflict: An Enduring Rivalry*. New York: Cambridge University Press.

Puri, Balraj. 1993. *Kashmir: Towards Insurgency*. New Delhi: Orient Longman.

Report of the Working Group. 2007. *Strengthening Relations Across the Line of Control,* January.

Shekhawat, Seema. 2006. *Conflict and Displacement in Jammu and Kashmir: The Gender Dimension*. Jammu: Saksham Books International.

Shekhawat, Seema and Debidatta Aurobinda Mahapatra. 2006. *Kargil Displaced of Akhnoor in Jammu and Kashmir, Report*. Geneva: Internal Displacement Monitoring Centre.

———. 2009a. *Contested Border and Division of Families in Kashmir: Contextualizing the Ordeal of the Kargil Women*. New Delhi: WISCOMP.

———. 2009b. *Contested Border and Division of Families in Kashmir: Contextualizing the Ordeal of the Kargil Women*. New Delhi: WISCOMP.

Shewly, H. 2013. 'Abandoned Spaces and Bare Life in the Enclaves of the India-Bangladesh Border'. *Political Geography* 32: 23–31.

Van Houtum, H., O. Kramsch and W. Zierhofer (eds). 2005. *B/ordering Space*. Burlington: Ashgate.

Van Schendel, W. 2001. 'Working through Partition: Making a Living in the Bengal Borderlands'. *International Review of Social History* 46: 393–421.

———. 2005. *The Bengal Borderland: Beyond State and Nation in South Asia*. London: Anthem Press.

Wastl-Walter, D. (ed.). 2011. *The Routledge Research Companion to Border Studies*. Routledge.

Widmalm, Sten. 2002. *Kashmir in Comparative Perspective: Democracy and Violent Separatism in India*. London: Routledge Curzon.

Wilson, Thomas M. and Hastings Donnan. 1998. 'Nation, State and Identity at International Borders'. In Thomas M. Wilson and Hastings Donnan (eds), *Border Identities: Nation and State at International Frontiers*. Cambridge: Cambridge University Press.

Zartman, W. (ed.). 2010. *Understanding Life in Borderlands: Boundaries in Depth and Motion*. Athens: University of Georgia Press.

VI

Internally Displaced or Refugees?

Politics, Identities and Citizenship Experiences

Mohita Bhatia and Mamta Sharma

Introduction

Sukh Ram, a Partition refugee in Jammu, points to the unfinished project of Partition and its continuing impact on the lives of people when he remarked, 'Partition has not ended, it is continuing with our problems. Our present lives and uncertain fates are shaped by what happened back in 1947.' His words also convey something more—Partition has continued to shape some of the present identities and concerns in Jammu and Kashmir. While historians and other Partition scholars have engaged in profound research on 'Partition as an unfinished process' and its influence on the post-Partition period, their inquiries stop much before contemporary times. The ways in which our contemporary subjectivities are fashioned and influenced, at least to some degree, by the Partition project are not powerfully foregrounded. This chapter argues that we must also look beyond 1947 and its immediate consequences towards the contemporary period to unravel the newer manifestations of Partition and border construction—newer forms of identities, ideas and pragmatic challenges that have links back to the unfolding of Partition in various ways and directions. It invokes the work of sociologists and anthropologists to engage in and unravel the contemporary, existing facets of Partition. This chapter explores these facets through the lens of Pakistan-controlled Jammu and Kashmir refugees, mainly Hindus, who migrated to India following the Partition violence in 1947. It focuses on the formation of new provisional borders and the 'temporary' status attached to the POJK refugees. The study, carried out in the tehsils (administrative areas) of Sunderbani, Nowshera and Rajouri in Jammu province in 2018–2019, explores the ways in which these Partition-related developments affected the refugees' present-day identity performances, politics, and citizenship experiences.

While Partition has been an unfinished business for the Indian subcontinent, nowhere else have the continuities been so sharp and conspicuous as in the case of Jammu and Kashmir. There has not been any formal closure to Partition, as manifested in the *de facto* nature of the India–Pakistan border that divides the two parts of J&K. While the eastern and western borders of India are permanent and considered international boundaries, large parts of the J&K borders are transient in the absence of any final resolution. The Partition conflict thus continues till the present day in varied forms, including frequent cross-border battles, insurgency, multiple displacements and military surveillance (Bhatia 2020). The POJK refugees have also formed a continuing part of the Partition conflict since 1947. Since the division of Jammu and Kashmir was not formally finalised and India always considered the POJK as part of the Indian Union, these Hindu refugees were regarded as internally displaced people and not 'Partition refugees' per se. They did not receive similar rehabilitation packages or compensation as their counterpart Hindu refugees in other parts of India did (Chowdhary 2015; Tremblay 2016). These various events have shaped their identities, memories and citizenship narratives in specific ways. Their struggles—to be identified as 'refugees' and treated in the same way as other Partition-based refugees deserving of material support and the state's empathy—remain unresolved till date.

The recent outstanding scholarship on Partition and refugees has illustrated the privileged position of Hindu refugees within India (Chatterji 2012; Zamindar 2007). Despite their struggles and internal hierarchical differences that defined their strained and differential relationship with the Indian state, the Hindu refugees were an influential voice with respect to the rehabilitation and citizenship discourse in India, in contrast to Muslims and other minorities. This chapter will partially concur with this position, but will go beyond to argue that regional variations in terms of demography and regional politics also intervened to set the discourse, and in a few cases such as J&K, turned it upside down to the disadvantage of some Hindu refugees. This chapter does not in any way deny the majoritarian intent of the post-Partition Indian state and its privileging of Hindu refugees over Muslims and other minorities who were affected or displaced by Partition and post-1947 boundaries and borders. However, it will expand and to some extent unsettle that debate. It will also argue as to how the similar majoritarian intent of the state was reflected even within Jammu and Kashmir *in an inverse manner*. This being a Muslim majority state, it privileged the majority Muslims over the Hindu refugees. Taking the example of POJK refugees, it will foreground the inconsistencies in the functioning of the Indian state in relation to the Hindu refugees, contingent on varied regional, political and territorial situations.

While pointing out the marginalised status of the POJK refugees and their citizenship navigations, this chapter will also argue that besides their actual hardships, the tone of entitlement set by the majoritarian pro-Hindu national discourse exacerbates their feelings of neglect. Before elaborating on these concerns, it is crucial to point out that we will be focusing on the Indian part of J&K, which until recently was a state of the Indian Union and since August 2019 stands reorganised into two Union Territories (of Jammu and Kashmir, and Ladakh). This erstwhile state was divided into three main regions—Jammu, Kashmir and Ladakh.[1] Mention of J&K in the chapter is mainly in relation to the Indian side, unless a reference is made to the POJK or both sides of the region.

LINE OF CONTROL: DE-FACTO BORDER AND 'TEMPORARY' REFUGEES

The Line of Control or LoC is closely connected to the POJK refugees' experiences of displacement and rehabilitation. As mentioned above, in contrast to the other international India–Pakistan borders, the LoC is a provisional boundary between Jammu and Kashmir on the Indian side and Pakistani-controlled Jammu and Kashmir. The temporality of the boundary implies that conflict between India and Pakistan over J&K is still belligerent and alive. It also points to the fact that J&K is caught up in multiple and intertwined layers of conflict. One, there is an unfinished project of the partition of the Jammu and Kashmir region, as symbolised by the LoC. This is manifested in prolonged and ongoing India–Pakistan skirmishes over the region, resulting in continuing socio-political uncertainty and turbulence for the people on both sides of Kashmir (Bhatia 2020). Two, the partition of J&K also overlapped with the Partition of the Indian subcontinent, with violent outcomes. The former took place a few months after the latter, and the intensity of communal violence, killings and displacement that the division of the subcontinent witnessed was also part of the J&K partition experience. Muslims were targeted in Hindu majority areas and so were Hindus who were residing in Muslim-dominated regions, thus unleashing huge waves of migration as people tried to move to safer places to survive the most callous human onslaught (Bhatia 2020; Bose 2005: 40; Chattha 2011). Three, another related and intertwined layer of conflict has been the domestic aspect of the dispute, symbolised by contentious Centre–state relations (Chowdhary 2015: 61). As a result of the domestic Delhi–Kashmir political friction, experienced more intensely in the post-1980s era, various parts of J&K have witnessed extreme political unrest, insurgency, loss of human lives, and internal displacement.

Diverse communities of J&K have been enormously affected by these intermeshed layers of conflict in many different ways. One, Kashmiri Muslims have been seeking to assert the Kashmiri ethnic identity, and in the process have often suffered violent consequences, especially during the period of militancy. Two, another community of Kashmiri Hindus or Pandits has suffered exile as they were displaced from their homes in the Kashmir region to Jammu and other parts of India during the period of militancy in the 1990s.[2] Three, the border residents of Jammu, both Hindus and Muslims, have been facing the direct brunt of frequent India–Pakistan animosities in the form of cross-border firings, land mining and military surveillance. Four, the Partition-displaced Hindu refugees in Jammu, both from POJK and West Pakistan, have suffered specific problems due to the temporality of borders and the unresolved nature of the conflict. This chapter is particularly looking at POJK refugees to understand the ways in which these multiple dimensions of the conflict have affected their post-1947 existence and the process of their becoming Indian citizens.

The LoC, initially known as the Ceasefire Line (CFL), came into existence in 1949 following the India–Pakistan war over Kashmir. Amidst the violence, many Muslims went from the Indian side of the state to the Pakistan side. Likewise, escaping Partition unrest, large numbers of Hindu and Sikh residents of POJK migrated to the Indian side, mainly the Jammu region, though some also went on to settle in other parts of India. Luv Puri states that, 'In 1947, 31,619 Hindu and Sikh families reached present-day IAJK from various parts of PAJK' (Puri 2012: 30). However, unlike other Hindu refugees from Punjab or Bengal who moved from Pakistan to the Indian side, the POJK refugees were not given an official 'refugee' recognition in India, as mentioned above. India claimed that the border between the two parts of J&K is only a transient one and laid its claim over the entire region. Since India did not consider POJK as a 'foreign' territory, the POJK refugees were viewed as internally displaced people or 'temporary migrants' who would eventually go back to their homes (Chowdhary 2015: 204). They could, however, never go back to their homes due to the ongoing conflict, and had to build their lives and identities anew in India.

Rajiv Chunni, Chairman of SOS, an organisation of POJK refugees in J&K, remarked that 'Even though the Government of India talks of retrieving PoK territory, it has practically closed the case of PoK refugees as a non-issue and is going to the extent of treating the holocaust of 1947 as a non-event and PoK refugees as non-entities' (IPCS 2007). While refugees were offered token rehabilitation support and some land to resettle, their resettlement amounts were insignificant as compared to the packages that many Partition refugees received in other parts of India[3] (Guha 2017: v). Satya Saraf, a POJK refugee whose family migrated from Muzaffarabad region in POJK, is now resettled in Jammu. He looks old and frail but still has many strong memories of the Partition times. While describing the troubles he confronted to resettle in a new, unknown place in Jammu, he gets teary-eyed. Saraf remarks:

> We lost our culture, our roots and had to adapt to a new place. It was difficult as we were not the priority for either the Indian government or Kashmiri leadership. The Indian government was busy with other groups of refugees, and the Kashmiri government always prioritised the interests of Muslims.

Saraf further stated that 'the POJK refugees wanted the moral and sympathetic support of the Indian governments … we never got that.' Pointing to the specificities of POJK refugees, Rekha Chowdhary (Chowdhary 2015: 204) states:

> POK refugees … are the political victims of the unsettled claims over the territory now under the control of Pakistan. Though they had gone through the same experience of displacement in 1947 as a large number of 'partition refugees' of Punjab and Bengal had gone through, the process of their rehabilitation and resettlement has not followed on similar lines. As per the

> official Indian position, the territory from which they have been displaced belongs to India and hence, they cannot be treated at par with those who were displaced from Pakistan. They are the residents of the same state and hence can be considered as internally displaced people. It is for this reason that unlike other partition refugees in India whose claims over land and property left back in Pakistan were settled, the claims of these 'POK refugees ' have neither been assessed nor settled. The process of their rehabilitation, therefore, has not been completed.

Describing the half-hearted resettlement measures taken by the national and state governments, Rajiv Chunni (IPCS 2007), Chairman of SOS, maintains that 'Neither the Union nor the state government has been sincere in settling these displaced persons. There were schemes, but the administrators of these schemes have been confusing relief measures and small ex-gratia grant with rehabilitation.'

Unlike other Partition refugees in India whose claims over property and land left behind in Pakistan were compensated for, the claims of the POJK refugees were not assessed. These refugees have not been compensated in lieu of their properties left behind. As Reeta Tremblay (2016: 101) notes:

> Because India did not accept the Partition of Jammu and Kashmir, India's Displaced Persons (Compensation and Rehabilitation) Act, 1954 and the Administration of Evacuee Property Act, 1950 were not made applicable to the state of Jammu and Kashmir. Thus, the Govenment of India did neither register them nor invite this group of people to request claims for compensation in lieu of the properties left behind.

Consequently, the relief measures provided to the POJK refugees were insufficient and on an ad-hoc basis. Although they were provided some land in rural areas, and small plots and quarters in urban areas, these rehabilitation offers were nothing in proportion to the material losses these communities had incurred due to their displacement. While some refugees were allotted land owned by the state, others were allocated the custodian or evacuee properties.[4] In the former case, the land has been transferred in the names of the refugees. However, in the latter case, Jammu and Kashmir's leadership did not allow the refugees to register the evacuee properties in their names (Chowdhary 2015: 204–205; IPCS 2007; Tremblay 2016). Consequently, many refugees are still living as tenants in the evacuee properties, unable to claim ownership of their houses and lands.[5] The Kashmiri leadership, that dominated the political power structure of J&K, had allocated to itself the task of protecting the evacuee property and often proclaiming the evacuees, who are now in POJK, as the rightful owners of these properties (Tremblay 2016). Voices of the POJK refugees, in the process, were marginalised and their land rights remained uncertain in many such cases.

It is in this context that the community argues that they do not enjoy equal citizenship rights—indicating issues such as recognition as refugees, land rights, and material support—as their counterpart refugees in other parts of India. 'Are we lesser citizens than the others that our most basic demands are not met by the Indian government? We never felt included in the way other refugees were made to feel in India after Partition. We feel as orphaned or stepchildren of the nation,' protested Ram Dayal, an elderly POJK refugee respondent. Another middle-aged respondent, Satpal, who is the son of a POJK refugee and also a political activist, alleged:

> Our fates have been linked with the unresolved politics and conflict of the state. Just like the temporality of the LoC, our rights have been left pending by the Indian state as well as Jammu and Kashmir government. Our lives, our properties, our experiences have been marked by uncertainty and determined by the ongoing Kashmir–India politics.

Here, Ram Dayal and Satpal are pointing to the citizenship experiences and grievances of the POJK refugees who are caught up in a unique post-Partition situation arising out of the *de facto* nature of the LoC. On the one hand, the national leadership did not fully support their resettlement or compensation issues and on the other hand, the local J&K government did not give sufficient consideration to this section of the population. Both these entities have prioritised the politics of conflict, borders and territories, and have been oblivious to the concerns of the POJK refugees.

While the POJK refugees have moved on since the time of their displacement, their cultural and political identities still manifest strong links with their past. 'Our family is well settled here. Yet, I feel as if I belong nowhere. I know that we can never go back to our homes in POK. India, Jammu is our home. I have spent my life here. But even in Jammu sometimes we feel as outsiders.' stated Mohan Lal, whose family migrated to Jammu when he was about 15 years old. His younger son, Suraj, was born in India but still refers to himself and his family as 'refugees'. 'Our culture is Mirpuri (now in POK). Our culture is very hospitable and soft, different from the culture of Jammu. We are proud that our families rebuilt their lives themselves. Not much was offered by the government,' Suraj remarked. He added, 'Our community has lost its identity, our homes and cultures were left behind. My father often says that a part of him is lost.' As expressed by Mohan Lal and his son, their sense of cultural alienation and being 'outsiders' still lingers on. Their contemporary political and cultural identities have strong associations with their Partition memories and the way they were accommodated and treated in the post-Partition period. An intricate mix of their past and present defines their contemporary identities and struggles. Before elaborating further on the post-Partition lives of the POJK refugees and their citizenship experiences, it is pertinent to briefly describe the conditions of Partition that led to their displacement.

Partition Violence: Tragedy of Hindus and Muslims

After the Partition of India, the fate of the erstwhile princely State of J&K was still undecided. Meanwhile, a local Muslim revolt in the Poonch district of the state against the Maharaja and Hindu landlords, which was joined by tribal invaders from Pakistan, turned into a communal frenzy (Bhatia 2020; Bose 2005: 32–35; Puri 2012: 28–30). Many Hindus and Sikhs in various Muslim majority districts were targeted and were compelled to move to what they thought were safer places.

As far as POJK refugees are concerned, they were at that time spread out in different districts of J&K that are now under Pakistan's control—Mirpur, Muzaffarabad, Kotli, Bhimber and the Poonch. In the situation as it had developed in the wake of Poonch revolt and tribal invasion, there was panic in these areas and other parts of the erstwhile princely state. These circumstances compelled Maharaja Hari Singh to accede to India, and seek the support of the Indian Army to push back the invaders and rescue the targeted minorities. However, before the Indian Army could rescue people in the POJK areas, tribal invaders and other communal elements had already created devastation there. The most haunting memory for these refugees is the Mirpur massacre of November 1947. Raghunandhan Singh Bali, a Sikh POJK refugee originally from Mirpur, describes the situation of panic brewing in the town at the time:

> After the Partition of India, the Hindu and Sikh refugees from adjoining Jhelum district of Punjab (Pakistan) came in sizeable numbers to the predominantly Hindu town of Mirpur, 25 miles from Jhelum town. Its population rose to 25,000 approximately. These refugees thought Mirpur, being part of the Maharaja's state, to be a safer place, little knowing that its borders were most vulnerable to attacks by Pakistani raiders.

Many POJK respondents narrated that as panic grew, some Hindu and Sikh families started to leave for Indian-administered parts of Jammu. Harmit Singh, an 85-year-old Sikh POJK refugee in Jammu, stated, 'Not many could escape as the Pakistani army and the tribal invaders had closed roads and would kill people trying to escape by buses. People were left with no option and they started wandering aimlessly with their families. There was panic all over.'

POJK refugees collectively recall 25 November 1947 as the ill-fated day when Mirpur town was raided and devastated by the raiders, killing Hindus and Sikhs in huge numbers. C. P. Gupta, originally belonging to Mirpur, recounted the tragedy in *Daily Excelsior* (Gupta 2019):

> ... more than 18000 unarmed citizens of Mirpur which included men, women, and innocent children, were brutally killed unprecedentedly by the Pakistani raiders. This was not the end of [the] misery of the people of Mirpur. At night of the same day at about 12 P.M. [*sic*] an ill-fated group of about 2,000 captured persons, was brought at a place known as 'Kas Gumma' ... they were tortured and killed brutally in batches during the night. The women and girls were taken to unknown places by the Pathans ... Next day, the enemy drove another group of about 2000 persons and brought them to another village known as 'Thithal'. They also met the same treatment as at 'Kas Gumma' during day-light. Finally there was a massacre at Alibeg where about 4,000 captives were huddled up in an old deserted and unhygienic ruined Gurdwara building ... Out of the total population of 25,000 of Mirpur city, luckily or unluckily a group of about 3000 persons which included the author also, could find right way and after walking on bare feet for seven days and nights without food and water, reached Jammu in a very miserable condition which too is very difficult to be explained in words even now. In the middle [of] January, 1948, a team of ICRS (International Committee of Red Cross) arrived there and took charge of the Alibeg camp and supplied much needed food and

> medicines to the captives. On March 18, 1948 they managed to get the captives liberated in exchange of the same number of Muslims who were in India and willing to go to Pakistan. These liberated captives were not more than 1600 as the rest were either killed, died or kidnapped.

This is a shared Partition narrative recited by the refugees belonging to the Mirpur area. Similar stories of communal violence against and displacement of Hindu or Sikh refugees are told of other POJK areas like Kotli, Muzaffarabad, Poonch and Bhimber. While many of these refugees may point to these Partition tragedies as unique and specific to their community and religion, a massive number of Muslims living in different parts of Jammu province that had a substantial Hindu population suffered a similar traumatic fate (Snedden 2007). While communal violence against Hindu and Sikh populations resulted in POJK areas being totally wiped out of these communities (Hindus and Sikhs); communal violence against Muslims and their migration resulted in changing the demographic character of Jammu region—from Muslim majority to a predominantly Hindu region (Puri 2012; Snedden 2007). As Luv Puri (2012: 31) notes:

> The scale of Muslim migration (due to Partition violence) can be ascertained from the changes in the data. In Jammu district alone, 37 percent of the population was Muslim in 1941. By 1961, it had come down to barely 10 percent .... On 5 and 6 November, many trucks and lorries carrying Muslim migrants from Jammu city on their way to Punjab province of Pakistan were attacked and massacred.

Till today, the academic and political discourse on the Partition of J&K has not offered a relatively impartial analysis of the violence that occurred. While some discourses selectively and exclusively talk about the tragedy of the Muslim 'massacre', others highlight and exaggerate only the stories of 'elimination' of Hindus from POJK areas. As is evident from the Partition narratives, memories and official accounts, there was nothing specific about the communal violence committed against any one particular community. What was specific and unique was the most horrific Partition violence itself that was committed against members of different communities which were minorities in the areas most powerfully affected by the Partition. However, for the purposes of this chapter, we will focus on the Partition journey of the POJK refugees that has shaped their politics, contemporary lives and citizenship experiences.

Partition Memories and Post-Partition Lives

These past accounts of physical and sexual violence and displacement are deeply imprinted in the memories of the POJK refugees, and they pass on parts of these narratives to their succeeding generations. Consequently, Partition lives on and thrives in the memories of POJK families and takes on multiple expressions. It is through Partition memories that these families express their sense of shock and trauma. Despite moving on and building their lives anew, the refugee communities do express shock that their 'perfect' homes and 'peaceful' lives of the past were abruptly ruined. They cling on to the Partition memories to explain their sense of alienation and loss of cultural identity. 'Anywhere we go in this world, anywhere we settle down in India, we feel like outsiders. Because our culture and our homes were taken away from us. We are outsiders forever,' remarked Rupa Devi, an elderly woman who migrated from Mirpur during the 1947 chaos. Memories of trauma are often also manifested in their distrust for Muslim communities, hardened political positions, and in many cases, support for right-wing Hindu politics. Vikas Gupta, son of a POJK refugee in Jammu, explained:

> Our families were deeply disturbed to know that not just raiders or Pakistani army but local Muslims were involved in killings of Hindus, rape of Hindu women and plunder of our houses. We lost our trust in local Muslims. It was a big shock for our communities.

Vikas, who is middle-aged and owns a grocery shop in Jammu, upholds the Hindu conservative political ideology. When asked whether Muslims of Jammu had not met a similar fate and were targeted by some communal-minded Hindus, Vikas stated:

> I am sure all minorities were targeted. I also know that many Muslims saved Hindus and many Hindus saved Muslims. But I and my community cannot forget the wrongdoings of local Muslim men. These were the people we trusted .... Some Muslims are good. I have some good friends. But we cannot trust this community as a whole.

In the absence of any kind of healing processes, the feelings of mistrust and stereotyping of Muslims have been reinforced over a period, and are often stoked by the activities of right-wing organisations working at the grassroots. Such sentiments are further intensified by the fact that Hindus of Jammu, including these communities, are a minority in J&K and share the feeling of being discriminated against by the dominant Kashmiri Muslim leadership (Bhatia 2020). While many districts of Jammu region have an overwhelming Hindu population, Hindus form a minority in the Muslim-majority J&K region. Since the post-accession period, Hindus of Jammu have blamed the Kashmiri leadership for prioritising the Kashmir region and discriminating against 'Jammu' and 'Hindus'—a perception that is reflective of the dominant political narrative of the Jammu region. In this background, the fears and sense of discrimination felt by the POJK refugees feed on minority insecurities and political perceptions. However, the refugees' experiences are also driven by their actual and genuine grievances vis-à-vis the Kashmiri Muslim leadership. The latter has often replicated the Indian state in asserting its majoritarian character and de-prioritising the interests of the minorities and non-Kashmiri communities (ibid.)—a theme that is elaborated in this chapter below.

For now, it is pertinent to mention here that though many among the POJK refugees have supported Hindu-oriented politics, they are also perhaps aware of its limitations. This community alleges that the Hindu political organisations have not powerfully voiced its demands, and in many instances have used its grievances for political propaganda. It argues that both the Indian state and Hindu-based political parties have made use of the 'Hindu refugee' issue to gain political sympathy and expand their Hindu constituency, and have not demonstrated any serious effort to reach out to and support the community. Ranjit, a middle-aged man belonging to a well-settled and educated refugee family, is a college teacher in Jammu. He is married to Sangeeta, who also belongs to a POJK refugee family and is a school teacher. In an interaction with the couple, Ranjit stated:

> We have been used as a political vote bank. Hindu-based parties voice our concerns but do not do anything for us in reality. We have been treated as secondary citizens by the Jammu and Kashmir leadership as well as by Indian governments. All elected Indian governments have simply looked the other way, overlooking our problems.

Sangeeta agreed with her husband's views and nodded all along. She added that 'India is a Hindu majority country but when it comes to Jammu and Kashmir, it is Kashmir that comes first. The Indian government has not even considered us as "refugees" ... till now.' Throughout the conversation, both Ranjit and Sangeeta were foregrounding their genuine grievances vis-à-vis the Indian government, but were also using the Indian majoritarian and pro-Hindu discourse to make their claims. For instance, Ranjit stated:

> We are very proud as a community ... that we are self-made. Our displaced elders started from the very scratch ... from working as menial labourers to opening shops to doing all kinds of hard labour ... Today many of us are successful. We have established ourselves in the education sector, in bureaucracy, in business. But we also feel that we were treated unfairly by the Indian government. We didn't get justice. Now we hear about Kashmiri Pandits, their exodus, and huge displacement packages they got. We, on the other hand, have grown up listening to stories of dislocation, hardships, adversities, and rebuilding our lives. We were not aware of any displacement packages. While Kashmiri Pandits were offered attractive packages, we were left to fend for ourselves. Aren't we Indians, Hindus, just like them?

When most respondents talk about the pre-Partition days, Partition violence, and the manner in which they rebuilt their post-Partition lives, they chaotically navigate between these memories. Without following a linear time-flow, they often switch from talking about their contemporary lives to abruptly recalling their immediate post-Partition distress of settling down, and then perhaps go further back to narrate their trauma of Partition violence. There is no particular sequence, as they go back and forth rupturing the linearity of the events. It is this messy and non-linear sense of narratives that link their past and present lives. They hold on to the chaotic, often fragmented, and unresolved memories of violence, trust, distrust, self-sufficiency, pride or injustice to make sense of their lives and collective identities.

Partition violence and dislocation aside, the politics of territorial conflict—of both the Indian state and the J&K leadership—in the post-Partition era has been instrumental in shaping the citizenship experiences of the POJK refugees.

As discussed before, both political entities remained stuck in the territorial aspect of the Kashmir conflict, overlooking the concerns of people affected by the conflict, including these refugees. This will be elaborated in the section below.

Caught between Indian and Kashmiri leaderships

The situation of POJK refugees remains complicated due to the fact that India has from the beginning contested the division of J&K. Since J&K officially acceded to India, the entire J&K, including POJK, is an integral part of India and depicted thus in the official maps. This territorial political claim clearly indicates that India does not consider the residents of POJK as foreign nationals. Therefore, the people who left the Indian side of J&K and migrated towards Pakistan's side of the state during Partition or the India–Pakistan wars are entitled to return, and claim back their lands. In this context, the POJK refugees are not allowed to register the evacuee lands in their names, as the evacuees still remain the original owners. As Reeta Tremblay observes:

> The Government of India has, on an off-and-on basis, allocated funds to the state government so that temporary relief could be disbursed to the PoKDP [Pakistan-Occupied Kashmir Displaced People]. The state government also took measures to allot the PoKDP temporary accommodations over which, however, the latter exercise no ownership rights. They were assigned the 'Evacuee Property' left behind by Muslims who had fled to (occupied) Kashmir and other parts of Pakistan. The Evacuee Properties are being held in custody by the department of the Custodian of Evacuee Property, Jammu and Kashmir. Its major duty is to look after these properties and ensure they are restored to their rightful owners upon their return (Tremblay 2016: 101).

The same goes for Pakistan, which reserves the rights of the Hindu evacuees to return and claim their evacuee lands in Pakistan-controlled Jammu and Kashmir. This has created an intricate, unresolvable problem as displaced people actually living on either side of the LoC are not offered any pragmatic solution. They are neither recognised as refugees nor offered any systematic material support for their resettlement. At the time of their arrival in 1947, these displaced people were not even officially registered by the Indian or state governments, as was done for Partition refugees in other parts of India. Recognition of these displaced people as refugees or taking away the ownership of people who had migrated to the other side during Partition weakens the territorial assertions of India and Pakistan over the issue of Kashmir.

On the Indian side, the nation-state has in many ways prioritised the rights of the Hindu Partition refugees in general, enabling them to shape the discourse on resettlement and citizenship. Yet, in Jammu and Kashmir, it diverges from this majoritarian discourse and instead, it has made territorial politics a primary concern, even at the cost of abandoning the concerns of POJK refugees. The POJK-displaced people have been caught between the Indian and the J&K leadership, and their uncompromising politics of conflict.

The political approach adopted by the J&K leadership is similar to that of the Indian state in many respects. To briefly trace the history of the J&K government, one needs to go back to the post-accession era. In the post-accession period, there was a drastic change in the political leadership of J&K. Hindu Dogra monarchical rule was replaced by a constitutional democratic setup, led by the educated and progressive Kashmiri Muslim leadership. The National Conference, headed by the popular leader Sheikh Abdullah, formed the government and undertook radical political and economic reforms. Although the National Conference was known for its progressive and secular values, it also had major limitations as its focus remained exclusively on Kashmir and uplifting the downtrodden communities among Muslims of this region. This led to other regions and communities of the state being overlooked (Bhatia 2020).

Over the years as the antagonism grew between Indian nationalism and Kashmiri identity politics, the Kashmiri leadership became increasingly and narrowly focused on asserting the identity of Kashmiri Muslims. This in the Kashmiri leadership almost mirrored the majoritarian approach of the Indian state. With the cultural and political autonomy of Kashmir as its main ideological agenda, and Kashmiri Muslims as its primary political constituency, the aspirations and grievances of other sections were largely sidelined. Kashmiri identity politics, in general, prioritised the concerns and aspirations of the majority, while obscuring the diversity of the Jammu and Kashmir region and suppressing voices of difference and dissent (Chowdhary 2015). Even the interests and political demands of the non-Kashmiri Muslim communities living in Jammu or Ladakh were brushed aside. Many marginal groups within the state, such as the Muslims of the border areas of Jammu, Gujjars living on the peripheries of the state, or refugees from POJK and West Pakistan, were largely overlooked.

The discussion above is not to argue that the Kashmiri leadership completely shunned the refugees or did not offer any support, as some form of aid in terms of allotment of land, loans or financial support was provided by the state government. However, the material support was too inadequate and the demands of the refugees remained unaddressed (IPCS 2007). Only nominal attention was given to refugees, and their problems did not find space in the political narratives of the J&K leadership. The Kashmiri leadership prioritised the displaced Muslim community, which is now residing in the Pakistan side of J&K, over the refugees. A focus on people who had left rather than on those still residing in the region was part of the nationalist politics of the Kashmiri leadership. Many constitutional formulations, policies and official narratives of the J&K government point to their majoritarian bias, at the cost of neglecting the grievances of refugees and other minority communities. In this context, Tremblay states:

> [T]he Jammu and Kashmir Constitution recognizes as citizens, as defined by the 1927 promulgation, all Muslims who, because of communal violence, abandoned their homes and property in the state and moved across the border to (occupied) Kashmir. To that effect, Article 48 of the J & K Constitution has reserved 24 out of 87 legislative seats for Pakistan administered Kashmiri citizens. It stipulates that these 24 seats will remain vacant till Pakistan ceases the 'occupation' of Kashmir. In addition, in order to assert Kashmir's distinctness and its autonomy, the Jammu and Kashmir Legislative Assembly passed the Resettlement Bill in 1982 to allow refugees from the state of Jammu and Kashmir, who were then settled in Pakistan and (occupied) Kashmir, to return freely to the state and allow them to reclaim property. The bill was opposed by the Hindus of Jammu, particularly those who had been seeking full citizenship rights for the WPR (West Pakistan Refugees) and the PoKDP (Pakistan Occupied Kashmir Displaced Persons). Although the bill was returned by the then Governor B. K. Nehru, citing inconsistencies, the Kashmir government referred the bill to the Supreme Court the same year, seeking its opinion on the legality of the Act. Over thirty years later, the Supreme Court is yet to act upon it (Tremblay 2016: 99).

The POJK refugees had to navigate these multiple layers of legalities, nationalist politics, and intricacies of conflict to carve a space for themselves in Jammu. Their neglect by the J&K state leadership enabled them to drift towards and be appropriated by the Hindu-right politics in Jammu. Consequently, many refugees from the community tend to 'Hinduise' their victimisation and sufferings, and look at their concerns, rights and entitlements from a religious perspective. Echoing the Indian majoritarian citizenship discourse, they believe that they have been betrayed by the Indian state and are entitled to privileges due to their Hindu identity, as also mentioned earlier.

Satish Gupta is a vocal and progressive leader of the POJK community. Opposed to the Hindu conservative politics, he blames the Kashmiri leadership for abandoning the refugees and offering a free space to the Hindu organisations to capture the POJK political constituency. He remarked:

> Jammu and Kashmir government gives more consideration to Muslims of the region. The Muslim Kashmiri leadership has set the debate on rights and entitlements, which doesn't favour us. Land reforms, redistribution of land were all carried out to benefit the poor condition of Kashmiri Muslims. This is a good thing as Muslims of the state were oppressed and needed attention. But this government started neglecting concerns of all others. All other peripheral communities were not paid any attention to. In our case, all policies regarding ownership of land were made to benefit displaced Muslims who went to the Pakistan side of Kashmir, in case they decide to return. But we were left vulnerable. Even the Government of India has overlooked our claims and rights. We don't have equal rights as other Indians when it comes to property rights or political rights.

The issue of the Resettlement Bill, mentioned by Tremblay, was also appropriated by the Hindu-based political parties. Known as The Jammu and Kashmir Grant of Permit for Resettlement in (or Permanent Return to) the State Act, 1982, this bill allowed the residents of Jammu and Kashmir and their successors who had moved to Pakistan from 1 March 1947 to 14 May 1954 to return to India. This bill was finally abolished by the NDA-II government in 2019 using the J&K Reorganisation Act. However, the discourse around the Bill/Act clearly reflected the majoritarian tendencies within the Kashmiri nationalist discourse. Representing the interest of the Muslims who were forced to leave J&K in 1947, the

National Conference and its leadership have been seeking to raise passions in Kashmir without even raising the implication that such an Act might have on the POJK refugees.

Conclusion

As already stated, the POJK refugees have been looking to the Indian state for their outstanding issues of compensation and settlement. As Hindu refugees, their claim on the Indian state follows not the logic of citizenship as much as the majoritarian logic of being 'Hindu' and not getting their due within the Hindu-majority Indian state. With the Bharatiya Janata Party (BJP) forming the government since 2014, their expectations from the state have increased. The state has also been symbolically and tangibly responding by focusing on the issues of some of these groups so far 'neglected' by the Kashmir-centric political elite in J&K. To address the outstanding issue of resettlement and compensation, in between the financial period 2018–2019 to 2023–2024 a compensation of Rs 5.5 lakh was given to each displaced family to cover a large number of POJK refugees (GoI 2023). However, this is not seen as enough and there is expectation that a full-fledged compensation will eventually be provided to them.

More recently, the NDA-II government has used the agenda of POJK refugees to justify its intervention in J&K. As mentioned earlier in this book, the government took the major initiative of modifying Article 370 and doing away with the special constitutional status of J&K; taking away Article 35A which safeguarded the special privileges for the permanent residents of the state; and reorganising the State of Jammu and Kashmir into two Union Territories. Though the abolition of Article 370 and 35A has been part of the ideological commitments of the BJP for a long time, yet in providing the justification for introducing these drastic changes, the government has referred to the interest of 'discriminated groups' and communities. Among the 'discriminated groups', the POJK refugees, along with the West Pakistan refugees, Balmikis[6] and women, have been named. Referring to the discriminatory approach of the respective Kashmir-based government using the provisions of Article 370 and 35A, the NDA-II government specifically mentioned the J&K Resettlement Act and described how these governments favoured 'those Kashmiris and their descendants who had migrated to Pakistan, or POJ&K during Partition in 1947' and the Muslim refugees from Xinjiang and Tibet who had migrated to Kashmir following the Chinese occupation of their countries in 1949 and 1959' over the 'POJ&K refugees and their descendants numbering about 1.5 million', who were not only 'kept out of this legal provision but the state government consistently refused to let them or their descendants settle in J&K as "State subjects".' One of the arguments therefore given to discard Article 35A was that 'the state was being turned into a state for Muslim only and Article 35A was the instrument to carry out such a nefarious act' (*The Hindu* 2019).[7]

Will the reorganisation of the state, and particularly the abrogation of Article 370 and 35A, satisfy the POJK refugees? This is a difficult question to answer. Though they have been named as the beneficiaries of the changes that took place in August 2019, their basic issues remain pending. They are not happy with the '5.5 lakh rupees' package as they find it to be too little and too late. Terming this settlement as 'peanuts', they have already declared this as a mockery of their claims and injustice to their long struggle (Sharma 2019). Though the refugees did express happiness over the abrogation of the special constitutional status of J&K, mainly because they viewed this as an act against the Muslim leadership of Kashmir, their sense of celebration has soon given way to disillusionment as their basic issues remain unaddressed.

Notes

1. Three broad regions of the erstwhile J&K state on the Indian side—Jammu, Kashmir and Ladakh—are culturally, politically and demographically different from one another. Kashmiri identity politics mainly represents the Muslim community of the Kashmir Valley. This political sentiment is not shared by Jammu and Ladakh. Jammu often takes a pro-Indian position and at times its politics takes on a parochial and ultra-nationalist approach. Ladakh, culturally and politically divergent from both these regions, often feels sidelined by the vocal politics of Kashmir and Jammu. Despite these differences, the three regions engaged in mutual interactions and cultural sharing. However, J&K ceased to be a state since August 2019. The NDA-II government used the Jammu and Kashmir Reorganisation Act, 2019 to abolish Article 370 and bifurcate the state into two Union Territories—Jammu and Kashmir, and Ladakh.

2. The late 1980s mark the phase of insurgency when the Kashmiri struggle against the Indian state entered a phase of armed resistance. It later spread to the Jammu region. In the initial years of insurgency, amidst fear and violence, Kashmiri Pandits fled *en masse* to Jammu and other parts of India.

3. A total of 31,619 registered with Rehabilitation Organisation, 26,319 families opted to settle down within J&K and 5,300 families settled outside J&K. Of those settled in J&K, 22,719 families were allotted land while 3,600 were allowed quarters/plots (Sharma 2018: 155).

4. Evacuee properties in the J&K borderlands were those left behind by Muslims who migrated to Pakistan. The Government of J&K is the custodian of such properties.

5. As per the Government Order No. 913 of 1951 and as per the Administration of Evacuee Property Act, those holding the evacuee property were obliged to restore the possession of land to owners who may return from POK (Sharma 2018: 156).

6. The Balmikis are SC groups in Jammu who are not natives and originally belong to the Punjabi Balmiki community. This community is categorised as 'non-native' as it was relocated from Punjab to Jammu in 1957 to replace its sanitation workers, who had gone on an indefinite strike.

7. One of the major political benefits given to the POJK refugees after the reorganisation has been a few reserved seats in the J&K Assembly. The report of the Delimitation Commission has recommended that 'the Central government may consider giving the Displaced Persons from Pakistan occupied Jammu and Kashmir some representation in the Jammu and Kashmir Legislative Assembly, by way of nominations of representatives of Displaced Persons from Pakistan Occupied Jammu and Kashmir.' (Election Commission 2022).

References

Bose, Sumantra. 2005. *Kashmir: Roots of Conflict, Paths to Peace*. Cambridge, US: Harvard University Press.

Bhatia, Mohita. 2020. *Rethinking Conflict at the Margins: Dalits and Borderland Hindus in Jammu and Kashmi*r. UK: Cambridge University Press.

Chatterji, Joya. 2012. 'South Asian Histories of Citizenship, 1946–1970', *Historical Journal* 55(4):1049–1071.

Chattha, Illyas. 2011. 'Escape from Violence: The 1947 Partition of India and the Migration of Kashmiri Muslim Refugees'. In Panikos Panayi and Pippa Virdee (eds), *Refugees and the End of Empire: Imperial Collapse and Forced Migration in the Twentieth Century*. UK: Palgrave Macmillan.

Chimni, B. S. 1998. 'The Geopolitics of Refugee Studies: A View from the South'. *Journal of Refugee Studies* 11(4): 354–374.

Chowdhary, Rekha. 2015. *Jammu and Kashmir: Politics of Identity and Separatism*. UK: Routledge.

Election Commission. 2022. 'Delimitation Commission Finalises the Delimitation Order Today', 5 May. Press release, PIB. Available at https://pib.gov.in/PressReleasePage.aspx?PRID=1822939 (accessed January 2024).

Ganguly, Sumit. 2002. *Conflict Unending: India–Pakistan Tensions Since 1947*. Columbia: Columbia University Press.

GoI. 2023. 'Financial Assistance to West Pakistan Refugees', Annexure 3, Ministry of Home Affairs. Available at https://www.mha.gov.in/sites/default/files/2023-07/Annexure3_28072023.pdf (accessed February 2024).

Guha, Ramachandra. 2017. *India After Gandhi: The History of the World's Largest Democracy*. New Delhi: Pan MacMillan India.

Gupta, C. P. 2019. 'Mirpur Mahyhem'. *Daily Excelsior*, 24 November. Available at https://www.dailyexcelsior.com/mirpur-mahyhem/ (accessed January 2024).

IPCS (Institute of Peace and Conflict Studies). 2007. 'The Forgotten People of Jammu and Kashmir: "Refugees" from PoK' (An Interview with Rajiv Chunni). Available at http://www.ipcs.org/comm_select.php?articleNo=2182 (accessed January 2024).

Malkki, Liisa. 1995. 'Refugee and Exile: From "Refugee Studies" to the National Order of Things'. *Annual Review of Anthropology* 24: 495–523.

Puri, Luv. 2012. *Across the Line of Control: Inside Pakistan-administered Jammu and Kashmir*. London: Hurst Publishers.

Sharma, Mamta. 2018. 'Rehabilitation of POK Displaced Persons of 1947 in Jammu Province: A Comparative Study of Jammu and Rajouri Districts', PhD Thesis. Dept. of Political Science, University of Jammu.

Sharma, Vikram. 2019. 'PoK refugees: One-time Central package peanuts'. *The Tribune*, 10 October. Available at https://www.tribuneindia.com/news/archive/j-k/news-detail-845125 (accessed January 2024).

Snedden, Christopher. 2007. 'What happened to Muslims in Jammu? Local identity, "the massacre" of 1947, and the roots of the "Kashmir problem"'. *Journal of South Asian Studies* 24(2): 111–134.

The Hindu. 2019. 'Full Text of document on govt.'s rationale behind removal of special status to J&K', 5 August. Available at https://www.thehindu.com/news/national/full-text-of-document-on-govts-rationale-behind-removal-of-special-status-to-jk/article28821368.ece (accessed January 2024).

Tremblay, Reeta Chowdhari. 2016. 'Protracted Displacement in Conflict Zones: Refugees and Internally Displaced People in Jammu and Kashmir'. *Migration, Mobility, & Displacement* 2(2): 91–109.

Zamindar, Vazira. 2007. *The Long Partition and the Making of Modern South Asia: Refugees, Boundaries, Histories*. USA: Columbia University Press.

VII

Marginalisation and Borders

What Does it Mean to Live on the LoC?

Chakraverti Mahajan and Sandeep Singh

Introduction

> Nabeel: *Ek jaise log, ek jaisi zubaan, ek jaisa rehan-sehan, bas in siyasatoon ne humein lakiro mein baant diya* (One people, one language, one way of life; only the politics has separated us from each other through lines).
> Sujaan: *Inhi lakiro ne to sab kuch cheen liya hamara* (These lines have snatched everything from us).

One evening, in a nondescript village situated on the LoC in Poonch district of Jammu and Kashmir, as Nabeel sits around the fire with Sujaan and Billa, he expresses his amazement at the similarity between people, language and lifestyle on either side of the LoC. Nabeel, a young Muslim man, was visiting along with his paternal grandmother from Mirpur, which is a border district on the Pakistani side of the LoC, to meet her sister on the Indian side of the LoC. Sujaan, a middle-aged Hindu man who lost his father and young sisters during the Partition carnage, exclaims that these lines had snatched away everything from them. Billa, a young Muslim man, orphaned due to the ongoing conflict, attempts to lighten the mood by asking Nabeel and Sujaan to stop talking about 'lakeero-shakeero' (lines) and rather concentrate on the drink that he had offered.

The above scene is from the film *Lines* (2021) directed by Hussein Khan, which shows multiple aspects of people's lives on both sides of the LoC. The movie is set in the late 1990s, before the Kargil War of 1999. Though the movie is primarily a romanticised tale of love and marriage across the borders, it also manages to capture genuine moments from the day-to-day lives of the borderlands. Scenes of intermittent shelling and firing, dislocation from the villages to makeshift camps, accidental civilian deaths, separated families, sustained kinship ties across the borders and navigating the layered bureaucracy intersperse the movie. The aspects that we want to underscore in this chapter are those depicting the peculiarity of the LoC, in terms of the cultural continuity among the people living on either side of this border, lived kinship and the fuzzy nature of the border which, despite the decades of conflict and antagonism, allows people to feel connected.

Before excavating the everyday lives of people living close to the LoC, it is crucial to comprehend its meaning. Borders are 'lines' separating one country or state from another. However, these borders are not just 'visible lines' on the land, they are complex creations with manifold meanings and functions (Haselsberger 2014). The term 'border' does not identify itself just as a physical boundary that separates the sovereign writ of one state from another, but also as another fault line generated or accentuated by a conflict (DasGupta 2012) that separates people living on either side of it. This chapter moves away from analysing the complex relationships that nation-states and borders share. It is given that imagining a border without a nation-state and a nation-state without a border is impossible. However, borders are also peculiar spaces and institutions, established and sustained by the exceptional interplay between border communities residing on either side. Borders are 'vibrant and have their internal dynamics that influence, and are influenced by, the patterns of social, economic and political developments in surrounding landscapes' (Kliot and Newman 2000: 9). People living across the LoC are affected by the more significant socio-political processes between two nations and yet manage to lead their lives through a web of local social ties, cultural continuity and lived kinships.

In this chapter, we shift our focus away from the International Border (IB), the settled border between India and Pakistan. Instead, we focus on the Line of Control, the unsettled border between Jammu and Kashmir and Pakistan-controlled Jammu and Kashmir that runs through all the three regions of the erstwhile State of Jammu and Kashmir (or now, the UTs of Jammu, Kashmir and Ladakh). To be more specific, the chapter talks about the borderlanders living in the Poonch and Rajouri districts of the Jammu region. These areas have borne the major brunt of the conflict between India and Pakistan. The chapter is based on field observations since 2011—especially trips to Poonch and Rajouri in June and August 2014—and supplemented by focus group discussions, and interviews with elders, youth, women, traders and the intelligentsia of the areas as well. The primary respondents comprise the people residing in the villages along the LoC and key towns of the sub-region. Recent telephonic interviews were also conducted in 2021 with people from the region.

The chapter aims to study people living along the LoC in terms of the cultural continuities and kinship with those living across the border. Living on the margins of the state should not be understood in terms of an absence of the state. On the contrary, these borders are where the state becomes extremely visible, and the process of state-making remains active in these areas, especially the LoC.

Poonch and Rajouri: The History and the People

Poonch and Rajouri are the twin hill districts of the Jammu region that lie in the Pir-Panchal mountain ranges and form a significant part of the divided Jammu and Kashmir. When the princely State of Jammu and Kashmir faced local rebellion and war in 1947, a substantial part of the state came under the control of Pakistan. The division of the state impacted all the three regions of the state (Jammu, Kashmir and Ladakh); however, the impact was most deeply felt in these two districts. The LoC runs through these districts and forms around 60 per cent of its total length. The history of the Partition dates back to October 1947 when the invaders plundered the nearby regions of the town, and the present-day Poonch town turned into a refugee camp overnight and remained so for years to come, up to 1952 when policies of refugee rehabilitation and resettlement were implemented (Sharma 2021b). The erstwhile Poonch district of the undivided Jammu and Kashmir was mainly affected, and except for one tehsil that remained on the Indian side, most of this district came under the POJK.

Meanwhile, present-day Rajouri was part of Bhimber and later Reasi districts. Like the Poonch town, the Rajouri town was also under siege by the tribal invaders, and it was after a few months that the Indian Army recaptured it. However, a substantial part of the area contiguous with Poonch and Rajouri, particularly a large part of erstwhile Poonch district and Kotli and Mirpur, were separated and formed the POJK along with the Muzaffarabad district. While Muzaffarabad district is contiguous with Kashmir Valley, the rest of what forms the POJK is physically and culturally contiguous with the districts of Poonch and Rajouri.

Poonch is surrounded by the district of Baramulla and Pulwama of Kashmir Valley in the northeast, Pakistan-occupied areas of the state in the northwest and by Rajouri in the south. The Poonch district in the north flanks Rajouri district, Jammu district in the south, Reasi district in the east and POJK in the west. While Sundarbani, Nowshera, Rajouri, and Manjakote are the major towns of Rajouri district, Surankote, Mendhar, Poonch and Mandi are the major towns of Poonch district. The people across both sides of the LoC fall into three categories: the Pothwari-speaking Paharis, the Gujjars and the Kashmiri-speaking Hindus, Muslims and Sikhs. Among the Muslims, a crucial element for stratification in this region is the biradari. 'Biradari is a caste-like kinship corporate entity that is the primary factor amongst the primordial loyalties which govern social organization' (Alavi 1972: 27), 'through which most people attempt to gain access to power and resources' (Loureiro 2015: 314).

Regarding religious demography, the Poonch district comprises of Muslims (90.45 per cent), Hindus (6.84 per cent) and Sikhs (2.35 per cent). The Rajouri district, meanwhile, is much more mixed—62.71 per cent of people here are Muslims, 34.54 per cent are Hindus and 2.41 per cent are Sikhs. All these communities have elements of caste and biradari among them, and they operate even in the borderland populations of LoC. The presence of caste and biradari structures has allowed for cultural continuity and sustained kinship ties across the LoC communities in this region, which we shall discuss in detail in the next section.

From the data presented above, we can reflect on the cultural and religious demography of the two districts along the LoC and find its complex diversity. While travelling in these two districts, one finds multiple diversity patterns. As we cross the Jammu district and enter the Rajouri district, we find that the towns like Sundarbani and Nowshera and even Rajouri town are dominated by Pothwari-speaking Pahari Hindu refugees who migrated from Mirpur, Kotli or Poonch area under the control of Pakistan. Apart from these Paharis, nearby towns and villages are also populated by the Jammu Dogras and local Muslims, mostly Gujjars. The demography changes as one crosses Rajouri town and joins the Thanamandi area in the Rajouri district. This area has a large Gujjar Muslim population. Moreover, as one enters the towns and villages of Poonch district, including Mendhar, Surankote, Poonch, Haveli, one finds a mix of Muslim Gujjar and Pahari populations.

A large part of the population of these two districts, especially the villages near the LoC, forms the chunk of 'divided families' and comprises the refugees. These people were part of various towns and villages in what came to be known as POJK. They were forced to migrate in the context of the communal violence that accompanied the division of the princely state in 1947. While a more significant part of the divided families is Muslim (Hindu-Muslim divided families[1]), the refugees are mostly Hindus and Sikhs. As discussed earlier in the book, the refugee families and the divided families are not limited to 1947 alone. Along the LoC, migration continued until the Indo–Pakistan war of 1965 and later in 1971. The borders remained porous for a long time, and mobility was possible until 1971. This phenomenon resulted in more divided families and kinship ties across the LoC. In the next section, we talk about the nature of the LoC and the multiple displacements that took place across it, resulting in divided families and sustained kinship ties.

A Border without Borders: LoC before 1971

> *1947 se 1965 tak ye jo borders the ... lines thi ... ye meaningless the. Inka koi bada role nahi tha ... ye barricade create nahi kar rahe the ... matlab log yahan aate the, wahan jaate the ... shadiyo me, maut pe, janaze pe ... easy access thi unki* (Since the Partition in 1947 and up until 1965, the borders were meaningless. They did not play a significant role, did not create a barricade. People could move across for weddings and funerals and had easy access).

Ramiz, a young Muslim man from Poonch, thus recalled movement across the LoC, which has become highly monitored since the advent of militancy in this area in the 1990s. He explains a great deal about the nature of the LoC and how it allowed people to maintain their kinship ties for many years after the Partition.

Though a large part of the inhabited areas of the LoC runs through the Jammu region, it does not exhaust itself in this region only. A substantial part of it runs through Kashmir and Ladakh as well. It starts from Munawar near Akhnoor in the Jammu region and runs through the approximately 798 kms range of the Himalayas, and ends at Indira Col in Siachen (Ladakh) in the Karakoram range. Through its whole length, the LoC travels through various cultures, languages and climatic zones. At one end lies the Dogra lingual-cultural zone of Jammu, followed by the Pahari-Pothwari linguistic area of Poonch and Rajouri districts of Jammu, then passes through Kashmir and reaches Ladakh, which has an entirely distinct lingual-cultural environment. The line consists of almost all climatic zones of the state—fertile plains of Akhnoor followed by *kandi* (dry areas), the lower and middle Himalayas and the cold hilly terrain of Ladakh while navigating the upper Himalayas. The part of the LoC that passes through the Poonch and Rajouri districts of Jammu is the most densely inhabited, and a large number of villages of these two districts lie around the LoC. Thus, a total of 65 villages of Tehsil Haveli and 50 villages in Mendhar (Poonch district), and 50 villages in Nowshera (Rajouri district) are located around the LoC.

As we have discussed, the history of the LoC starts with an indigenous revolt by locals in Poonch against the oppressive practices of the Hindu monarch of the erstwhile princely State of J&K, Maharaja Hari Singh, which was joined by tribal invaders from Pakistan after the Partition in 1947. Maharaja Hari Singh acceded to India soon after and received military assistance of the Indian forces in the subsequent months (Behera 2006: 74). It is during this period that a large area of the erstwhile princely State of Jammu and Kashmir, including the towns of Bhimber, Kotli, Muzaffarabad and a large part of the Poonch district as well as the whole of Gilgit-Baltistan, was separated from the Indian side of J&K and came under Pakistan's control. In 1948, the formal ceasefire was declared, and the *de facto* border was drawn.

This saga of border formation had diverse political ramifications for various cultural/ethnic/geographical zones and sections of society of J&K. The way the line was drawn between the two sides was entirely arbitrary. Because of this invasion, the Hindu–Sikh families, who were around 4 per cent of the total population of Poonch, had to flee to Tehsil Haveli, the only portion which remained on the Indian side (Sharma 2021b). Whether it be in Jammu province or the district of Poonch, communities, villages and families were divided. The bordering process had severe economic, political, psychological and security consequences for the borderlanders. As has been discussed in the previous chapters, with the division of the state, there was an influx of Hindu and Sikh refugees from POJK who came to settle in the various towns of Rajouri and Poonch.

Meanwhile, many Muslims migrated to the other side of the LoC. Some of them returned after some time while others stayed back. However, not all Muslims who chose to come back were reinstated in their original property, as some of their property was considered evacuee property and was allotted or taken over by the Hindus and Sikh refugees (Sharma 2021b). Consequently, there was a substantial number of Hindu–Muslim divided families. Many Muslim families had their members living in the Pakistan side due to the chaotic manner in which the displacement occurred. Similarly, a few Hindu family members or relatives were left behind in POJK, and eventually they converted to Islam (Bhatia 2020).

The uncertainty of life during Partition in 1947 and the subsequent war of 1965 divided many families. Ramiz narrated the story of his grandfather, who remained on the Indian side of the LoC. His grandfather's brother had left for Pakistan, and Ramiz's grandfather and father continued to await the return of their relatives from POJK. In Ramiz's words: *'Hamare paas jo land hai … bahot jyada land hai … lekin wo hamare dada ne ya hamare father ne apne naam iss liye nahi karayi ki wo hamare relatives aayenge to wo apna hissa sambhal lenge'* ('We have much land, but our grandfather or our father never got it registered in their name, hoping that our relatives may arrive someday and manage their share'). Another instance is of Nazir, a resident of the border village in Poonch, and he narrated to us how his grandfather migrated to Pakistan in

1947 with his entire family, assuming their stay on the other side would be temporary. Later, he sent Nazir's father back to Poonch. Nazir said,

> My father has struggled a lot as he had been forced to go to POJK and come back. My uncle also returned to Poonch in a volatile situation in 1966. However, the others could not come back. Now, the rest of our family is spread over different parts of Pakistan and POJK.

Apart from war and fear of army violence, livelihood and the lure of land were the main reasons people migrated to this or that side of the LoC. For instance, Abid and his brother Akbar of Chandok migrated to Tatrinote (POJK) in 1947 with a group of seven families. After some time, four families (including their own) returned to Poonch. 'Some men of those families who got jobs/work settled on the other side of the fence,' they said, 'We were jobless there, and soon this joblessness became the impetus for us to come back to Poonch.'

With borders remaining porous for a long time, people could move from one side to the other. Since kin, home and land were on both sides, and people moved to-and-fro across the border, there was much interaction across the LoC. People would move from one side to the other to attend funerals or in the event of marriages in the broader family, as Ramiz had noted at the beginning of this section. 'It was common for our previous generations to cross the border and visit our relatives during marriages, death and even for economic purposes. My uncle who lives with us got his bride, our aunt, from Pakistan side,' said Guftar, a 32-year-old Muslim school teacher and resident of the border village, Poonch. Most respondents told us that cross-LoC marriages were also a pretty recurring phenomenon, and mainly done between families separated by the LoC but joined by the same biradari or caste. A culture of shared ties and traditions continues to even this day, though in a reduced manner. The bus service, which was started when somewhat cordial relations existed between the two nations, also facilitated the maintenance of cultural continuity between the people on either side of the LoC. Ramiz described this during his interview in the following words:

> When the bus service started, families began to meet. People would go from here, and families would come from there. The Hindu and Sikh families that are here have relatives in POJK. When those people (who were Muslim) visited here, they would visit Sikh households. They would address people as Sakina Fufi, Sakina Bua, Qulsom Aunty or Nazia Baaji. So, religions might have changed, but our culture and relations have not.

He also explained that the culture and traditions in Poonch are very similar to POJK and people across the LoC continued to identify with each other for a long time. Ramiz noted,

> The reason behind us continuing with the same rituals and the way of life is that the division in Jammu and Kashmir, particularly in Poonch and Rajouri, was unclear. The majority of Poonch district is, even today, near POJK. Because of the proximity, our relations did not perish. Relations perished in Punjab because the Hindus arrived here and the Muslims remained there. They moved with their families. If anyone was abducted, they did not remain in touch with each other, which is not the case with us. For us, those who left in 1947, their chapters were closed. They did not bother much with us nor did we with them. However, those in POJK, who moved in 1965, still identify themselves as being from Poonch. They could not absorb Pakistan's culture but we were able to absorb India's culture. We had a special status here, so most of our culture remained intact. We have blood relatives on the other side of the border, and our culture, our traditions are still the same. We have not changed, and we have maintained continuity. This continuity lies between the people who live in POJK and us. For example, my sympathies do not lie with Pakistan or POJK in my case. The attachment that I feel is for my relations, my people who live there.

Thus, it can be gauged that prior to 1971, the nature of the LoC was very different from what it is today, and this history of shared cultural traditions have lived on to some extent.

LoC After 1971: Militarisation, Restricted Mobilities and Everyday Challenges

The LoC border started becoming stringent and less permeable in the 1970s. After the 1971 India–Pakistan war, the kind of movement that used to take place across the border was gradually but significantly controlled. In the post-1970s era, people witnessed a newer and more severe form of border control. The villages near the border were mined, which held severe consequences for those seeking to move across. The LoC border became even more uncompromising and sealed after the onset of Kashmiri militancy in 1989 (Bhatia 2020; Puri 2012). Since the militants were using the LoC route to infiltrate from the POJK to the Indian side of J&K, the border surveillance became very strict. According to a respondent, Khurshid: 'The area provided a very congenial environment for the militants to infiltrate through Poonch and Rajouri route of LoC due to the hilly terrain, dense forest cover as well as the availability of the guides and overground workers.'

Hardening of boundaries and fencing techniques have significantly altered people's mobilities and relationships with the borders. From being transcendent, borders have come to be seen as sealed, surveilled and non-negotiable. After several warlike situations and conflicts, the nature of this border changed over time. For a period, e-passes were issued to people who wished to cross the border for their work or for meeting their relatives (*Kashmir Observer* 2019).The security along the borders has strengthened over time, and at present various thermal detection technologies have taken over. The border security forces have deployed anti-drone technologies at vital installations as drones are emerging as a new frontier of warfare (Kweera 2023).

However, the LoC symbolises uncertainty, internal displacement and violence, which are far from stability. Due to frequent India–Pakistan tensions at the borders, including intermittent firing, shelling and mining, the residents of the LoC have been witnessing a perpetual cycle of displacement and return. Escalated firing along the borders has resulted in waves of displacement in Rajouri and Poonch. Residents living near the border areas in these districts informed us that the frequency of India–Pakistan ceasefire violations along the LoC has substantially increased from 2013 onwards. These ceasefire violations have been so fierce in the last few years that the people living in the border villages have been time and again forced to move away from their homes to safer places in the villages closer to towns and cities. The ceasefire violations had not stopped even in the COVID-19 pandemic. Since mid-March 2020, both countries had been virtually under lockdown, but border lives still continued to be struck by firing and shelling. People now have to struggle doubly with the pandemic and the displacements due to ceasefire violations.

This situation of unsettled life has its implications for the overall socio-economic stability of the areas near the LoC. Though it is right to say that cultural and religious similarities bind the people across both sides of the border, the problems the people face during conflict cannot be invalidated.

These areas remain cut off from the fruits of progress and development and provide a low quality of life, and therefore, many people leave these villages along the LoC to settle in towns and cities. Economic development and opportunities are low in the villages very close to the LoC and overall in Poonch and Rajouri districts. The situation becomes worse in the LoC areas. One can illustrate this from the example of Kerni village (Rajouri), which lies on the LoC. This village has a population of 600 and has only one ex-serviceman, a working clerk in a government department, and an ReT teacher.[2] The rest of the villagers are BPL (below poverty line) cardholders. 'Due to our children's lack of educational facilities, they cannot study beyond the eighth standard. How can they get government jobs, although there is provision for reservation for the inhabitants of LoC?' said a local, adding that those who originally belonged to this village but now live in cities appropriate all the benefits and reservations (Sharma 2013b). There is not much access to education beyond the school level for the people living in these villages. Asif of Pukharni village (Rajouri) thus informed, 'Our children in Std 11th and 12th have to travel more than 20 kms to attend their classes in Nowshera town.' Such long distances deter children from getting a higher education. According to the residents, the school education is not up to the mark, mainly because of extensive absenteeism among the teachers and lack of administrative supervision.

During the conflict in border areas, children's rights, that is, the right to life, the right to education, the right to be with family and community, the right to health and the right to be nurtured and protected, are severely violated and compromised (DasGupta 2012). Childhood is the most crucial stage of human development. Children living on the borders experience conflicts regularly, which jeopardises their childhood and future (Kousar and Bhadra 2021). At times of stress, the people living along the border have to evacuate their homes and seek shelter in schools, which are converted into refugee camps during such times, thus underlining the negligence of education and the effect on the future of children residing in these places.

Another trend seen in the Poonch–Rajouri border areas is that people from both sides of the border have moved to the Gulf countries in search of employment (Chandran 2013). 'Unemployment is quite high in this area, and the kind of agricultural work we are doing is full of risk with no returns; therefore, it is better to go out and earn for the family,' says Jigar, a 75-year-old resident of Digwar Terwan village of district Poonch. He remarked, 'In fact, there are villages here that are known for their "Gulf money" as most men in families have sought and found work in different parts of the Middle East.' Hussain told us that his son and nephew are working in the Gulf. Though he did not share the details of the kind of jobs they are doing, he mentioned that they work in some factories in the Gulf and can make a decent amount of money. Many respondents told us that a region called Mendhar in Poonch, in particular, had seen the highest volume of migration to the Gulf. The money generated in the process enables people to buy land and build houses, both in and outside the border villages and nearby towns if they prefer to do so, especially when they already own sufficient agricultural land there. 'Families with men who work in Saudi Arabia or with government jobs can afford to shift from the border villages; many have even shifted to towns,' says Zayed, a government employee and resident of Salotri village, Poonch. People of Salotri village added that many people are constructing houses in towns as alternative accommodations, even as they continue to stay in their native villages. One of the incentives for the locals to stay in their village is the government scheme of appointing local people as school teachers, known as Rehbar-e-Talim (ReT). Such schemes encourage educated people to stay in the village.

One issue linked to the backwardness of the people in this area relates to the question of land. Due to the overwhelming number of refugees and divided families inhabiting these two districts, there is a peculiar pattern of ownership of land. In areas like Sundarbani, Nowshera and some other parts of Rajouri and Poonch, where Hindu-Sikh refugees from POJK have been settled, each family has been allotted 48 kanals[3] of land area. Local Gujjars who shifted from the hilly areas have been allotted 24 kanals per family. In both cases, there is no entitlement to the ownership of the land. In the case of Hindu-Sikh refugees, the land allotted to them is the 'evacuee' land which is still registered in the original owner's name, although he has already shifted to POJK.

Moreover, in the case of Gujjars, the land allotted to them is classified in the revenue records as illegal (*kabza najaiz*).

This kind of relationship with the land has many implications. Without land ownership, people are debarred from seeking state benefits like loans from banks, even for small enterprises or small self-employment initiatives. Further, in case of such land coming under mining or fencing, the issue of compensation remains unresolved. In the absence of land ownership, they are not compensated at par with those who have ownership rights.

Sandwiched Villages and Marginalisation: Life between the Lines

Although the LoC borders were made relatively more militarised and surveilled in the 1970s, fencing of the LoC started in 2003. However, the fence is not constructed precisely where the LoC is, but is around 2–3 kms away. Consequently, many villages are sandwiched between the fencing and the LoC at various points in Rajouri and Poonch—known as the fenced-out villages within Jammu and Kashmir. The process has created multiple quotidian problems for the villagers as they feel severely restricted and confined because they cannot cross the fence and go to cities and towns whenever they want. There are specific securitised gates that they have to cross at particular times to travel to other places within their districts. Villagers belonging to the fenced-out villages need to carry their IDs at all times and sometimes feel humiliated during security checks at various points. Rasheed, an elderly resident of a fenced-out village in Poonch, said,

> Many security people that are regulars here know us and do not harass us. However, sometimes we can be humiliated. Our mobilities get severely restricted. We have to live with these problems that make our lives very uncomfortable. While other parts of the country are progressing, we live an altogether different life here. It is not easy ... whether it

> is maintaining our timings to go to town or managing the health-related emergencies or free movement and education of girls. Fencing has created many problems for us. It also affects our marriage alliances.

Zoona, a 75-year-old woman respondent from a fenced-out village in Poonch, stated that

> People prefer not to marry their children in fenced-out villages. The custom of marrying within our relations, which our religion allows, is essential for many. However, now our relatives may not want to have marriage alliances with our families who live in the villages that are fenced-out.

However, Rasheed also mentioned that people are happy with the fencing since earlier, militants and other infiltrators from POJK would cross the borders and come to their sides. He said that the 'people of these villages would get harassed by the infiltrators, and the security people would also look at the villagers with suspicion. With fencing, we do not have to be afraid of outside threats.' However, these layers of fencing and living-in-between have created many other problems for people here. The most critical disadvantage of fencing along the LoC is the restriction on the daily movement of people, and interruption in their agricultural and other allied activities. Many people have their lands divided due to fencing. 'Even though it is our land and on our side, still we cannot go freely to till a piece of land. We have to go through several layers of security checks. It feels miserable,' said Rasheed.

The large chunk of land taken over by the Army for fencing has set in a structural change in the land–farmer relationship, not just in fenced-out villages but all along the LoC. The residents cannot go to their fields because they have been fenced or fall beyond the fence. In addition, the loss of the land fosters a feeling of being an outsider in one's land. 'I have a patch of around 50 kanals of land on both sides of the fence, including this crossing point (designated gate), and it hurts me when I am asked to show my identity on my land,' said Zameer, who lives in Digwar Terwan village very close to the LoC in Poonch. Zameer is a middle-aged Muslim who owns a small grocery shop in the village. The shop business does not meet his economic needs, and he has to depend on his agricultural land. 'Division of my land due to fencing makes me feel like a refugee in my land,' Zameer added. Another resident of this village, Kalu, a Hindu respondent, told us that

> [T]he village forest and its pastureland is organically associated with the agrarian economy and the life of the people, now disturbed and distorted by the fencing and mining. Be it collecting firewood or various forest produce, timber and so on, fencing and mining have made these tasks much harder.

Fencing agricultural land has led to a dip in production, impairing an already meagre income. Also, as the sustenance of livestock depends on the fodder procured from the remains of agricultural produce and on immediate grazing land (common land/state land) in and around the villages, rearing cattle has become quite impossible.

Apart from war and conflict, LoC areas face multiple marginalisation and neglect. A society that labels certain people as outside the norm marginalises those people, edging them out. Marginalisation based on geographic isolation has severe repercussions for the families residing there. The entire Poonch and Rajouri districts are marked by economic backwardness, lack of educational and health facilities, and low job opportunities; however, the lack of economic progress and infrastructural neglect as one gets closer to the LoC within these districts become much more noticeable and glaring. Compared to other borders of India, the LoC border between India and Pakistan has been the most disputed and talked about owing to its history. India's relationship with Pakistan has also been complex and largely hostile due to several historical and political events. Though there have been numerous attempts to improve the relationship, the sourness remains.

Although Poonch and Rajouri have been allowed 'reservations for border regions' in the context of government jobs and access to education in Jammu and Kashmir, locals of the remote villages close to the LoC allege that the benefits of the reservations go to people who live in towns, or in villages that are close to the towns and have better access to economic and educational facilities. The presence of conflict and violence has taken a toll on the economic lives of the people of border areas. The conflict has resulted in decreased access to schools, preventing the opening of schools in certain situations, threatening children's security and well-being while travelling to school, and increasing teacher absenteeism. Asif of Pukharni village in Poonch said,

> Our children have to study in a difficult situation ... a situation marked by fear, uncertainty and border disturbances. The long distances to schools further deter children from receiving higher education. In case they can somehow complete higher education amidst conflict and uncertainties, they cannot compete with others for admissions in professional institutions and later while applying for jobs. This situation is especially limiting for the girl students, who often drop out because the schools in their immediate vicinity do not offer higher education.

The plight of women, too, is noticeable in these villages. Women of all ages work in the fields and do household chores. At the age when she should be studying, a woman has no other option than to earn bread for her family and support them through tough times. This is the story of innumerable girls and women residing in these border villages. Due to the condition of their families and lack of access to better facilities, they lag behind in education.

The Government of India has introduced the Border Area Development Programme (BADP)—a scheme that invests in infrastructure, education, health and agriculture and other facilities in various bordered regions of India, including Jammu and Kashmir. The order of priority in terms of coverage and allocation of funds is clearly defined in these programmes—the villages closest to the border are top priority, followed by those within the next 10-km radius. Although people benefit from the scheme, residents of the remote villages alleged political manipulation and divergence of funds. Despite the laid down priorities based on which villages are to be covered by this scheme, in reality, these rules are often reversed and manipulated under the influence of local politics. The core border is often bypassed in favour of towns, creating a sense of dissatisfaction and anger among the residents of the deserving villages.

Conclusion

Borderlands are generally seen in terms of their territoriality and strategic worth. For a nation, borders are a romanticised symbol of national power. However, borders are rarely seen through the perspectives of border communities and their gruelling lives. People residing in the border areas are often rendered invisible, and the problems they face in their day-to-day lives are no one's concern. The border areas, especially LoC, face shelling and firing as a matter of routine. In recent years, the frequency of border shelling and firing has increased, and in many cases, civilian areas are targeted. Although this makes 'news', rather than generating much sympathy for the loss of lives or injuries or insecurities of the people around the LoC, it generates a media frenzy favouring a militaristic response. Such a militaristic response further increases the vulnerability of the residents of the LoC.

This chapter has demonstrated that the LoC has been a border of a unique kind, evolving across times of conflict. When the Partition of Jammu and Kashmir took place, the LoC was an indecisive and unclear border. Unlike the Partition of Panjab and Bengal, lines in J&K remained fuzzy, allowing borderlanders in Poonch and Rajouri to continue their mobilities and way of life. People moved across the borders, and so did their relatives, creating a continuum of culture and kinship ties. In the 1965 and 1971 wars, more families were displaced and fractured. The 1971 war took away the porosity of the LoC. It became more monitored, and with the onset of militancy, it was heavily militarised. However, the people still remembered their old ways of life and the memory of their separated kin still resides in their hearts. A similarity of traditions and cultures continues to exist between people from Poonch–Rajouri and the borderlanders from POJK, owing primarily to the presence of social structures of biradari and caste.

In recent times, the LoC has been facing increased instances of cross-border firing. This has resulted in greater LoC fencing, and various sandwiched villages have emerged across the lines. These villages face challenges concerning livelihood, land, health and education. What has added to their suffering is that they have not received the required attention of the state, society and the international community due to various factors.

On the whole, the issue is not simply the capacity of the state to reach out to people, but its overall focus on these bordered areas as 'militarised areas'. Furthermore, for the state, these are, at best, the 'securitised' zones and therefore need to be defended militarily. Economic development and the creation of jobs and infrastructure are not the state's top priorities. Even for the local or J&K administrations, the priority is to develop more affluent and already prosperous cities and not the border areas. The peripheral and backward situation here is justified under the pretext of the border situation, conflict and insurgency.

It becomes vital to look at the border areas as sites of conflict and war and cultural and social lives. People living on the borders of LoC have their way of life and challenges. Be it the film, *Lines*, or the accounts provided by various locals from Poonch and Rajouri, borderlanders collectively demand the attention of the state authorities to live a life beyond conflict and hopelessness. These borderlanders await a future with better living opportunities and a fulfilled life. They hope for a future with cordial relations between India and Pakistan to once again meet those they had seen decades ago. These sentences from the film aptly depicts the aspirations of the people residing on the LoC:

> *Mai kyun bhula du Mehdi Hassan, Fehmida Riyaz ya Malika-e-Pukhraj ko...*
> *Hum nahi chahte do ek jese pahad ke bich ke faasle ko samjha jae—antarrashtriya seema...*
> *Hum nahi chahte aman or milan ka bhavishya likha jae rajneeti ki gandi chaalo par.*
> *Ghulti huyi mombattiyon par...*
> *Hume ladna chayie ab...*
> *Hum ladna chahte bhi hai ab har hathiyar se...*
> *Waise bhi hamare buzurgo ne kaha hai ki apne haq ke liye ladna jaayaz hai*
> *Jung aur ishq me sab jaayaz hai...*
>
> (Why must I forget Mehdi Hassan, Fehmida Riyaz or Malika-e-Pukhraj? ...
> We do not want the roads between the same hills to be labelled as international boundaries...
> We do not want the future of peace and reunions to be written on the foul tactics of politics.
> Now, we must fight over dying candles...
> We must fight against all weapons...
> Because our elders have decreed that fighting for one's rights is fair
> All is fair in love and war!)

Notes

1. Hindu–Muslim divided families refer to those Hindus who found themselves in POJK and had to convert to Islam and vice versa, that is, those Muslims who found themselves on the Indian side who may have also converted to Hinduism.

2. The Rehbar-e-Taleem (ReT) scheme was launched in 2000 by the J&K government for meeting the requirements of teachers in primary and middle schools in inaccessible and far-flung areas, where teachers posted from other places were ordinarily reluctant to join.

3. A kanal is equivalent to one-eighth of an acre in India.

References

Aggarwal, R. 2004. *Beyond Lines of Control: Performance and Politics on the Disputed Borders of Ladakh, India*. Durham and London: Duke University Press.

Alavi, H. 1972. 'Kinship in West Punjab Villages'. *Contributions to Indian Sociology* 6(1): 1–27.

Behera N. C. 2006. *Demystifying Kashmir*. Washington D.C.: Brookings Institution Press.

Berg, E., and H. V. Houtum. 2003. *Routing Borders between Territories, Discourses and Practices*. Aldershot: Ashgate Publishing Limited.

Bhatia, M. 2020. *Rethinking Conflict at the Margins: Dalits and Borderland Hindus in Jammu And Kashmir*. Cambridge: Cambridge University Press.

Chalfin, B. 2010. *Neoliberal Frontiers: Ethnography of Sovereignty in West Africa*. Chicago: University of Chicago Press.

Chandran, S. 2013. *Making Sense of LoC: Internal Politics & Bilateral Firings*. New Delhi: IPCS (Institute of Peace and Conflict Studies).

Choudhary, Z. 2012. *Locating Jammu Muslims in Kashmir Conflict*. New Delhi: Centre for Dialogue and Reconciliation.

Chowdhary, R. 2012. *Border and People—An Interface*. New Delhi: Centre for Dialogue and Reconciliation.

DasGupta, S. 2012. 'Borderlands and Borderlines: Re-negotiating Boundaries in Jammu and Kashmir'. *Journal of Borderlands Studies* 27(1): 83–93.

Eilenberg, M. 2009. 'Negotiating Autonomy at the Margins of the State: The Dynamics of Elite Politics in the Borderland of West Kalimantan, Indonesia'. *South East Asia Research* 17(2): 201–227.

Farfan, M. 2009. *The Vermont-Quebec Border: Life on the Line*. South Carolina: Arcadia Publishing.

Haselsberger, B. 2014. 'Decoding Borders: Appreciating Border Impacts on Space and People'. *Planning Theory and Practice* 15(4): 505–526.

Jamwal A. B. 2004. 'Auditing the Mainstream Media: The Case of Jammu & Kashmir'. In *Three Case Studies: Media Coverage on Forced Displacement in Contemporary India*. Mahanirban Calcutta Research Group. Available at http://www.mcrg.ac.in/mediareport2.htm (accessed January 2024).

John, P. 2016. 'Understanding the lives of those living along the LoC'. *The Wire*, 3 March. Available at https://thewire.in/uncategorised/understanding-the-lives-of-those-living-along-the-loc (accessed January 2024).

Kashmir Observer. 2019. 'With State Subject Law Gone, Cross LoC Bus Becomes History', 28 October. Available at https://kashmirobserver.net/2019/10/28/with-state-subject-law-gone-cross-loc-bus-becomes-history/ (accessed February 2024).

Kliot, N. and D. Newman (eds). 2000. *Geopolitics at the End of the Twentieth Century: The Changing World Political Map*. London: Routledge.

Kousar, R. and S. Bhadra. 2021. 'Border Conflict: Understanding the Impact on the Education of Children in Jammu Region'. *Journal of Peace Education* 18(1): 48–71.

Kweera, Rakshit. 2023. 'Drones in Modern Warfare: Utilization in India–Pakistan Cross-Border Terrorism and Security Implications'. *Strategic Analysis* 47(4): 376–388.

Loureiro, Miguel. 2015. 'The Boundary Within: Equality, Hierarchy and Exclusion in Azad Jammu and Kashmir'. *Contemporary South Asia* 23(3): 314–333.

Manchanda, R. 2012. *When Home is the Edge of the Nation: Dialogue with 'Border' People of Rajasthan, West Bengal and Bangladesh*. New Delhi: South Asia Forum for Human Rights.

Mahapatra, D. A. 2011. 'Positioning the People in the Contested Borders of Kashmir'. Research Working Paper 21, Centre for International Border Research. Belfast: Queen's University.

Maini K. D. 2009. *Poonch, the Battlefield of Kashmir*. Srinagar: Gulshan Books.

Mau, S. 2012. *Liberal States and the Freedom of Movement: Selective Borders, Unequal Mobility*. Palgrave Macmillan.

Nazir, P. 1993. 'Social Structure, Ideology and Language: Caste among Muslims'. *Economic and Political Weekly* 28(52): 2897–2900.

Newman, D. 2011. 'Contemporary research agendas in border studies: an overview'. In Doris Wastl-Walter (ed.), *The Ashgate Research Companion to Border Studies*. Aldershot: Ashgate Publishing Limited.

Puri, L. 2012. *Across the Line of Control: Inside Pakistan-Administered Jammu and Kashmir*. London: Hurst.

Sharma, A. 2011a. 'Justice denied?' *Tribune News Service,* 22 July. Available at http://outofsomething.blogspot.in/2011_07_01_archive.html (accessed January 2024).

———. 2011b. 'Life Behind Barbed Wires'. *Tribune India*, 27 July. Available at http://www.tribuneindia.com/2011/20110727/jkplus.htm#1 (accessed January 2024).

———. 2013a. 'Kashmir: Childhood under threat'. *Countercurrents.org,* 9 July. Available at https://countercurrents.org/asharma090713.htm (accessed January 2024).

———. 2013b. 'The exploding reality.' *The Hindu*, 14 June. Available at https://www.thehindu.com/news/national/other-states/The-exploding-reality/article12073512.ece (accessed January 2024).

Sharma, Malvika. 2021a. 'Identity, Religion and Difference in the Borderland District of Poonch, Jammu and Kashmir'. *Borders in Globalization Review* 3(1): 24–34.

———. 2021b. 'Nodes of Marginality: Identity, Displacement and Migration in the Post-Partition Borderlands of Kashmir'. *Journal of Immigrant & Refugee Studies* 20(4): 486–500. Available at https://www.tandfonline.com/doi/full/10.1080/15562948.2021.1949656 (accessed May 2024).

———. 2022. 'Remaking of Ethnic-Boundaries: Identity and Religion among Sikhs in the Borderland of Poonch, Jammu and Kashmir'. *Asian Ethnicity* 23(2): 279–297.

Shaw, A. 2000. 'Conflicting Models of Risk: Clinical Genetics and British Pakistanis'. In P. Caplan (ed.), *Risk Revisited*, 85–107. London: Pluto Press.

Shekhawat S. and D. A. Mahapatra. 2006. *Kargil Displaced of Akhnoor in Jammu and Kashmir: Enduring Ordeal and Bleak Future*. Geneva: Internal Displacement Monitoring Centre.

Suri, K. 2014. 'Impact of Armed Conflict on the Seasonal Migratory Practices of Gujjar and Bakkarwal tribes in Jammu and Kashmir'. *IOSR Journal of Humanities and Social Science (IOSR-JHSS)* 19(2): 54–62.

Wastl-Walter, D. (ed.). 2011. *The Ashgate Research Companion to Border Studies*. Aldershot: Ashgate Publishing Limited.

Wilson, Thomas M. and Hastings Donnan (eds). 1998. *Border Identities: Nation and State at International Frontiers*. Cambridge: Cambridge University Press.

VIII

Irrelevance of Borders?

Cross-LoC Interactions, 2005–2019

Rekha Chowdhary

Introduction

Though the Partition has become history for millions of people in the Indian subcontinent, yet for a large number of people of Jammu and Kashmir, it still forms a 'present' and a 'day-to-day reality' with no closure in sight. As we have seen, the Line of Control is a permanent reminder of the unsettled nature of the border, with implications not only for the people living close to this line, but also for a large number of people affected by it—including the POJK refugees and divided families. It forms one of the most volatile borders without much distinction between 'war time' and 'peace time'. For the people living close to the LoC, life is full of uncertainties and their 'normal' life can be disrupted anytime by firing and shelling. Meanwhile, a different kind of uncertainty is faced by thousands of refugees, who were forced to abandon their homes and land in the wake of the 1947 violence. Unlike the 'refugees' who came from various parts of Pakistan, these dislocated people were not even granted the status of 'refugees'. Since they had come from Pakistan-controlled Jammu and Kashmir, they were treated differently. With POJK being officially treated as part of India, the residents who moved from any part of POJK are seen as 'internally displaced people'. They are therefore not entitled to the kind of compensation for the loss of land and other property that other Pakistan refugees have been entitled to. If there is another class of people whose fate is similarly linked to the unsettled nature of LoC, it is the divided families. Across the LoC, there are lakhs of families who were separated from their near ones in the period between 1947–1965, and they have been the worst sufferers of the borders being drawn between the two sides of the erstwhile princely State of Jammu and Kashmir. With stringent travel restrictions, they have been unable to meet, to share the happy moments of the members of their families, or to mourn the loss of their dead on the other side.

The fate of all these people is linked with the LoC. The LoC by its very nature reflects an unending tentativeness. It signifies not only the division of the state that was superficially imposed on the people of J&K, but also the 'unresolved' and 'ongoing' nature of the conflict. Both India and Pakistan have taken a resolute stance and claimed the whole of Jammu and Kashmir and not recognised the division, and this has had precarious consequences for the people who are bound by it. It makes the conflict intractable and unending. Is there a way out for the people who are bound by the fate of the LoC, especially the refugees and divided families? Can the families divided by the border here communicate with each other in a relatively 'normal' manner? Can the refugees ever go back to visit the land which is still officially their home? Is there a possibility of the LoC losing its volatility that endangers the life of thousands of people living in the firing range of the 'other' side?

Most of these problems seem to be insurmountable for the simple reason that these cannot be resolved without resolving the pending issues between India and Pakistan. This is more so as both the countries have been emphasising the territorial nature of the borders and adopting a maximalist position over the conflict and division of J&K.

However, in the post-2001 period, a very interesting idea of the 'irrelevance of borders' was officially promoted by India and Pakistan. This idea was linked with the confidence-building measures (CBMs) that were offered by both the countries in the wake of the peace process initiated by the then Indian Prime Minister, Atal Bihari Vajpayee. It was in pursuance of this approach that an effort was made to address the problems of the people affected by the borders by starting the cross-LoC bus service in 2005. In 2008, the LoC trade was started. These initiatives have functioned quite smoothly, until very recently. Despite the fact that the peace process, of which these initiatives were a part, had started losing its steam (since just a few years after these were put in place, there was an increase in India and Pakistan hostilities), these initiatives remained more or less intact. The cross-LoC bus service and trade were temporarily suspended at times, but were soon resumed.

The Peace Process and Confidence-Building Measures

It was in 1997, under the initiative of Prime Minister I. K. Gujral, that the first steps were taken towards the peace process and engagement with Pakistan. It was at this time that a decision was taken to have a composite dialogue on all outstanding issues between India and Pakistan. However, it was after a lot of fits and starts that the peace process could be practically initiated by Prime Minister Vajpayee in 2002. Though initial steps were taken vis-à-vis Kashmir, it was in 2003 that Vajpayee laid down the contours of comprehensive dialogue involving Pakistan.[1] Among the multiple steps that were agreed upon between India and Pakistan, the most important related to giving some relief to the people affected by the prolonged conflict situation and offering them crucial confidence-building measures. The 'composite dialogue', as the process came to be known, represented a major shift in India's approach to conflict. Rather than a territorial approach based on militaristic means, a people-oriented approach based on dialogue and engagement was initiated.[2] While trying to find a way by which some movement forward could be made in the peace process, the emphasis was placed on people-to-people interaction between the two sides of the LoC. The opening of routes across the LoC, a bus-service, and trade across a few points between the two sides of the erstwhile princely State of Jammu and Kashmir were therefore offered as the most important CBMs.

In the context of the intractable and maximalist positions being taken by the two countries, cross-LoC interactions provided a possibility for taking a path towards peace. Initially, a proposal was made by India to enable the meeting of families divided by the LoC at five places on 'designated days and time'. These five places were situated in the LoC and included Mendhar and Poonch in Poonch district (in Jammu division), Suchetgarh in Jammu district (in Jammu division), Uri in Baramulla district (in Kashmir division) and Tangdhar in Kupwara district (in Kashmir division). All these were the traditional points that people would use to travel before the LoC existed. However, soon a more structured response of starting a cross-LoC bus service to facilitate travel from one side of the LoC to the other was initiated.

In April 2005, a bus service between Uri in Kashmir region and Muzaffarabad on the POJK side was started, which was followed by another bus service between Poonch and Rawalakot (in Jammu region) in June 2006. Five foot-crossing points were meanwhile opened in October 2008 for the purposes of relief and rehabilitation after the massive earthquake that affected large parts of POJK. A few months earlier, in May 2008, the proposal for cross-LoC trade was initiated and on 21 October the same year, trade was started on both the routes on which the cross-LoC bus service was running.

The whole idea of cross-LoC interaction was based on an innovative concept of 'the Irrelevance of Border'. This concept, going beyond the conventional categories of 'sovereignty', 'territory', 'boundaries' and 'borders', sought a movement forward through 'people', 'economy' and 'trade'.

Concept of Irrelevance of Borders

In specific terms, the concept of irrelevance of borders, in the words of Chari and Rizvi, include 'wide range of measures ... proposed to promote interactions across the LoC and enable the two parts of Kashmir to develop a multifaceted relationship.' Classified into four categories, these measures include: 'Promoting people-to-people contact, increasing trade and commerce across the LoC, encouraging humanitarian aid and development, improving governance, including security administration ... ' (Chari and Rizvi 2008: 6–7).

This concept of irrelevance of borders made it possible to break through the non-negotiable and maximalist positions of India and Pakistan and find a way out of competitive nationalisms—the Indian, the Pakistani and the Kashmiri—which had made the conflict almost impossible to resolve. With India and Pakistan making claims on the whole of Jammu and Kashmir, a negotiable resolution would not have been possible. The problem had to be resolved in such a manner that the interest of all parties was taken care of and the concerns and anxieties of each were also addressed.

Thus, right in the beginning, the contours of the peace process were clearly formulated. These contours were based on Pakistan's urge that the resolution of conflict should go beyond the status quo then and India's condition that no borders would be redrawn and no sovereignty compromised.

Going beyond the status quo and yet not changing the borders provided the most important challenge to the peace process, which was sought to be met by subverting the very idea of 'borders' itself. Those borders over which there were conflicting claims and which were the most 'problematic' in the conflict were to become the basis of conflict resolution. Accordingly, it was resolved to work on making the borders irrelevant and reducing their significance, in the words of Manmohan Singh, Prime Minister of India (2004–2014), to 'just lines on a map'. The free movement of people on both sides of the LoC and trade between the two sides was therefore suggested as the way forward.

Assuming a more 'soft' character, borders, rather than inhibiting the movement of people and goods, were to become the basis for facilitating the same. Irrelevance of borders, therefore, was a pioneering idea through which new possibilities could be explored and the question of Kashmir could be resolved in radically new directions.

The most interesting aspect of the concept of irrelevance of borders was that national sensitivities were respected. In no way did the concept challenge the 'nationalistic sentiments' and while maintaining these sentiments, sought to accommodate the aspirations of people divided by the national boundaries. By implication, this concept sought to define the conflict from an alternate perspective which 'calls for retaining the relevance of nation-state, yet making space for fluid overlapping identities and accommodative nationalisms' (Bhatia 2020).

The concept of irrelevance of borders implied that the Line of Control that symbolised the division of the State of J&K as well as its unsettled and unresolved status was to assume a more dynamic character. Rather than being a barrier, it was to be so animated that the interaction between the two sides of J&K could become possible through the free movement of people, goods and services. In its application, this concept had wide-ranging implications and could change the internal relationship between the two sides of J&K in such a drastic manner so as to mitigate, if not undo, the harsh implications of its division. For the divided families, it had a humanitarian angle. Since the time the LoC was drawn in the 1948–1949 period, the two sides have been totally cut off from each other with not much possibility even of communication, not to talk of visiting each other. The implication of this situation had been grave for the large number of such families located on both sides of the LoC. Their most important aspiration, therefore, relates to the opening of the borders.

Opening of the borders, as Bhatia argues, does not necessarily mean a borderless world, but a world in which the borders exist but are 'soft' enough to allow the movement of people. Referring to the divided families in the district of Rajouri, she notes that a reading of the demand to open the borders reflected that people

> ... were not particularly insisting on a 'fenceless border zone' or complete dissolution of borders. Aware of the fact that the current geo-political realities may not warrant a 'borderless world', they aspired for softening of borders and uninhibited movement of people across the borders so that they could meet their relatives more frequently and without much bureaucratic hitch (Bhatia 2020: 75).

Hence, their desire was for 'porus borders'. '*Milne ke raaste khol do*' (open routes for visiting). As per Bhatia, it was 'their unanimous demand' (ibid.: 75).

This concept also offered a humanitarian approach for the refugees who had been uprooted and displaced in 1947 and had a strong sense of belonging to their ancestral places. Due to the barriers put in place by the borders, they had not been able to revisit these places. The idea of 'soft' borders made it conceptually possible for these people to visit their original homelands and to interact with people on the other side. Although this would not give them a complete sense of closure, it would give them the satisfaction of tracing their roots and visiting their native places as and when they wanted.

One could also see the humanitarian angle of the 'soft border' at play when the area was affected by a massive earthquake in October 2005. Though J&K on the Indian side was impacted with some loss of life and property, in POJK, it had a devastating impact with huge loss of life, injuries and destruction of whole cities, towns and villages. To help in the process of relief, rehabilitation and reconstruction, India and Pakistan decided to open crossings at five points across the LoC. These points were Nauseri–Tithwal; Chakoti–Uri;

Hajipir–Uri; Rawalakot–Poonch; and Tattapani–Mendhar (Government of India 2005).

As the Rawalakot–Poonch border was opened as one of the five crossing points for the convenience of relief operations, there was a surge of people, mostly the divided families, who wanted to cross the border to meet their relatives. These people were so emotionally charged that they did not feel the need for formal travel papers to visit the other side. They had to be restrained by force. As an *India Today* report notes:

> The emotional significance of the moment was evident when 25 truckloads of relief materials were ferried across the first Loc entry point at Kanchaman Post in Poonch on November 7. Anxious and bereaved residents of Pakistan-occupied Kashmir (PoK) attempted to breach the police cordon to cross over to the Indian side where their relatives waited with tears in their eyes ... The Pakistani Police had to fire several rounds of tear gas shells to stop the citizens from crossing the line (Hussain 2005).

However, the concept of the 'irrelevance of borders' was not limited to its humanitarian angle. In the context of the static positions taken by India and Pakistan towards Kashmir, it offered a very dynamic concept of conflict resolution, not only for India and Pakistan but also for the Kashmiris who were impacted by the conflict politics. Opening of the borders, with the possibility of free movement and greater interaction between the two sides of J&K, definitely meant a movement forward.[3]

What captured the imagination of Kashmiris, in this concept of irrelevance of borders, was the idea of 'unification' of the state—even when it was not a physical unification but rather a 'notional unification'. One could see how the concept of 'notional unification' of the state flowed both in the idea of the movement of people across the two sides of LoC through the bus service as well as in cross-LoC trade.[4] The underlying idea was to recognise the two sides in continuity and to treat them as part of a single unit. With a special provision made for the people of undivided J&K to move from one side of the LoC to the other, it was notionally accepted that the erstwhile princely State still formed a single continuous unit. It was in the economic and trade-related activities that the recognition of a singular/continuous entity of Jammu and Kashmir across the two sides of LoC took shape in a more concrete manner. With the opening of trade between residents of the two sides of divided J&K, the discourse was opened for the economic 'integration' of this erstwhile princely State.[5]

The concept of opening the border could lead to not only strengthening of the relationship between the two sides of J&K but also could strengthen the relationship between India and Pakistan in the process. While starting the bus service, the state actors had begun indicating future possibilities in the process. The Indian Prime Minister, for instance, spoke of joint mechanisms in socio-economic cooperation between the two sides of the LoC. To quote then PM Manmohan Singh,

> I also envisage a situation where the two parts of Jammu and Kashmir can, with the active encouragement of the governments of India and Pakistan, work out cooperative, consultative mechanisms so as to maximise the gains of cooperation in solving problems of social and economic development of the region (cited in Pattanaik and Anant 2010: 3).

Meanwhile, the then Prime Minister of POJK, Sardar Sikandar Hayat, referred to educational and employment opportunities for the people of the two sides. Since Jammu and Kashmir on the Indian side had many educational institutions, its benefit could be availed of by the residents of POJK, whereas their side could offer employment opportunities to the people on the Indian side. How this idea was catching the imagination of Indians could be seen during the Round Table Conferences (RTCs) of Prime Minister Manmohan Singh. A specific group with the purpose of promoting greater interaction between the two sides of the LoC was constituted during these RTCs. Named as the Prime Minister's Working

Group on Strengthening Relations Across the LoC, it was headed by M. K. Rasgotra, the former Foreign Secretary of India. In the final report that it submitted, it suggested various measures. It emphasised the 'importance of people-to-people contacts and freer travel facilities for the persons residing on the two sides of the LoC to promotion of friendly and beneficial cooperation and strengthening of peace in the region.' It also suggested that contacts between special interest groups and professionals be encouraged and recommended visits of university students and faculty members, exchanges of groups of journalists, academicians, lawyers and other groups (*Report of the Working Group* 2007: 2).

What was most interesting about the softening of the borders was the investment that both India and Pakistan made in this process. The concept, when it was introduced, reflected the enthusiasm of both the countries. This enthusiasm was reflected in the Government of India's terming the initiation of the bus service between the two sides of the LoC in 2005 as historic. The government not only took ownership of the initiative, but also reflected a sense of pride in it.[6]

Throughout the post-2005 period, the Governments of India and Pakistan continued to reflect their keenness to support the cross-LoC interactions. Even after the peace process was formally stalled, these countries continued to provide support as well as reiterate their commitment to further improve the process, remove the bottlenecks and provide better infrastructure. In 2011, much after the peace process had already been derailed, a joint statement was issued after a meeting of the foreign ministers of the two countries that showed their mutual intent to expand the cross-LoC travel and trade. It was decided to expand travel to include visits for tourism and religious pilgrimage. It was also resolved to facilitate the frequent travellers by issuing six months' multiple entry travel permits. During this meeting, a number of decisions to improve trade were also taken. For instance, it was decided to enhance the number of days for trade from two to four, and it was also agreed to strengthen the existing telephone facilities. A decision was also taken in favour of a biannual review of the existing arrangements related to cross-LoC travel and trade. The joint statement highlighted 'the importance of early establishment of a non-discriminatory trade regime between the two countries, including reduction/removal of tariff and non-tariff barriers' (Government of India, Ministry of External Affairs 2011).

Cross-LoC Bus Service

The cross-LoC bus service that was started in 2005–2006 at two points—one in Jammu division (Poonch-Rawalakot point) and the other in Kashmir division (Uri-Muzaffarabad point) allowed the people to cross the LoC by road. Thus, while the residents of Jammu and Kashmir on the Indian side could use the bus service to visit Pakistani-controlled Jammu and Kashmir, the residents of the latter could similarly use the bus service to visit J&K on the Indian side. What was unique about such visits was that the permission to POJK residents was given only to visit the Indian side of Jammu and Kashmir and not any other part of India. Similarly, the residents of the Indian side of J&K could visit POJK but not go to any part of Pakistan beyond that. To cross the LoC and avail of the bus service, there was no requirement of passport or visa. The only requirement was an entry permit from the respective administration. On either side, the permit was given only to the permanent residents of J&K. The permission to stay on the other side of LoC was for a duration of 28 days, which could be extended by another 15 days (Reddy 2005).

These peculiar conditions—first, that the cross-LoC visit was limited only to the residents of J&K; second, that the permission to visit was restricted only to the areas of undivided J&K and not to other parts of India or Pakistan;

and third, that there was no requirement of passport or visa—provided a new basis for recognising the continuity of J&K across the LoC.

The cross-LoC travel was officially termed as *Karvan-e-Aman* (Caravan of Peace) and was a boon for the divided families. It allowed people who had been separated from their close relatives since 1947 to meet them and to close the gap that had developed between them for such a long time. This is why, though theoretically the bus service was open for all the permanent residents of J&K, priority was given to those residents who had a close relative across the LoC. Referring to its impact, Pattanaik and Anant noted that it enabled families 'to unite' after a prolonged gap. 'Some of them have even traveled to visit family graves as they were not able to visit their near and dear ones when they were alive. The process has brought together parents divided from their children and united brothers and sisters after many years' (Pattanaik and Anant 2010: 9). This has been especially true of many divided families around the border districts of Jammu, specifically the Poonch-Rajouri area. This area has felt the biggest impact of the division and has a large number of divided families. Around two-third of the Muslim families of this area have relatives on the other side of the LoC. For these people, the opening of the bus route has been a great relief (Maini 2010: 1). There are lots of stories about siblings who were separated for 60 years and due to this CBM, could meet each other after such a long period. There are stories of separated children meeting their aged parent/s. Luv Puri has noted some cases where people who came to meet their close relatives refused to go back to the other side. He has, for instance, noted the case of 99-year-old Nawab Din, who had travelled to Rajouri from Mirpur in POJK to meet his son. After spending the permitted time on the Indian side, 'he refused to return to POJK and moved the court to stay his deportation. He said he had no family in POJK and begged to be allowed to stay with his son. He was granted an interim stay by the court.' He similarly mentions the case of 70-year-old Syed Alam Shah, who refused to go back and filed a writ petition in J&K High Court in this regard. He was also given an interim stay order (Puri 2012: 89–90).

One peculiar reality that came to the fore during the visits of the cross-LoC bus service was the existence of many inter-religious divided families, comprising mostly of Hindus and Sikhs on the Indian side of J&K and Muslims in POJK. In the midst of the chaos, while these Hindu and Sikh families were leaving their homes, many members of their families were separated and had to stay back in the area now under the control of Pakistan. They eventually settled in that area and were converted as Muslims, and had no means of communicating with their families on the Indian side in the years prior to 2005. They grabbed the opportunity to cross the LoC to visit. Many of them travelled with their children and grandchildren. Many women who were abducted or left behind for some reason could also come to meet their kin. Usually, such meetings were quite emotive, notwithstanding the difference in religion and nationality. [7]

As per the data provided by the Ministry of Home Affairs, from April 2005 to March 2019, 25,725 visitors from POJK used the bus service and came to the Indian side (for a maximum of three months). During the same period, 11,028 visitors from the Indian side used this service to visit POJK (Government of India 2019). Of the two routes, it is from Poonch-Rawalakot in Jammu region that a large number of people visited the other side.[8] The travel across the LoC, it may be noted, was limited during this period mainly to the members of divided families. There were many who were not part of these families but who would have liked to visit the other side, including the POJK refugees, but could not do so. The enthusiasm for the travel persisted despite the rigorous process of applying for the permit.

Cross-LoC Trade

Economic integration across the Line of Control remained central to the peace process. It was considered a very important process for generating the mutual interest of people on both sides. The idea, according to Moeed Yusuf, was to create so much economic stake in the peace process that a 'bottom up pressure' could be built to 'hasten up the process of normalisation between the two parts of the state' and also to sustain it on a long term basis. 'Ultimately, permanent improvement in intra-Kashmir relations,' argued Yusuf, 'presupposes substantial economic interdependence across the LoC such that the costs of reversal become unbearably high' (Yusuf 2009: 9). Seen in this context, the cross-border trade served a greater political purpose of conflict resolution. Rather than merely providing a point of exit from the conflict, it offered a new paradigm of mutual dependence and mutual development. The importance of cross-LoC trade as the basis of conflict resolution was seen as having substantial potential since it had both symbolic and real value. Also, it was considered to have a lot of future possibilities. Referring to these possibilities, Yusuf noted that: 'Although critical in their own right, all stakeholders, including the Indian and Pakistani governments, acknowledge that these steps are only the beginning of a process of economic collaboration that could ultimately make the LoC irrelevant for economic and human exchanges.' That this logic was also officially dominant in India at that time was reflected in the *Report of the Working Group* on 'Strengthening Relations Across the Line of Control'. This Report noted: 'The opening up of routes for trade and commerce would help in not only improving the economic conditions on both the sides but would also be an important step towards normalization of the situation' (*Report of the Working Group* 2007: 2).

That initiation of trade, to begin with, would have more instrumental than real value had been generally acknowledged. At the time that the trade was started (on 21 October 2008), many people emphasised that it was one of the ways to lead to a resolution of conflict[9] (Sardar Attique Khan, then Prime Minister of Pakistan-occupied Kashmir, cited in *Dawn* [2008]).

However, despite its symbolic value, the cross-LoC trade had a strong economic logic, mainly due to the economic backwardness of this erstwhile state.[10] There were a number of constraints under which the economy of the state was operating.[11] Of these, the first emanated from the over-dependence of the state on the federal government, and its debt liabilities. After subsidising the economy of the state for a long time, the Central government reversed its policy of liberally financing the state's economy and substituted the aid being given so far with loans. As a result of this policy, debt and interest repayments began comprising a very large part of the budgeted expenditure of the state.[12]

On the whole, it was believed that cross-LoC trade made lots of business sense and had much to offer to the static and backward economy of the state. Besides providing trade opportunities across the LoC, if run to its full potential, it would tap into the markets along the traditional silk route up to Central Asia. It was speculated that while the state would benefit from finding alternative markets for Kashmir's handicrafts, carpets, shawls and fruits, etc., there would also be the possibility of the state becoming the central point for trade between India and Pakistan on the one hand and India and Central Asia on the other (Chandran 2009).

As a crucial CBM for sustaining the peace process, the cross-LoC trade had stakeholders all over the state. In Kashmir particularly, there was a positive response to the opening of the LoC the trade purposes, mainly for its sentimental value and psychological implications.[13] The biggest stake in the cross-LoC trade in Kashmir was that of the fruit growers and those Kashmiris linked with the horticultural industry. Among others with expectations of the opening of new trade routes were those linked with the carpet and furniture industry. For them, the idea of an alternative route as well an alternative market was quite attractive. The opening of this route also meant a reduction in the transportation time. As compared to the average time of 36 hours to reach the nearest market in Delhi, it would take merely six to eight hours to reach Islamabad (Mirani 2007).

While there were political and emotional reasons for the support of the cross-LoC trade in Kashmir, in Jammu, on the other hand, one could find solid economic logic.[14] Jammu is a trading city controlling the wholesale trade not only of the far-flung parts of the region, but also of Kashmir. For the traders, therefore, the opening of routes across the LoC made a lot of business sense.[15] Besides the wholesale trade, there is also the industrial base with many manufacturing units located in areas such as Gangayal (Jammu), Brahaman ki Bari and Samba (Samba). These manufacturing units, though provided with incentives by the federal government to boost the economy of the state, find it difficult to sustain themselves due to the location disadvantage of the state. Both in terms of transportation of raw material and the market for their manufactured goods, the manufacturing units feel constrained. These manufacturers, therefore, saw a large potential for business across the LoC. Since manufactured goods were not included in the list approved for trade items, they demanded the expansion of the list and saw a great future in the cross-LoC trade.[16]

The stakeholders of the cross-LoC trade were not limited to the urban centres of Jammu and Srinagar (Kashmir) but were also located in far-flung areas like Poonch and Uri and many other points, especially those lying around the LoC. Since both these areas were the crossing points for trade purposes, there was sufficient enthusiasm here for the trade. People in Poonch, for instance, saw the trade as an opportunity to revive its backward economy. On the whole, there was a positive response to the cross-LoC trade and hence there were demands to open routes in other parts of the state as well. For instance, there was demand in Ladakh for opening the Kargil-Skardu border route and in Jammu, there was demand for opening the Suchetgarh-Sialkot route.

The cross-LoC trade could never reach its full potential. This was mainly due to the fact that it was a CBM linked with the peace process. However, as the peace process itself had slowed down and later stalled, trade continued to operate at a minimum pace and the traders involved in the process were quite discontented.[17] The list, limited to 21 categories of items, remained limited and could not be extended. [18] On the contrary, in the process of the trade, a number of items which were bringing good business were banned over the period, either by the Indian or Pakistani side.[19]

The most important constraint on the trade, however, was defined by the absence of a financial arrangement. No decision had been taken on the currency to be used for the trade and no banking system had been provided. Hence, the trade was taking place through the most medieval barter system. Moreover, there was a problem of communication. Due to non-availability of direct connection with the traders on the other side, the traders on the Indian side of J&K had to follow a circuitous route for communication. Citing security reasons, the government has banned the direct dialling system from within J&K to any part of Pakistan, including Pakistan-controlled Kashmir. Later on, some limited communication channel was provided by the Government of India.[20]

On the whole, trade was taking place at a symbolic level and was limited in its nature. As Dar and Gul (2009) pointed out, the trade had

> lost most of its sheen, leaving it for divided families to sustain the trade. Barring a few who visited Muzaffarabad personally and settled terms with their counterparts, most of the traders either deal only with their relatives living across the line of control (LoC) or seek a counter guarantee from relatives of PaK traders living here.

The reason why the trade could be sustained, especially on the Kashmiri side, was not because of economic reasons but because of the involvement of the divided families.[21] Since a large number of people 'involved in the trade have blood relations across LoC', it is 'an inter-relations trade', according to Dar and Gul (ibid.: 16–17).

Conclusion

It was the fuzziness of the CBMs related to cross-LoC linkages that enabled it to engage different stakeholders in J&K at their own levels—whether the divided families, the Kashmiris, the Ladakhis, the refugees, or the traders of Jammu. Thus the strength of the cross-LoC CBMs lay in the fact that these were not only approved by both India and Pakistan and adopted and implemented as the state policies, but these also had the active consent of the people of the state—the major stakeholders in conflict politics. Of course, the most enthusiastic were the members of the divided families located mostly in Jammu region, as well as some in Kashmir. The Ladakhi divided families wanted a similar initiative for Ladakh as well and constantly made demands for the opening of the Kargil-Skardu road. There was also the demand to open the old Nowshera-Mirpur route and other routes on LoC that were operational in Jammu region.[22] For Kashmiris, it offered a movement beyond status quo and a recognition of the unified entity of J&K; for the refugees, it offered a chance to link themselves with their homeland and develop their cultural bonds with people they had left behind; for the trading class of Jammu region, it offered very good business opportunities; for Ladakhis, an opportunity to connect with their relatives on the other side of the border. Being an important CBM, it therefore filled the very important purpose of bridging the divide created by the hostilities of the two nations and generating an environment away from conflict and towards peace.

The CBM related to the cross-LoC exchanges have, on the whole, proved to be quite resilient and despite the highs and lows of India–Pakistan relations, it has been sustained. It was only after August 2019, when India sought the abrogation of the special constitutional changes and a reorganisation of J&K that both the bus service and trade were suspended by Pakistan.[23] Even so, officially these have been 'suspended' and not stopped.[24]

For those who availed of the bus service, the whole process was quite satisfying, as they were given the opportunity to cross the LoC and meet their relatives after a half-decade of no communication. Their connections were reignited, enabling them to reassess their own situation. For those dealing in trade, there was an added economic advantage. The role played by the divided families meant that despite all the obstacles and problems faced by the traders, there was sufficient enthusiasm and vigour in the trade, especially on the Poonch-Rawlakot side. The number of the trading companies, which was restricted to a few local traders in the beginning, had been expanded, and new actors from Jammu as well as from the local areas had also joined.[25] The traders were quite innovative and found ways to serve their interest. In many ways, they had been quite successful in extending the trade activities beyond J&K.[26] In the light of the scope they saw in such trade, they continued making new demands, including those related to rationalising the trade and extending the list of items to be traded.[27]

Cross-LoC interactions were considered important not only for the people of Jammu and Kashmir, but also for the whole of South Asia. In this context, it was assumed that once these interactions were institutionalised and entrenched, the political hostilities between India and Pakistan would be eased. The border, which till now was known as the *nuclear flashpoint*, was now seen as a *bridge* through which peace could be established between India and Pakistan. The assumption underlying the cross-LoC travel was that it would open up new opportunities for interactions and thereby create a congenial environment for a better relationship between India and Pakistan. Similarly, there were also expectations that with the institutionalisation of the cross-LoC trade, new possibilities would be opened up for engagement and cooperation between the two countries. The Working Group on Strengthening the Cross-LoC Relations had recommended a number of joint activities which could be undertaken by both the sides. It also talked about exploring 'scope for co-operation on subjects of common interest like environment protection, water management, natural disaster management and forestry'. Suggestions were also made about joint tourism and power projects.

However, for all their positives, the cross-LoC exchanges remained hostage to conflict politics. And despite the overwhelming demand for expansion, it remained confined, mainly due to security concerns. As Yusuf points out, 'both Pakistan and India, despite having moved away from their traditional maximalist stances, remain wedded to a security-centric paradigm in their outlook toward the dispute. The two countries see each other through a zero-sum lens whereby granting unilateral concessions is a sign of weakness' (Yusuf 2009: 7–8). Despite the paradigm shift in the approach to the conflict resolution, even during the heydays of the peace process, the conventional approaches continued, as did the fear that these routes on the LoC would be used for the purposes of infiltration of militants and arms from the other side. The fear that the route could be used to smuggle contraband goods, especially drugs, also remained paramount. This seemed to be one of the major reasons for the Indian government going slow on the trade process. Right from the beginning, there was a lot of media hype around the few detected cases of contraband goods being smuggled in by a few passengers crossing the LoC. As the tension between India and Pakistan started increasing after 2014, the concerns about the misuse of the routes became much more vocal. In 2017, there were numerous cases of arms and ammunition being seized. As per the authorities, seizures were made of 'pistols, grenades, spares and ammunition, including one particularly large cache concealed in a consignment of bananas. The drug hauls have been sizeable too' (Haider 2019).

Notwithstanding this concern for security, one can still make the point about the relative resilience of this CBM. In the uncertainties characterising the India–Pakistan relationship, there are not many such instances of any mechanisms, with the exception of the Indus Water Treaty, which have stood the test of time. Various ceasefire agreements that seem to be resilient at one point in time, are violated quite soon. The last such example is of the 2003 ceasefire agreement that seemed to be quite effective for the few initial years, but started crumbling very soon. Much before a decade had passed, ceasefire violations were taking place with impunity. Going by the history of the cross-LoC bus service and the cross-LoC trade, one can see the investment made by both the countries, and an intention to prolong it despite the relations deteriorating very badly. This is perhaps because this CBM was pushed by the suffering/interest of people on both sides of the LoC. Whatever the reason, this provides a good example to be returned to whenever the two countries wish to resume the thread of dialogue and peace process.

Notes

1. It was during his visit to Kashmir in April 2003 that Prime Minister Vajpayee laid down the basis of the comprehensive dialogue. Among other things, he offered friendship to Pakistan. Later, after receiving a phone call from the Pakistan PM, Mir Zafarullah Khan Jamali, Vajpayee made a statement in the Lok Sabha:

> ... we have repeatedly expressed the need to create a conducive atmosphere for a sustained dialogue ... an end to cross border terrorism and the dismantling of its infrastructure. ... I emphasized the importance of economic cooperation, cultural exchanges, people-to-people contacts and civil aviation links ... PM Jamali suggested resumption of sporting links between the two countries. We agreed ... (PM's Statement in Parliament, 2 May 2003, https://archivepmo.nic.in/abv/speech-details.php?nodeid=9219 [accessed July 2024]).

2. The environment for the various initiatives towards the peace process was generated by the offer of a ceasefire by the then Prime Minister of Pakistan, Jamali. This was followed by a formal ceasefire agreement between India and Pakistan in Novermber 2003. In response to PM Jamali's offer for a ceasefire, India formally agreed to observe a ceasefire with effect from 25 November 2003. The ceasefire was effective on the International Border (the working boundary for Pakistan), the Line of Control and the Actual Ground Position line (AGPL) in Siachen. It was following this agreement that India and Pakistan committed to resolve all outstanding issues between the two countries. This commitment was formalised during the South Asian Association for Regional Cooperation (SAARC) meeting in January 2004 (Sharma 2003).

3. How the whole process of cross-border movement was linked with larger peace in the subcontinent was reflected by Prime Minister Manmohan Singh after the initiation of cross-LoC trade. In a press conference, he stated,

> When I inaugurated the Srinagar-Muzaffarabad bus service in April 2005, I had said that this is the first step on a long road of peace .... Notwithstanding the many difficulties which have come, we have taken several steps. The start of trade on the Srinagar-Muzaffarabad and Poonch-Rawalakot roads on 21st October is a major initiative that has been taken. History will judge how big these steps were. The fact is that they have taken place after many lost decades of mutual recrimination, violence and war.

PM Singh emphasised that winds of change were rife in the subcontinent with economics, travel and technology changing rigid and hostile mindsets. He further remarked that for India and Pakistan, of late: 'Trade, people to people contact, cultural exchanges and most of all the desire to move on are altering the landscape of our relationship. I would like the entire state of Jammu and Kashmir to be part of this wider process.' He stressed that both India and Pakistan needed to approach issues with an open and amicable mind so that the past could be overcome and a basis for enduring peace and prosperity could be laid in the future. He said, 'Within this framework, borders become doors to cooperation as we shun violence, condemn terrorism and embrace the spirit of a new approach to bilateral relations' (PM's Opening remarks at the Press Conference in Srinagar', 10 October 2008. Available at https://archivepmo.nic.in/drmanmohansingh/speech-details.php?nodeid=703 [accessed February 2024]).

4. Haseeb Drabu, the well-known economist and political leader from J&K, used the term 'functional unification', meaning thereby 'a de facto unification without disturbing the sovereignty claims and the de jure political status of either side'. In his article written for *The Indian Express*, Drabu focuses on the potential relevance of this idea of functional unification. He suggested three progressions in making best use of this idea—interactions, interdependence and institutionalisation. 'Suspension of J&K LoC trade is a regressive step and a lost opportunity,' he had remarked (Drabu 2019).

5. The idea of economic integration of the two sides of LoC had been integral to the local discourse of Kashmir. The concept had been given a concrete shape, for instance, by Sajad Lone in his *Achievable Nationhood* (2006: 10). According to this document,

> [T]he concept of J&K economic union is a process of unification of the two parts of J&K by producing a 'single economic entity' out of 'two distinct geographical and political sub entities of J&K S and J&K M [Lone describes J&K S as J&K under Indian administration and J&K M as J&K under Pakistani administration] having separate severity linkages with two separate sovereign entities of India and Pakistan. A single economic entity would mean free flow of capital, trade, services, labour, economic operations across LoC and the removal of barriers to movement are perhaps the most profound visible indicators of change—psychological unification. The 'J&K Economic Union' would be an economically boundary-less J&K. The economic union of the state of J&K would be a separate custom territory, internal barriers to trade would be removed while external barriers to trade would be harmonised. Both Indian and Pakistani currencies would be the legal tender.

6. Referring to the disruptions made by militants before the start of the bus service, the Report of the Home Ministry stated that the militant attack 'failed to dampen the popular enthusiasm and the bus was cheered all along its route. The people of the State, mainstream political parties and the Press have welcomed the successful re-opening of Srinagar-Muzaffarabad road despite the shadow of terrorist threats' (GoI 2006: 10–11).

7. Ashutosh Sharma narrates the story of three brothers, two on the Indian side (Bopinder Singh and Ujagar Singh) and one on the POJK side (Neck Mohammad), who were able to meet after the cross-LoC bus service was started (Sharma 2013).

Mahapatra narrates the story of Savitri, who was abducted in 1947 and was later converted to Islam. She was married in Kotli, and could meet her brother after decades when her elder brother Vishnu Mohan travelled to Kotli through the cross-LoC bus service (Mahapatra 2011).

8. The division of Jammu and Kashmir in 1947 affected Jammu region more than Kashmir and it is here that a large number of divided families are to be found. Within this region also, it is Poonch which has the largest number of divided families, for the simple reason that this district itself was divided and a large part of it became a part of POJK. Also, till the inception of armed militancy, the border was quite porous and people could travel to and fro, and therefore families were settled on both the sides of the LoC.

9. Governor of Jammu and Kashmir, N. N. Vohra, said the trade link was a major step in a slow-moving peace process: 'Today is a historic day….The trade volume will increase. I'm completely hopeful that this will remove a lot of difficulties and create an atmosphere of friendship on the two sides' (*Dawn* 2008).

10. Though agriculture remained the primary source of livelihood, the only opportunities provided to the expanded middle class was the state employment sector. However, the state was already running an overloaded administrative structure with around four lakh employees in the state sector. The salaries and wages of the government employees had been the biggest liability of the state. Much of the state budget went into financing the wage bill of these employees. Industry suffered not only from lack of capital investment but also a lack of infrastructural resources. The problems of power, expensive raw materials and the cost of transportation had worked as disincentives for private-sector investment.

11. Due to the backlog of economic problems and political uncertainties, the processes of globalisation, liberalisation and privatisation seemed to have escaped this state. Ironically, the period of liberalisation in India coincided with the period of militancy in J&K. The weak economic infrastructure on the one hand and political uncertainties on the other dissuaded private capital from investing in the state. While states like Andhra Pradesh, Karnataka and West Bengal were competing with each other for FDI, this state was starved even of Indian private capital. This was despite the fact that all the successive political regimes had been making special efforts to attract investment from the private sector of India.

12. Referring to the 'backwardness trap' of the state due to 'a weak resource base, poor infrastructure, sparse population density, shallow markets and most importantly a law and order situation threatened by militancy', the Working Group on Economy had identified the following implications for economic development of the state:

> First, the internal market is too small to take advantage of scale economies in production. The alternative of scaling up production to viable levels by exporting to markets outside the state is infeasible because of poor connectivity. Second, unit costs of service delivery are high because of high costs of inputs as also low population densities. Third, the private sector, which should be the engine of growth, has not taken off because of low supply and demand linkages and in part because of inhibition of the private sector on account of security concerns (*Report of Working Group III* 2007: 2).

Stating that all these factors having resulted in economic activity being dependent mainly on the public sector, the report further argued that 'the beneficial impact of public expenditure has been lost to some extent'. Meanwhile the continued dependence of the state on the central assistance has resulted in 'a complacent attitude towards resource generation, fiscal responsibility and accountability for results' (ibid.).

13. With this region being linked with the rest of the world only through the Jawahar Tunnel, there persisted a feeling of being 'psychologically suffocated'. Being the only route linking Kashmir with the rest of India gave it not only a sense of isolation but also a feeling of dependence on the Centre, especially for trade purposes. The fact that the highway was becoming fragile in many places

and would get blocked in poor weather conditions made this feeling of psychological suffocation more intense. Hence, the idea of an alternate route for trade from Kashmir was quite appealing to Kashmiris.

14. As Zafar Choudhary noted about the interest of Jammu's trading class in the cross-LoC trade, '... Jammu business people lobby for stronger trade and for opening more routes because local markets within Jammu and Kashmir are very limited' (Choudhary 2010: 33).

15. How the cross-LoC trade had impacted the people and helped them change perceptions about the 'other' across the LoC and how this trade helped develop common perceptions and mutual interdependence was noted by Pawan Kumar, a Jammu-based trader. To quote him:

> I had never imagined that so much would change in Poonch in a short span of less that two years .... Life in Rawalkot, Hajeera, Bagh or other parts of Pakistan-administreed Kashmir (PaK) is now part of our daily talk. We have traced our forgotten relatives, made new friends and discovered collaborations for mutual growth in business. Despite odds, there is no looking back. Our feelings have changed (Anand 2010: 8).

16. Even as recently as 2020, the demand for including locally manufactured goods in the cross-LoC trade was made by the local industrialists and entrepreneurs (PTI 2020).

17. One major reason underlying their discontent was that the list of goods to be traded did not have any economic rationale and did not follow the economic realities of the erstwhile state. As pointed out by Yusuf, 'goods on the positive list do not seem to correspond to market realities. A number of items defy trade rationale as they are already available at lower cost within the importer's market or the exporter has a more lucrative market available domestically' (Yusuf 2009).

18. The 21 items approved for import and export included: carpets, shawls, namdas, gabas, embroidery items, fruits, vegetables, dry fruits, saffron, imli, rajmash, Kashmiri spices, foam mattress, medicinal herbs, jahnamaz, tasbeehs, precious stones, Peshawari chappals, maize, maize products, honey and rice.

19. For instance, a ban on the import of garlic from the Pakistani side was imposed by the Government of India and later, the former banned the export of Moong Dal.

20. There was also no possibility for the traders to visit their counterparts on the other side of the LoC, as a matter of course. Theoretically, they could avail of the bus service mainly meant for the residents of the state to freely move to the other side, but in practice the service had not been opened to the general public and remained restricted to the 'divided families'.

21. Sengupta et al. (2012) state that the cross-LoC trade was sustained mainly because of the sentiments of the people living close to LoC, particularly the divided families. In their report titled *Cross-Line of Control Trade: Peacebuilding and Economic Potential*, they note that:

> ... emotional attachment to the other part of the LoC ... played a major role. It is not easy to justify the risks taken in the absence of a proper dispute settlement mechanism if the business parter on the other side of LoC decided to renege on a deal. Thus businessmen located close to the LoC became pioneers not because they were the best suited but because they were the most eager.

22. The refugees from POJK, who were otherwise seen as having quite extreme views, were also quite enthused by this process and not only wanted to visit their homeland but also sought to restart cultural relationships with people across the LoC.

23. It was due to security concerns that the cross-LoC trade was suspended in April 2019. As per the Ministry of Home Affairs, the trade route was being used by 'terrorists based in Pakistan as a channel to smuggle arms, ammunition, narcotics, counterfeit currency and funds to support anti-India activities within J&K.' The government also stated that a number of trading companies were actually run by the Kashmiri militants who had crossed over in the 1990s and had settled in POJK (Haider 2019).

24. As per the Home Ministry's annual report, the trade has been suspended and not terminated. 'Cross LOC trade between India and PoK has been suspended from 19.04.2019 till a stricter regime is put in place to ensure that only bonafide trade takes place for the benefit of the people of J&K' (GoI 2019).

25. By 2019, 'more than Rs. 6000 crore trade had been conducted over the LoC points, and a total of 1.6 lakh job days created because of it' (Haider 2019). On the whole, about 662 traders were registered for conducting this trade and at least 110 traders were regularly and actively involved in the trade activities (ibid.).

26. The goods sent from the Indian side, especially fruits, were not restricted to those available in J&K. There was a lot of trade taking place in items like banana and coconut, which the traders procured from other parts of India.

27. In the Jammu region, for instance, there was a demand for opening the trade to the manufacturing sector. In Poonch, meanwhile, there was a demand for trading in local agricultural products. There was also a demand for freedom to trade on the basis of market logic, and for permission to visit the 'mandis' across the border so that they can assess the nature of demands of items to be imported or exported.

References

Anand, Pawan. 2010. 'The Gains of Cross-Line of Control Trade'. *Jammu and Kashmir—Trade Across the Line of Control*, Discussion Papers, December. Conciliation Resources. Available at https://rc-services-assets.s3.eu-west-1.amazonaws.com/s3fs-public/JammuandKashmir_DiscussionPapers_201012_ENG.pdf (accessed January 2024).

Bhatia, Mohita. 2020. *Rethinking Conflict at the Margins: Dalits and Borderland Hindus in Jammu and Kashmir*. Cambridge: Cambridge University Press.

Chandran, D. Suba. 2009. 'Expanding Cross-LoC Interactions: Perspective from India', IPCS Issue Brief, 131. Available at https://www.ipcs.org/issue_briefs/issue_brief_pdf/IB131-Ploughshares-Suba.pdf (accessed February 2024).

Chari, P. R. and Hasan Askari Rizvi. 2008. *Making Borders Irrelevant in Kashmir'*, Special Report, 210. United States Institute of Peace (USIP).

Choudhary, Zafar. 2010. 'Cross-line of Control trade: Changing the mindset in Jammu region'. Jammu and Kashmir-Trade

Across the Line of Control, Discussion Papers, December, Conciliation Resources. Available at https://rc-services-assets.s3.eu-west-1.amazonaws.com/s3fs-public/JammuandKashmir_DiscussionPapers_201012_ENG.pdf (accessed February 2024).

Dar, Hamidullah and Rasul Gul. 2009. 'Cross Kin Trade', cited in Shamas Irfan, 'Cross-Kin Trade', *Kashmir Life*, 4 March 2010. Available at https://kashmirlife.net/cross-kin-trade-132/ (accessed February 2024).

Dawn. 2008. 'Cross-LoC Trade begins amid high hopes', 22 October. Available at https://www.dawn.com/news/amp/326518 (accessed February 2024).

Drabu, Haseeb A. 2019. 'Suspension of J&K LoC trade is a regressive step and a lost opportunity', . The *Indian Express*, 25 April. Available at https://indianexpress.com/article/opinion/columns/symbolism-over-substance-india-pakistan-loc-trade-ban-jammu-and-kashmir-5693069/ (accessed February 2024).

Government of India (GoI). 2005. 'Joint Statement, India-Pakistan discussion on Opening of crossing points across the LOC', Ministry of External Affairs. Available at https://mea.gov.in/bilateral-documents.htm?dtl/7005/Joint+Statement+IndiaPakistan+discussions+on+opening+of+crossing+points+across+the+LoC (accessed February 2024).

———. 2006. *Annual Report, 2005–06*, Ministry of Home Affairs. Available at https://www.mha.gov.in/sites/default/files/AnnualReport_05_06.pdf (accessed February 2024).

———. 2011. 'Joint Statement following meeting between the Minister of External Affairs of India and Minister of Foreign Affairs of Pakistan', 27 July, Ministry of External Affairs. Available at https://mea.gov.in/bilateral-documents.htm?dtl/87/Joint+Statement+following+meeting+between+the+Minister+of+External+Affairs+of+India+and+Minister+of+Foreign+Affairs+of+Pakistan (accessed February 2024).

———. 2019. *Annual Report 2018–2019*, Ministry of Home Affairs. Available at https://www.mha.gov.in/sites/default/files/AnnualReport_18_19.pdf (accessed February 2024).

Haider, Suhasini. 2019. 'Will closing LoC trade end terrorism', *The Hindu*, 27 April. Available at https://www.thehindu.com/news/national/other-states/will-closing-loc-trade-end-terrorism/article26967473.ece (accessed February 2024).

Hussain, Aijaz. 2005. 'Kashmir earthquake: Opening of relief points along LoC becomes high point of Indo-Pak ties'. *India Today*, 21 November. Available at https://www.indiatoday.in/magazine/states/story/20051121-kashmir-earthquake-opening-of-relief-points-along-loc-becomes-high-point-of-indo-pak-ties-786572-2005-11-21 (accessed February 2024).

Lone, Sajad Gani. 2006. *Achievable Nationhood: A Vision Document on Resolution of the Jammu & Kashmir Conflict*, Jammu Kashmir People's Conference. Available at https://www.slideshare.net/peoplesconference/achievable-nationhood (accessed February 2024).

Mahapatra, Debitalla Aurobinda. 2011. 'Positioning the people in the contested borders of Kashmir'. CIBR, Working Paper 21, 15–16. Available at https://www.humiliationstudies.org/documents/MahapatraContestedBordersKashmir.pdf (accessed February 2024).

Maini, K. D. 2009. 'Cross-LoC Trade: Prospects and Problems', IPCS, 20 January. Available at https://www.ipcs.org/comm_select.php?articleNo=2785 (accessed February 2024).

———. 2010. 'Rajouri and Poonch: Identifying Early Warnings and Addressing new Challenges', IPCS Issue Brief. Available at https://www.jstor.org/stable/resrep09170?seq=1 (accessed February 2024).

Mirani, Aaron. 2007. 'Line of Commerce'. *Business Line*, 14 September. Available at http://www.thehindubusinessline.com/life/2007/09/14/stories/2007091450020100.htm (accessed February 2024).

PTI. 2020. 'Industry seeks inclusion of locally manufactured items in cross LoC trade'. *The Week*, 2 April. Available at https://www.theweek.in/content/archival/wire-updates/business/2018/12/23/nrg18-jk-industry.html (accessed February 2024).

Pattanaik, Smruti S. and Arpita Anant. 2010. 'Cross-LoC Confidence Building Measures between India and Pakistan: A Giant Leap or a Small Step towards Peace', Issue Brief, Institute for Defence Studies and Analyses, February. Available at https://www.files.ethz.ch/isn/137394/CrossLoCCBMbetweenIndiaandPakistan.pdf (accessed February 2024).

Puri, Luv. 2012. *Across the Line of Control: Inside Pakistan-Administered Jammu and Kashmir*. Hurst & Company.

Reddy, B. Murlidharan. 2005. 'A Bus Ride for Peace'. *Frontline*, 11 March. Available at https://frontline.thehindu.com/the-nation/article30203827.ece (accessed February 2024).

Report of the Working Group. 2007. *Strengthening Relations Across the Line of Control*, January.

Report of the Working Group III. 2007. *Economic Development of Jammu and Kashmir*, March.

Sengupta, Dipanker, Ershad Mahmud and Zafar Iqbal Choudhary. 2012. 'Cross-Line of Control Trade: Peacebuilding and Economic Potential', Conciliation Resources. Available at https://rc-services-assets.s3.eu-west-1.amazonaws.com/s3fs-public/IPK_LoC_trade_peacebuilding_web.pdf (accessed February 2024).

Sharma, Rajeev. 2003. 'Ceasefire Begins, Infiltrators to be shot, India tells Pakistan'. *Tribune News Service*, 25 November. Available at https://www.tribuneindia.com/2003/20031126/main1.htm (accessed February 2024).

Sharma, Ashutosh. 2013. 'Along the Line of Fire'. *The Hindu*, 25 October. Available at https://www.thehindu.com/news/international/south-asia/along-the-line-of-fire/article5268980.ece- (accessed February 2024).

Schaffer, Terrista. 2005. *Kashmir: The Economics of Peace Building* (A Report of the CSIS South Asia Programme with the Kashmir Study Group), December.

Yusuf, Moeed. 2009. *Promoting Cross LoC Trade in Kashmir: An Analysis of the Joint Chamber.* USIP Special Report, 230, August.

NOTES ON THE CONTRIBUTORS

Mohita Bhatia is Assistant Professor in the Department of Sociology, Saint Mary's University, Halifax.

Rekha Chowdhary retired as Professor of Political Science, University of Jammu.

Chakraverti Mahajan is Associate Professor in the Department of Anthropology, University of Delhi.

Mamta Sharma is Lecturer in Political Science in the Directorate of Distance and Online Education, University of Jammu.

Seema Shekhawat teaches politics at the University of North Florida. She is an honorary research fellow at the Department of Politics, International Relations and Philosophy, Royal Holloway University of London.

Sandeep Singh is Assistant Professor in the Department of Lifelong Learning, University of Jammu.

INDEX